Acting On Camera
The Australian Way

Acting On Camera The Australian Way

Paul Parker (B.Ed.) International Acting Teacher/Acting Coach

Learn how to:

- Act on camera
- Do a self-tape audition
- Do detailed scene study
- Create characters
- Role play
- Cold read
- Improve movement
- Improve your charisma and attraction
- Discuss differences between Australian and American acting training

- And much, much more

Edited by:

John Mapps. Sydney, Australia.

Typesetting by:

Trisha Fuentes, California USA.

Front and back cover design:

Hollie Kirby, Melbourne, Australia,

Images and articles:

All images used in this book are either property of Paul Parker and his school AIDA, or have been used with permission of the copyright-holders, who are acknowledged in the captions. I thank all the organizations who have approved the use of their material in this book. all reasonable efforts were made to obtain permission to use copyright material, but if material has inadvertently been used without permission, the author welcomes information in this regard.

Publisher:

IngramSpark Publishing

Previous Books:

Acting The Australian Way – published 2022.

© Copyright:

Paul Parker, Melbourne, Victoria, Australia. 2023.

This book is dedicated to, and in loving memory of, my eldest brother, **Colin Michael Parker**. 19.09.1957 – 28.04.2010.

A man who was born to perform professionally but never did. Colin was charismatic. A showman. A singer with a tambourine.

Colin knew how to hold an audience. He would sing and dance away to songs from bands like The Bee Gees and Slade. He would sing the memorable songs Ferry Across The Mersey and the unofficial English Football theme song – You'll Never Walk Alone – both by English band, Gerry and The Pacemakers.

Everyone, especially women, loved him. This man had je ne sais quoi.

Colin also loved watching movies.

I am one of seven children. Of five boys and two girls. Colin would listen to me, respect my perspective and allow me to have my opinion. He also accepted me in my chosen vocations. What a wonderful gift this was to his younger brother. For that, he will always be in my heart. Miss you and love you, Colin.

About the author

Teacher, audition coach, on-set acting coach, guest teacher around the world, writer, director, producer – Paul Parker understands the actor's journey, and is dedicated to helping actors hone their craft. He has a wide roster of clients.

Paul worked as a professional actor in Australia and then later in America from 1977 to 2003. He won two acting awards.

His career as an acting teacher/coach began in 1990. He has taught acting at universities, colleges, TAFE (Tertiary and Further Education) colleges, as well as at acting schools and privately in Australia. This includes with his own school, AIDA – the Australian Institute of Dramatic Arts.

AIDA is a school that Paul founded in Hollywood, Los Angeles, in June of 2002. With AIDA, Paul taught, in person, in Chicago, Los Angeles, New York and San Francisco, for nearly 10 years between 2002 and 2011. The school is still operative today, albeit online.

Paul has taught, in person, across the USA, across Australia, in Osaka and Tokyo in Japan and in Beijing and Hainan in China.

Online, he has also taught in London, England, and Seoul and other cities in South Korea.

Paul published his first book, *Acting The Australian Way*, worldwide in 2022. It gives a full introduction to Paul's methods and includes many practical exercises.

For four years from 2007 in Los Angeles, Paul was an official professional judge of actors performing on camera. He was also a judge for theatre acting in 2014 in Australia.

Paul has been working as a theatre director since 1990 and a director for the screen since 2015.

He has written for the theatre since 1991 and for the screen since 1999.

Paul is a qualified teacher with a Bachelor of Education in Drama and English Literature and Language linguistics from Deakin University/ Victoria College – Rusden Campus, graduating in 1991.

He currently teaches worldwide on Skype and Zoom with AIDA. He also still travels the world to teach. His last teaching tour was to Japan in 2022.

Paul has attended six Academy Awards and two Golden Globes awards in Los Angeles. Paul was a voting member, in all categories for ten years with BAFTA – LA. The British Academy Awards from 2002 to 2011.

For more information about Paul, please see the curriculum vitae at the back of this book or listed in full in his first book.

Alternatively, see the following websites:

www.aidaacting.com

www.player-productions.com

www.paulparkerpc.com.au

In addition to Paul's student successes, Paul states his *greatest achievement* for his resume is the work that he does in class with his students.

Above: Paul Parker on the red carpet at the 2007 Academy Awards at the Kodak Theatre in Hollywood. Entertainment industry icon Joan Rivers, chatted with Paul shortly after this photo was taken. Paul was seen on the red carpet on NBC television on Entertainment Tonight on the pre-Oscar afternoon show and later on that evening, February 25th, 2007.

All Academy Awards photos were approved to appear in the book in January 2022, by Kristen Ray - Senior Specialist, Clearance. Academy of Motion Picture Arts and Sciences. 8949 Wilshire Blvd. Beverly Hills. CA 90211

Contents

Foreword 1
Introduction 11
Prologue 19

Part 1
Theory 25

Chapter 1: Acting on Camera. 27
Chapter 2: Audio excerpts from classes 71
Chapter 3: Self-tape Audition 91
Chapter 4: Detailed scene study. 107
Chapter 5: Create Characters. 121
Chapter 6: Differences between Australian and American acting training, Part 1. 139
Chapter 7: Differences between Australian and American acting training, Part 2. 165
Chapter 8: Training Japanese actors 215

Part 2
Practice 223

Chapter 9: On-camera research 225
Chapter 10: Acting exercises – a way of thinking 241
Chapter 11: Improve movement 247
Chapter 12: On-camera exercises 251
Chapter 13: On-camera work: Conclusion. 263
Chapter 14: Role-playing exercises 269
Chapter 15: Cold-reading exercises. 277
Chapter 16: Improve your charisma and attraction 283
Chapter 17: Case scenarios 289
Chapter 18: Self-evaluation form 297
Chapter 19: A checklist of your professionalism 301
Chapter 20: Review of your audition 313

Appendix 1 Handouts 325
Appendix 2 Lesson plans 333
Appendix 3 People who influenced my teachings in Book Two 337
Appendix 4 Successful students 339
Appendix 5 Paul Parker Curriculum Vitae 343

Foreword

Three of my former AIDA students read this book before publication and agreed to share their impressions of it and their experience of being taught by me over the years.

Chris Ivan Cevic

My friendship with Paul Parker began as early as 2004 while I was studying at the Australian Institute of Dramatic Arts and then throughout my acting career in Los Angeles.

When I met Paul, I was looking for something different in a scene study class. More specifically I was looking for an edge. In a business that seemingly celebrates fast and loose, I was looking for tools to help with consistency... something that was more tangible and repeatable, but that could also help to deliver more believable and memorable performances.

What caught my attention at the time was Paul being the only person really talking about believability, risk taking, and memorable performances in concrete terms. He did this in a way that felt was achievable through mindset, mechanics and preparation. I found most coaches to be heady and ethereal about acting, choosing instead to direct actors.

Paul's approach is very disciplined. He wants you to be directable, yes, but also to empower you first with specific processes, skills, and techniques so next time your work is elevated from the get go. His approach to acting is always clear..., no matter the size of the role, even ones with few words. And it's because he simply asks of you, *'Did you do the work? Did you do your breathing exercises before you came into the room? Did you break down what the scene is really about? What about the character... do you know their gait? How about their secrets? Did you make a choice about their want? Not what the scene wants, but what that character really wants ... in life and from the other person?'*

I was always amazed how often new actors came in the door dull and predictable, but were soon leaving awestruck by how alive and vibrant their work had become. It was inspiring. And when actors came in the door strong, Paul could always find something to sprinkle in that would make scenes soar to the next level. Just really interesting risk taking. Like, 'Try a whisper instead of yelling. Say that with your eyes first, or say that line to yourself.' Paul was also always coaching us to bring more risks. I found this alone became a great source of confidence. A game changer in this business.

Looking back, I can see Paul has been an enthusiastic scientist all these years in the classroom, and this book is the culmination of every lesson learned and every breakthrough earned along the way. He has clearly broken down what makes someone watchable, and how you can go about achieving that in every role, every time. From simple mindset rituals, to camera angle mechanics, building characters, making strong choices, and how to introduce yourself in an audition. It's truly comprehensive.

And yes, refreshingly, this book speaks candidly about the business. Paul never shied away from any of it. We actors are people too, navigating a career in a business that prides itself on being insular and throwing out the rule books, so being in the class meant we were all collaborating in that sense. Paul had us bring everything into the room, our auditions, our projects, our successes, our failures. We turned over every stone to find the silver lining. The gem we could all benefit from. How to break into Hollywood and be a working actor was just as much on his mind as being someone who consistently creates memorable performances. Paul has been hitting on these questions for years and from all the different angles. I'm happy to see this book delivers on all accounts.

From a performance perspective, no matter your skill level, this book offers plenty to elevate your work. From a professional standpoint, you will also elevate your career with the insights gleaned from Paul's take on the business. That is a rare combo, but then again, so is Paul.

As a producer, I meet a lot of people who want to be an actor and ask for advice. Paul's book is now at the top of my recommend list, and if you get the chance to work with him like I did, you'd be an even better actor for it.

Chris Ivan Cevic

2 x award winner on IMDB
21 credits as an actor
13 credits as a producer
A student for many years
https://www.imdb.com/name/nm2160048/?ref_=fn_al_nm_1

Cyanne McClairian (Martin)

Let me start by saying, I don't believe in coincidence. When I found Paul Parker's acting class in 2002, it was mere months after coming back to life. Literally. To say it had been a rocky year, would be an understatement. You see, I was born with a heart condition.

Due to some pain and other symptoms, I was dealing with in early 2001, I read that energizing my chakras might help – something that Paul goes into with his techniques in Book 1. So, I began activating them on a regular basis, just focusing on my heart chakra, of course. But it was the one thing that I could always count on to ground me and help with any discomfort that I was having. Especially if I needed to remedy it quickly in order to get to set or for a last-minute film or TV audition.

So, needless to say, when I ran across AIDA a couple months into my recovery after major surgery, I was immediately drawn to it! I mean, if my chakra work had been helping my heart so much ... what could it do for my acting? Then, once I experienced Paul's teaching and techniques myself, it was not only refreshing, but eye-opening. And it got me really, really excited!

You see, prior to starting at AIDA, I was primarily known for my Shakespeare and other stage performances, as well as my European look that booked me quite a few indie film roles at the time. I actually would have relocated because of it if my surgery had been timed better. I was also one of the many actors here in LA who had maxed-out credit cards a couple times over from casting director workshops. Not only did that cause me to need multiple jobs to survive, it started making me very distrustful of compliments – something Paul goes into in this book.

I was regularly paired with a few male actors who booked film, TV, and series regular roles through the workshops. But while I received positive feedback every time, somehow, I was never even called in for an audition. That led me to doubt myself. A lot. I mean, I felt connected. I got great notes. Why would they gush over my scene work and my choices, bring in the guys I worked with, but never me? I knew it was partially dependent on if they needed my type, but...? There had to be something I could be doing better! And it got me in my head more and more, over time. But I stuck with it and just worked harder, because I loved the craft.

Once I was in class with Paul, however, I learned what my specific strengths really were, and how to build them up and intensify them even more. I am a character actress through and through, and I love to take risks and do the unexpected! Paul's class was no exception. But with his help, I stopped limiting how far away from centre I went with them and tapped deeper into my instincts and my emotions.

A couple years in, for example, we were coincidentally doing a month of CD workshop-style classes off of a reader Paul would bring in from another class. We were all handed a scene, worked on it individually for about 15 minutes using the techniques we were taught, then came back in and got called one by one. The scene was from the film *The English Patient*.

I don't remember much because I was totally in it and we were very connected. But at one point, I know I had the gut instinct to kiss the other actor. So instead of second guessing and getting in my head like I would have before, I kissed him. It completely changed the scene in the best possible way.

When we finished, the room was so silent you could hear a pin drop. On a side note, that actor is now my husband. Thank you, Paul. Your results may vary, lol.

In addition to deepening my risk taking, I could go on and on with things that Paul helped me to improve for film and TV – stillness for the screen, utilizing the space for self-tapes, creating characters, surprises (I love surprises! Shocker, I know). But I will stick to just two more, which have helped me immensely in my on-camera work.

You see, Paul is nothing, if not honest – a very rare and wonderful trait to find in an acting teacher. He's also very personal, which is incredibly different to what I had experienced before in most classes. Much less formal. During warm-ups one day, he commented on my clenched jaw. I had no idea what he was even talking about, so I asked him about it afterwards. He had me look into the mirror, and clench and un-clench my jaw. The difference was subtle, but it put me in a very specific category for TV and film characters I'd get cast as. And the camera catches everything!

By simply learning how to relax my jaw, I have been cast in so many more types of roles! Just that one moment changed my casting profile, and my life, immensely. To this day, if I am just sitting on a zoom or watching television, etc., you'll probably catch me stretching or massaging my jaw.

Lastly, when I started with Paul, I was working on accepting my inability to cry on cue – which is huge for film work, specifically. Especially if you can do it subtly, or hold the tears back right behind your eyes. I went to a Theatre Arts high school and have been in class with very reputable teachers in Hollywood. Yet, crying on cue was something I'd never been able to master. I had all these tricks I was taught to make it happen. But it never felt genuine because, well, it wasn't. Yet, after working with Paul for maybe eight months, applying his techniques and breathing into my chakras, it all came rushing out. Initially, I thought it was a happy accident, but nope! Now, not only can I cry on cue, I have full access to my emotions at any point, without even thinking about it. No tricks needed.

If you are anything like me, right now you are probably thinking, 'really?' My answer . . . yeah! Paul is a rare breed. And he's helped me with so much more than just my acting techniques! As a teacher and as a human, he is just different. Maybe they are less jaded in Australia, I don't know. But Paul is easily one of the most genuine people I have ever met. He really does want the best for all of his students.

His personable nature makes him so very easy to trust, which in turn helps him to help you even more. I truly believe he is an empath. He senses your struggles and feels your pain. He is definitely not a therapist by any means, but he has a keen eye to help you navigate self-doubts, insecurities, all that bullshit that blocks you from really trusting that you are enough and letting your truth come out. I love that about him!

As you would imagine, dealing with a heart condition, as well as dying and coming back has been difficult. It has caused me to feel broken at times and feel unworthy. One night after a hard class, Paul leaned over to me and said . . . 'I wonder if the universe knows you are alive? Why don't you consider doing a meditation exercise where you tell the universe that you are alive?' Looking back, I really don't think the universe did know I was alive. But who even thinks to ask those kinds of questions? Paul does! And we most definitely made sure the universe knew I was . . . and AM . . . alive! I even wrote and performed an award-winning one-woman show about it years later at the Hollywood Fringe Festival!

I cannot even express how grateful I am to have had Paul as a teacher. And I am completely honoured to have been asked to write this foreword! Wow! Reconnecting with him years later and reading his books, has been a trip. Not only am I a better actress thanks to him, I am much more confident in who I am and what I have to offer. So buckle up, breathe, be open and enjoy the ride.

And to Paul – I am forever changed by you. Love you so much, my friend. Thank you, a million times over!!

Cyanne McClairian (Martin)

24 IMDB credits

7 times award winner on stage in Los Angeles

A student from 2004 to 2019

https://www.imdb.com/name/nm0202563/?ref_=nv_sr_srsg_0_tt_0_nm_1_q_Cyanne%2520McClairian

Naama Kates

I first came across Paul Parker and AIDA in Manhattan, New York, as a 17-year-old aspiring actor in 2004. Paul had recently opened the branch in New York after two years of his school's success in Los Angeles.

I was so impressed with Paul's teaching from the outset. What impressed me so much was Paul's ability to connect with each and every one of us in class. Which soon became classes as Paul's New York branch soon grew from one night a week to three nights a week.

Like his Los Angeles branch, Paul also started creating social events for us to go to, usually at Aussie bars in Manhattan. I loved that!

I studied with Paul at the New York branch of AIDA until I moved to Los Angeles in 2009, where I then joined the Los Angeles branch of AIDA. Yep, I followed the teacher when he moved back to Los Angeles to live. The last time Paul taught me in person was in one of his touring workshops in 2019 in Hollywood.

Paul's acting techniques really worked for me. I booked Off Broadway theatre, commercials and film in New York – some with Paul prepping me for the roles, and then later film and television in Los Angeles. Paul's on-camera training was and still is profound and precise.

Two brief stories go like this:

At 17 years of age, I had recently broken off from my first boyfriend and I couldn't stop crying. I got an audition for a commercial in New York. Paul prepped me for the audition and talked to me about how to best handle my emotions so I didn't collapse into tears when in the audition because I couldn't stop crying. I did exactly what Paul suggested and I booked it. I booked the commercial.

In Los Angeles, Paul prepped me for a guest star role on NCIS for television. I booked that too.

Paul also came and watched me perform on stage Off Broadway in New York and created many opportunities to help me succeed as an actor on both coasts of America.

Most importantly, Paul is a dynamic teacher, a caring teacher, a bloody smart acting coach, who always improves actors' work.

Reading this *Acting On Camera The Australian Way* book brings back so many memories. There are so many fantastic exercises in this book that I have used over and over again.

Remembering Paul's first book on technique, Paul has a tried and trusted formula that really empowers actors' work. I recall watching with delight to see my peers, on both coasts of America, really improve with Paul's teaching.

Oh, I'm a professional singer too, and Paul's breathe and voice work really improved my vocal freedom, my vocal range and the quality of my voice.

Delve into the book, actors. Enjoy it. Do what Paul is suggesting in this book and you will improve. I guarantee it.

He is awesome!

One final thing I would like to mention: Paul encouraged us all to be writers, producers, directors, film crew – anything and everything to help us create work that we could put ourselves in. I took this to heart and taught myself to write and produce and I have become a multi-award-winning filmmaker.

Filmmaking is such hard work, but I've done it. I've made films that have won awards and I put myself in the lead roles, knowing that I could do them.

Paul has been encouraging all his students to create their own work for over 20 years now, I believe.

Bravo, Paul Parker! I love you and am so proud of what you have achieved as an acting coach around the world. Love this book.

Naama Kates
Actor/Producer/Singer
6 award wins on IMDB, including 2 x Best Actress winner
19 credits
A student from 2004 to 2019
https://www.imdb.com/name/nm0441809/?ref_=fn_al_nm_1

Introduction

Thank you very much for purchasing this book and thank you if you purchased my first book, *Acting The Australian Way*. My first book talks about five acting techniques for actors, including Australian acting techniques and the importance of breath and voice and how to teach yourself to learn to connect with the text that you are going to say. All as you create characters for film, television, theatre and commercials.

My books are an unabridged and relevant stream of educational consciousness. My mind is active all the time, my learnings, my readings, dissecting things, analyzing things, looking for connections and reasons. Looking for the *best way* to achieve great results and/or, to see how and why we do things and how things work. This includes what works and what doesn't work in front of the camera, with actors.

I wish to share my thoughts and experiences because I believe doing so can help me be a better teacher and, most importantly, help other people.

My aim in this book is to teach you how to act on screen, the Australian way. I like to think of it as a working guide for you in your on-camera acting training. It is Australian on-camera acting training as I class myself as Australian. I have lived in Australia, most of my life since 1968.

Am I an expert on on-screen acting?

I believe that I am simply doing my job with an astute eye and ear and with detailed observations of actors working on screen. I will draw on personal experiences as an actor and on my teaching experiences and on watching human behaviour, both on and off screen. My students ongoing booked work validates my teaching training in all areas.

I have been teaching acting since 1990 and teaching on-screen acting around the world since 1998.

Dozens of actors that I have trained have won awards. Most of these awards have been for work on camera and seen on the cinema or TV screen.

Some questions I encourage the reader to ask themselves are:

- How do the movie stars, or the people who book a lot of screen acting jobs, work? What is it about them that gets them ongoing work on screen?
- How come [please insert a successful actor's name here that you like] can be so brilliant on stage, but they don't get any, or very little, on-screen work? You don't often see them in film or television and if you do, their work is not so good?
- How come you audition and don't book work?
- How come you audition and don't make an impact with your work on camera?
- And, are there really such things as on-camera skills? And if so, what are they?

This book will answer all these questions and more as together we delve into the art and the skills of performing on screen.

I am, in particular, going to talk about drama – that is, dramatic acting on screen – although I will talk about comedy acting on screen as well.

Succeeding in the acting profession, becoming an established actor, having a public profile, performing great characters and earning lots of money, will not happen with acting on the stage alone.

As wonderful as theatre is, generally speaking, statistics tell us that less than five per cent of any population in the world go and watch theatre. So, as great as you may be at performing on the stage and being loved in theatre circles, you will not reach celebrity status or earn a lot of money if you work only on the stage.

On-screen work generally pays the actor so much more than theatre. If we think in terms of hourly rates, there is generally no comparison. Acting in front of the screen pays so much more.

For example, instead of rehearsing for months, then performing for months and being lucky enough to be paid $1000 to $1500 a week for performing in a theatre show, the irony is that if you do a national burger or supermarket commercial, which plays over and over again for six months on television, you may not need to work again for a while, and it may have taken only *hours* to shoot. And shooting the commercial could pay you four to five thousand dollars or, in some cases, a lot more, and then there are residuals.

Doing a commercial just may ignite your film/television acting career too. Take, for example, Aussie celebrity actor Lisa McCune. Ms. McCune was spotted and discovered by television producer Hal McElroy, of TV show *Blue Heelers* fame, while acting in a supermarket commercial.

I love theatre. I love theatre training and theatre acting. I have been on stage a lot as an actor and have directed a lot of plays. I have seen and read a lot of stage plays too. Like I said, I love it, but, and this needs to be emphasised, it may not pay the rent. It will absolutely help you get auditions for film and television work because of its rich actor training. But you will need more than this to succeed as a professional working actor – on screen.

An aside: Sir Michael Gambon died on 27 September 2023, well after most of this book was written and just as it was going through the final stages of production. In my comments about his work, I'd like to make clear that under no circumstances am I out to belittle Sir Michael. I am simply commenting, by comparison, on the impacts made by this amazing theatre actor on stage versus his work on screen. Naturally this is simply my opinion, at the time of watching his on-screen work around 2004 and 2005.

With my very strong history of both performing and watching theatre, in late 2000 or early 2001, I was lucky enough to see Sir Michael Gambon play the character The Caretaker in the play of the same name by Harold Pinter, at the Comedy Theatre in London's West End theatre district.

Introduction | 13

I was mesmerized. I'm a huge Pinter fan, and this performance, this character portrayal by Michael Gambon, was incredible. I could not take my eyes off him. His attention to detail, to all things relating to the manner of a man, his character, his connection to and then delivery of his text, were on show. I was spellbound.

Around this time, I had recently become a voting member of the Los Angeles branch of BAFTA which meant I could vote for the British Academy Awards. I held this position, as a member, for ten years until I returned to live in Australia in 2011.

Well around this same time, I started seeing lots of films and started receiving lots of invites to lots of film screenings; multiple dozens in fact each year.

The reason I bring this up is because over the next year or two, I saw Michael Gambon perform in three feature films: *The Layer Cake, The Life Aquatic* and *Being Julia*. But he was not so mesmerizing. I was not so impressed.

Please excuse me, Sir Michael, with your 172 IMDB credits as of September 2023, and your knighthood from Queen Elizabeth II for services to drama, here I was, not that impressed with his performances in these movies.

Upon reflection, I was not that impressed by his on-screen performances because I had seen him on stage, in person, and he was brilliant. Very powerful. But I also think that there was another reason why I was not so impressed with his work on screen. He was *too big*, meaning I felt his acting was too theatrical. His acting was too much for the screen, especially when he was acting in the mid-shot and the close-up shots in these films.

I waited a while and watched him again in these films, as I had the DVDs at home (they call the DVDs that BAFTA members receive 'screeners'), and well, same again, I was not that impressed.

One could say, he was being *directed* that way and so it is the directors' fault that his performances were too big for the camera shots. If the three films were directed by the same director, one could say this. But this was not the case.

I felt Sir Michael was pushing his performance down the barrel of the camera a bit. I felt, watching him, that I didn't believe him. I could see him acting and felt he would be best in children's films and comical television shows, where we often see over-the-top and slightly pushed or forced acting from actors.

Ta da! Soon Sir Michael Gambon started appearing as Dumbledore in the *Harry Potter* movies.

An aside: Casting directors are smart at casting actors, aren't they? Of course, this is a rhetorical question.

In support of this introduction to on-screen acting, what you as an actor must learn to do is act through the eyes. You must learn to have the inner monologue or inner story or inner feelings going on, on your face. Most importantly, in your eyes and in the tone of your voice and you must trust that what you are doing is enough.

As an actor, if you push your work on screen, the more you push, the more you will either:

- Work in comedy
- Work in children's film and TV
- Work in a stylized television show where they want you to pull faces, think: Arrested Development, The Office, Up Pompeii with Frankie Howerd
- Do television commercials where they want you to pull faces
- Not make an impression at an audition
- Not book the job

In my humble opinion, Sir Michael Gambon is much better on screen nowadays. He has improved his work a lot since the early 2000s on TV and film.

I will have a lot to say on the topic of improving your work on screen in this book.

My point in discussing Sir Michael Gambon's film work in the early 2000s is this: even some of the finest actors in the world can be too big when acting on screen. Some of the most coveted actors in the world can be too big, or too theatrical and/or push too much.

Unless it is comedy, actors, please don't push. Don't overact. *Less is more on the screen for drama.*

Casting directors and directors need to know that they can trust you on screen. If they give you the job, they need to know that you will do well.

This is why the beginner, the actor with no film and television credits, generally struggles to book their first job. As booking your first job on screen will, generally, always be the hardest gig to get. American actresses (and sisters) Elle and Dakota Fanning booking lead roles in feature films, seemingly straight from nowhere, is definitely not the norm.

A couple of other important points.

Be aware that in this book I will utter clichés, I will generalize, I will stereotype. This is because I believe clichés, generalizations and stereotypes are in existence in our language and in our thinking and our behaviour because there is validity in them.

In my first book when I referred to gender, I used the word he and asked actors to just assume I meant she as well. In this second book I will reverse that. So, when I mention she, just assume I also mean he. I will also use the terms they and their.

Also, Americans please excuse me but I have used Australian and English spelling such as theatre and colour and not the standard American spelling of words.

I will also use the word teacher more so than coach. So Americans please, when I say teacher, please assume that I mean coach.

I'm so excited. Here we go!

Above: Paul running an Audition Preparation & Training class at the AIDA School in Hollywood, Los Angeles, in 2003 with student Charley Allen. The invited guest this night was casting director Melinda Gartzman (pictured above). Melinda has five nominations and one win at the Casting Society of America, USA, awards, and 30 IMDB credits as a casting director and 10 IMDB credits as Casting Department. Melinda's credits include television shows: Charlie's Angels, Falcon Crest and Knots Landing, as well as many feature films.

"After reading with all the students and watching their work on tape, I would like to say, the collective work of the actors in the group is the best audition tape that I have ever seen! These techniques work and it is a credit to Paul Parker and his teaching staff at AIDA."

Melinda Gartzman, Casting Director, Los Angeles, USA, 2003.

Prologue

Let's look at some of my personal experiences for a moment to help exemplify an important point.

Even though I worked and have film and television credits in the 1970s up to 2003, including work on *The Young and The Restless* for CBS television in Los Angeles, and I have won an on-camera award at a competition in Victoria, Australia, in 1998, I never quite had the same power or made the same impact as an actor on screen as I did on stage.

I have performed as an actor in over thirty theatre productions and I have always felt very comfortable on the stage.

These theatre experiences, and my experiences of auditioning for film, television and commercials, is what led me to study camera/on-screen acting and to be teaching it in great detail.

What was my biggest concern as an actor when I was in front of the camera? I didn't trust. I didn't trust that what I did would be enough on the screen. I often pushed. Especially if I really wanted a particular job.

Remembering I am Australian, here are a few television shows that I auditioned for with characters with dialogue in the USA. Noting, that I didn't book them. I've also listed the number of times that I auditioned for some of the shows:

- *The Shield* – three times
- *Battlestar Galactica* – three times
- *Alias* – twice
- *Ally McBeal* – once
- *Malcolm in the Middle* – once (call back, but didn't book)
- And some other shows

An aside: I wanted to list how many times I auditioned for the shows as I must have been doing some things right. They must have seen my talent.

Because if they didn't, they wouldn't have kept calling me back for more auditions.

Why didn't I book any of these shows? Maybe because I pushed. I didn't trust. I didn't relax enough. To be fair on myself, I also struggled with sounding standard American when talking in an American accent.

I also wanted it too much and this is not a healthy way to think.

The best way for you to get the most out of my teachings in this book, the best way for me to make an impact with you, is to:

- Draw your attention to the mistakes that I made as an actor
- Draw your attention to the mistakes my students have or do make
- Teach you the skills that I teach my actors
- This will include drawing your attention to the following:
- My philosophy of performing on screen
- My curriculum
- Actors you know doing great work
- Successful actors personifying in their work what I want you to do
- Hearing about some successful students of mine

If you see recognized actors and booking actors doing what I talk about, along with the education in this book, you will most likely change and/or start to learn how to do the things that I talk about; and do them much quicker, and with much more confidence.

My humble beginnings

I began my observations of actors acting on screen in 1979 while working on an Australian television show called *The Sullivans*.

Originally cast as an extra, as the time rolled on, I was given some dialogue. I worked on this television show for approximately four months in 1979 with Crawford Productions. While on set, in a cold and wet Melbourne winter, at the old Gasworks in Port Melbourne, we were all trying to emulate Changi Prison in Singapore.

While I was not acting on set, I would often stand as close as I could to the directors, who included Lex Van Os and Pino Amenta.

Due to the cold weather, and with us wearing very little clothing as Changi prisoners of war, most actors, wearing old army coats, were huddled together around large steel-drum fire pits, and drinking coffee or hot chocolate to keep warm. But I would stand (including often under an umbrella), and watch actors Steven Tandy, Norman Yemm and Richard Morgan perform in the mid-shots and the close-up shots. I'll never forget it.

An aside: I mentioned this to Steven Tandy in 2021 when we became Facebook friends and we shared a laugh or two.

My on-screen analysis grew from this point. I'm still learning. Every day's a school day they say.

In this book I would also like to address the self-doubt that actors have. The constant thought of, am I really good enough? This *am I really good enough* complex encourages actors to put a lot of pressure on themselves. It is not good thinking.

I will offer alternative ways to think on this subject as well as exercises that you as an actor can do that will help you shift the focus from your frustrations and doubts, to empower yourself and become analytical and practical and hopefully calm and centred.

I find I am always talking to the student about what goes on in their minds. So much so, that I say to students, what goes on in your mind, the thoughts that you have, will profoundly influence whether you work or not, whether you book a lot of work or not.

But firstly, a reminder from Book One, I teach in three main human condition areas. All three of these areas are of paramount importance in all of your acting, including your acting on screen.

My experiences as an actor, teacher and director have led me into forming these three main areas of teaching study. They are:

Psychology

- What's going on in the mind
- How to eliminate self-sabotage and procrastination
- How to have a clear mind

Physiology

- How the body works
- How to use the body with breath
- Breath, thought, image, voice connection with text

Physiognomy

- How to use the head, the face and the eyes, especially for the camera shots: mid-shot, medium close-up, the close-up and extreme close-up

My curriculum teaches in three main areas: Structure (subjects)

- Acting Techniques x five levels
- Australian Techniques – how to connect with text x eight
- Creating Characters x four
- Role Playing x two
- Improvisation x four
- Breath and Voice x eight
- Movement x two
- On Camera x eight
- Performing for the Frame x two
- Self-tapes x two
- Neutral Mask
- Performance
- Risk-taking x two
- Your Style Appeal x two
- Business Side of Acting x two

Making choices

- Scene study/scene analysis x four levels
- Background to scene and character x two
- Surroundings – the start/moment before
- Character choices – including wants, opinions, attitude, points of concentration

Let go, relax, trust, play, enjoy

- Audition Preparation and Training x four levels
- The right mindset to relax, trust, play and enjoy yourself in performance
- Audition Performance x four
- Taking the re-direction in an audition x two

I find that with my philosophy and curriculum, I give the actor the best training that I can. I am working with them from the beginning, all the way to the audition.

Of course, for my private students, this includes prepping them for the work after they have booked the job and then reviewing the work, once it airs on stage or screen.

Along this path in this book, if you enjoy my teachings and find them educational, and I know you will, well then, that will be great! Let's go, shall we?

And so, let's begin ...

Paul at the 2011 Academy Awards above and at the 2007 Academy Awards below. Both at the Kodak Theatre in Hollywood.

All Academy Awards photos were approved to appear in the book in January 2022, by Kristen Ray - Senior Specialist, Clearance. Academy of Motion Picture Arts and Sciences. 8949 Wilshire Blvd. Beverly Hills. CA 90211

Part 1
Theory

Chapter 1: Acting on Camera

I took on a new student in September of 2022. A student who was referred to me by a Los Angeles manager. This actor was also reading and resonating with my first book.

After about six weeks of training, the actor asked me to look at a self-tape audition that she had done for a film. Of course, I said yes. This actor has a profile in IMDB, with credits, has representation, a showreel and was auditioning weekly and sometimes booking work in the difficult and overcrowded actors' market of Los Angeles.

I started to watch her self-tape. I stopped the self-tape viewing after two seconds and made a note. I considered stopping the tape again several times before finally stopping the tape viewing at fifteen seconds in, and writing down six things that I didn't like or that the student didn't do that I think she should have done.

Here were the six things:

- Didn't do something at the start of the scene to help establish where she was and what she was doing (Americans call this: the moment before)
- Dressed in a way that was distracting – way too much cleavage was showing
- Did not know how or where to look in the frame
- Often looked up in the air, showing us the whites of her eyes
- Leaned forward fast towards the camera
- Often had her chin up in the air

I watched the rest of the scene and then added this to my notes:

- Lifted her shoulders nearly every time she spoke
- Spoke too loudly for a while
- Didn't listen strongly enough
- The pitch of her voice was higher than normal
- When she did greet someone else in the scene, she didn't know how to place them in the frame. In fact, she placed them out of the frame
- She had the person reading the other character's lines in the script, on the telephone, and not in the same place that she was in

Fortunately, this actor had transition in the scene. Emotional transition from neutral to anger to vulnerability. She also had reduced her head nodding (since starting classes with me), and was breathing through the mouth as she was taught by me.

I saw all that, and more, in her ninety-second audition self-tape for a real job. I gave the actor positive feedback and then said, if I was the casting director, or the director, I would have ascertained this about the actor:

- There was no sense of where the location of the scene was taking place
- The actor was not listening strongly enough
- Doesn't know how to use the frame for effect
- Doesn't know how to place other people in the frame
- Doesn't realize her job is to draw the camera in, not push down it
- Doesn't realize you do not move vertically fast towards the camera
- Doesn't realize that on screen we don't need to yell – there is always a microphone nearby
- Doesn't realize that lifting shoulders is often a sign of no training or certainly no classical training
- Doesn't realize a higher pitch of voice is not only not liked (unless in a sitcom or comical commercial), but is also often a sign of no training or certainly no classical training
- Basically, doesn't know how to perform to make an impact

I went on and said that I wouldn't give the actor the part as I was unsure of how they would go on set because they lacked on-camera/on-screen acting skills and technique.

Can you resonate with this self-tape at all?

I have just explained what I didn't like about this actor's audition and I will explain *why* I want you to do the things I want you to do in this book. I will teach you how to not do some of these things and how to do things better, so that you do make an impact in front of the camera and in your auditions.

Before I do, I need you to know that this type of audition tape performance that I watched is *common* with actors. Even some experienced booking actors make plain and simple mistakes like some of these listed above, and thus their actions could be affecting their careers in a negative way.

We are always sending messages by what we do and by what we don't do. What message do you think you are sending if you audition like I have described above? The answer is, the subliminal message you are sending is: you don't know what you are doing in the frame.

So, let's go address all these points, and more, through this book. Before I talk in depth about acting on camera, the first thing I feel compelled to talk about is this.

The waiting time game

Some actors want success too much. Their self-esteem is dependent on it. Early on, I was one of those actors myself. Try not to think and act like this. It is not good for your mental or physical health. You can come across as needy or a bit desperate. If this is the case, it will affect your mind and your preparation and most often, your performance as well.

Nothing improves an actor's confidence more than being paid for their work. Will you, or have you already, had the experience of *the waiting time game* before booking professional work?

As already stated, in 1979 I was cast in a television show in Melbourne called *The Sullivans*. Originally cast as an extra, I was eventually given a few lines. I was very young. I was lucky. I worked on the show for approximately four months. People would recognize me from television and talk to me when I was walking down the street. They would also talk to me in other places like, at school, or in supermarkets and say things to me like, "You're on television, aren't you?"

The reason I mention this is because most actors starting today do not have this luxury. Most actors today play the waiting time game. The game, for want of a better phrase, of the actor often thinking: *Will I make it? Will I book work? Will I have a career? Will someone pay me for my craft? Will my break come?*

This is a terrible time for actors. In their minds, anxiety, fear, hurt, frustration, jealousy and sometimes resentment towards the industry, all occasionally surface for the actor. I know this because it surfaces with some of my students.

In my first book I talk about the actor needing to have a clear thinking and confident mind when they go into an audition or do a self-tape for an audition. They can't have their fears, worries or anxieties going through their minds. And they can't keep thinking they want to control what is going on. They need to have prepared the best they can in the timeframe permitted, and then, let go, play, relax and trust, and be affected by what happens in the scene.

Actors are beautifully candid with me about their frustrations, anxieties and worries. I say *beautifully* because this is the best way for the teacher and student to operate together.

I trained actor Tarnue Massaquoi from 2003 to 2021. Originally in group classes in Hollywood and then later on my teaching tours to the USA, and even online via Skype and Zoom. Tarnue used to say to me all the time, "Paul will I work? Paul, will I succeed?" I used to always reply, "Tarnue you will work. You will be paid to act." I believed this based on the following: Tarnue's work ethic, his talent, the work he was producing in class, his smartness, his creativity and his commitment. As of the writing of this book, Tarnue Massaquoi has 59 credits on IMDB and has won an award. He had no credits on IMDB when I started training him in 2003.

Actors must learn to trust, learn to let go, learn to open themselves up to the universe and say, "It will come to me when I am ready". I will trust.

All the negative thoughts of "Will I make it, am I good enough, will someone pay me for my craft" etcetera, are a waste of time. The worst thing that will happen to you, to any actor, is you won't have a career. If that is the case, it was never meant to be. Just because you want it, doesn't mean you can have it.

But, with very good training, you can try your damn best to be in the field of play, shall we say, to have a chance to get what you want. Trust. Improve. Think positively. Wait calmly. When you find a very good teacher and you know your work is improving and you start to make real impact in auditions and with the skills you are learning and implementing, then stick with that.

Above: Paul teaching a student in Australia.

What is acting on screen?

Let's begin talking about acting on screen with a question and a definition. On-screen acting is acting on camera. Whenever I use the words acting on screen or acting on camera, I mean acting in front of the camera.

Acting on screen is an ability to be believable and watchable as a human being when we watch you back on television, in television commercials, in films, in the movie theatres or online, and also, online in internet web series or web films.

When I say *believable*, I mean, you look like you are experiencing what is happening to your character and the journey your character is on, and we are watching your performance and believing it. Believing it like it is happening in life. Even happening to us, some people say, as an audience often gets caught up in the emotion of a story.

In the end, no matter which way you look at it, the audience makes two very simple, but profound, decisions about your work on screen: Do I want to watch you? And do I believe you?

No two humans are the same. Not even twins. Hence, some actors need to do less when in front of the camera. Some actors need to do more. It all depends on the individual. Some actors have habits or tension that needs removing. Some actors do not.

Lots of actors underact and do very little and don't look captivating or exciting to watch. Lots of actors overact and don't realize that less is more. They push or telegraph the points they want to make or do. With less is more, it is the *internal goings on* with the actor that help make us want to watch you. It's the *internal stuff* that draws the camera in.

As an actor, if you don't learn how to perform in the frame, make impact in the frame and not overact in the frame, you won't work that much professionally in film and television. It is that simple.

I teach within the five most important shots for actors. I want all my students to perform for the shots, within the frame and implement my on-camera acting techniques. I have no doubt that by doing these things, this will help them book work.

I say to my students, to what extent do we, as an audience, want to watch you? And to what extent do we, as an audience, believe you? As just said, the answer to these two questions will profoundly influence whether you work on screen or not, whether you book work or not, whether you will be a film or television working actor or star or not.

Your job is to make the percentages of watchability and believability be as high as they can be. Such as, nine or ten out of ten for watchability and nine or ten out of ten for believability.

Chapter 1: Acting on Camera | 33

Acting on screen is made to look easy by the movie and television stars. It is made to look so easy that so many people want to do it. So many people think they can do it.

Sadly, for most, they won't become major booking stars who only live off their acting work. This is because, generally speaking, acting on screen for most people is not easy. It is a craft. You need skills. You need to develop techniques, you need to know where to look, you need to know how big you can be, how loud you can be. You need to learn to perform for the different genres and styles of films and television and most importantly, the different camera shots. Then, you must develop clever ways of using the frame as the camera lens looks at you. What you do in that frame is paramount. Especially in the medium close-up, the close-up and the extreme close-up shots. More on the shots soon.

Actors need to develop a profound sense of the following when acting in front of the camera; especially in the close-up or in the extreme close-up:

- Stillness; especially of the head
- An ability to act through the eyes. Meaning, get your thoughts across through the eyes
- Develop different vocal tonal sounds and have an understanding of how to make impact with their voice
- Learn to control their facial expressions
- Learn to predominately look sideways as opposed to up and down
- Really, really listen
- Know where to look
- Know how to look
- Know how to cross the screen for effect
- Know how to multi-cam perform
- Know how to perform for the different shots
- Know when to move

An internal process

Acting for the screen in drama is an internal thinking process and an internal implementation. Meaning, it is the internal stuff going on that draws us, the viewer, in.

Think of the brooding leading man: Al Pacino – Robert De Niro – Russell Crowe – Harrison Ford – Marlon Brando.

Acting for screen in comedy is much more outgoing and exaggerated. The comic actor's work is captured easily by pulling the camera frame back. Whether you watch I Love Lucy from the 1950s or *Will & Grace* or *The Big Bang Theory* from today, the camera shots are much wider. These said shows are full of full-body shots, and two-person shots and group shots. Close-ups are a rarity.

What actors need to do is hone their skills and be able to perform in *front* of the camera. The camera captures our truth, or what looks like the truth, our magical moments, our nuances of human behaviour and our subtext. The latter preferably without the audience knowing what the subtext is.

In a generalized world, some people say the camera loves you, is ambivalent about you or dislikes you. This is an injustice because no matter how wonderful you are as an actor, if you fall into the *camera doesn't like you* category, this will, most definitely, affect your ability to get work in front of it.

Of course, production values can help you look good. Such as, by having specific lighting, or shooting you through panty hose (think Cybil Shepherd in the US television show *Moonlighting*), or, shooting you from specific directions or angles or by having you shot in wider shots as opposed to close-ups.

To help you look better on camera, the camera can even be as specific as: having the camera slightly move on you at the same time that you *move as you* act. The camera often does this if you have a false or lazy eye or an eye stigma. Think actor Forest Whitaker from the film *The Last King of Scotland*, for example. The camera slightly moves on this actor in close-ups, as the actor moves his head, so he doesn't look cock-eyed.

The camera does not lie is a cliché widely used, but I think there is a lot of truth in it. If you are being shot in a mid-shot or a close-up: if you are not totally tuned into the scene and/or not tuned into listening and interacting, the camera will pick it up in your eyes, as well as in your slight facial and body movements.

Genre and styles

An actor must always ask herself, what is the genre? What is the style of any particular show or film?

Examples of different genres and styles are:

Film

- Horror
- Romantic comedy
- Drama
- Period drama
- Comedy

Television

- Sitcom
- Drama
- Soap opera
- TV serial drama
- TV serial comedy

Some examples of styles are:
- Action
- Detective
- Love story/romance
- Science fiction
- For children (like from a Disney production)
- Farcical
- Educational
- Imaginative

As discussed in my first book, your preparation should be different for both comedic and dramatic work. One example of this is having the awareness that our breathing is different when we do comedy as opposed to when we act doing drama.

With comedy, you breathe into your upper chest and your shoulders and you generally can, and will, move quickly. The camera is generally full studio shots, or two- or three-person full-body shots. There are very few mid-shots and close-ups in comedy.

But with drama, you, preferably, and certainly with classical training, will breathe into your diaphragm, all around into your back and into your genital, pubic bone areas. Your pitch of voice is much deeper in the body too, and you often have to draw on your emotions and show vulnerability. These emotions are accessible by how deep you breathe into the body.

As said, you must also want us to want to watch you, hence your habits, the things you naturally do. Often, your habits need to be curbed, or restricted, or eliminated from your behaviour. I put these things under the heading of the word physiognomy.

Physiognomy

Physiognomy relates to what you do with your body, your face and your eyes. All as a part of your manner, your personality, your demeanour and your character. Physiognomy is also a word that I like to choose when we look at what you do, do with your head, face and eyes as an actor in any given scene.

Looking as pretty or handsome as possible on screen will help you get work. Looking pretty or handsome in two different ways.

Firstly, *pretty* in your general looks. While I acknowledge this thought of looking *pretty or handsome*, I think it is more important for me, and for you, that I talk about the *training of you on screen and* give you the skills for acting on camera.

Secondly, *pretty* in the sense of the way we, the audience, look at you, and see what you are doing in the frame. Preferably having what you do look appealing and not a distraction.

I grew up in Australia where, generally, you will get acting work if you are very good; much more so than if you are simply lucky enough to be born looking pretty or handsome. I am sure this is one of the reasons why cosmetic surgery is nowhere near as common in Australia than it is in, let's say, America, with actors.

And so, the actor has to be conscious of what they do on screen. Especially in their preparation and their training. They must also have to be open to change or alter or even eliminate some of these things relating to their manner, to be able to work and work consistently. All to help them look better on the screen. You could call this: *be more watchable.*

The judge of what the actor does is the viewer: the casting director, the director and ultimately the viewer on television, online or in the movie theatres.

Knowing what is good or applicable and what could be altered or eliminated, often creates a paradox. An actor must learn to let go, enjoy, play, relax and trust their work while performing, and yet, they must also know how to:

- Perform for the camera shot
- Perform for the genre

- Perform for the style of the show
- Perform as the character
- Perform for the particular role that they are cast in. For example, are you the series regular, the guest star or the co-star or the five-and-under actor in television? Or are you the lead actor – carrying the film, or an actor in a supporting role?

Many actors find it difficult and/or challenging to eliminate some manner or natural ways of behaviour that don't look good on screen. Actors must learn to work on these things that the camera does not like. This is where the teacher comes in.

How animated is your face?

Acting on screen is very different from acting on stage. This is because, on stage your aim is to be seen and heard by everyone at the back of the theatre. Whether the audience is in a small hall, a large theatre or even a concert hall, the actor's aim is to be seen and heard from the front row to the back row.

However, on screen, the microphone can be just out of the camera shot to catch the actor's voice, and the camera shot can be very invasive. Meaning, the camera shot could be an extreme close-up, where it focuses on the eyes or the eyes and the mouth only.

Hence, the actor needs to be still. The actor needs to be calm. The actor needs to have a relaxed body and head and face, in these close-up shots. The actor needs to learn to act through the use of their eyes and with the tone of their voice and learn how to use the frame in these different shots; all with an awareness of genre and style of the show.

Then, they have to, if they can, take into account, or have some awareness of, the style of each director who is directing them. I note, however, that this is not always achievable.

The closer the camera comes in on you, the clearer it sees everything that you do.

Think of watching a close-up of an actor's face on the big screen in the movie theatre. When in a close-up, if you lift your eyebrows up, according to Michael Caine's book on acting for the screen (which I have not read by the way), you, as an audience member, are watching an eyebrow lift of ten feet on the movie theatre screen, and if you, as an actor, keep doing this, it could very well become a distraction.

I agree with this. Hence, as a part of what I call physiognomy, if an actor's face is too animated, I ask her to tape her forehead. If actors cannot control their eyebrows from lifting every time they talk, or, they cannot stop frowning or lifting and wrinkling up their forehead, I encourage them to cut pieces of tape and put the tape on their foreheads.

In Australia, this kind of tape is called Scotch tape, which is clear and non-invasive. Many stores have it in the USA, and it's widely available in Australia too. Actors that I have been training around the world have been wearing tape on their foreheads for as long as it takes to control their forehead distractions. I have been teaching this technique for well over twenty years, and it works. The tape costs very little to buy.

I encourage actors to wear the tape on their foreheads as much as possible, in acting class, when at home, when driving in the car.

What the taping of the forehead does is let you know every time you frown or lift your eyebrows, particularly when you talk. By letting you know this, you learn to control these facial muscles and make the minor adjustments necessary to help you be more watchable on screen. You are more watchable on screen because your face is not so animated in the mid-shot and the close-up shots.

The reason actors work on this is because many of them cannot control these facial movements. There are always exceptions to the rule, but generally speaking, the best actors control these facial muscles, especially when the camera comes closer.

A very successful actor who frowns every time he talks is Leonardo DiCaprio, and yet, when in an extreme close-up in, say, the feature film

The Revenant, he has relaxed these muscles, so the stress tensed lines are not as prominent on the screen.

This is one of the main reasons many actors get Botox injections. They get Botox injections because they want to control their wrinkling forehead or the constant use of lifting their eyebrows when they talk. Don't get cosmetic surgery – I suggest you buy the tape instead.

The mark

Standing on the mark means simply just that. Standing on the mark. At an audition for film, television or a commercial, the person auditioning the actor gets the actor to stand on a mark that they have placed on the floor. This is usually a piece of black tape. But it could be a small book or even a piece of paper.

The reason the person casting actors does this is because they want to see what the actor does in the frame. They set the frame before actors stand in front of it. By having a mark to stand on, when the audition work is watched back, all the actors on camera skills, or lack thereof, are seen within the same camera frame.

The other reason there is a mark on the floor is to let actors know, generally, that that is where they want you to be. Not wondering off around the room. Not walking towards the camera. Not walking out of shot. Hence, an actor should ask, "What is my frame?" or "What's my shot please?" every time they audition in front of a camera.

Another reason casting people ask the actor to stand on the mark is because this is what actors have to do when on set. Walk to this mark, stand, then turn and walk to this mark, so the camera gets you in the shots that the director wants. You generally always do rehearsals for this before the camera starts rolling.

The frame

The frame is the whole picture, everything we see, when we watch a film or television or a commercial production. Whether we are watching actors on the big screen in movie theatres or on the small screen on television at home, what we see in the frame is what we see.

As an actor, your job is to light up that frame. Have us, or make us, want to watch you and believe you. It is that simple, but it is not easy to do.

I started analyzing actors using the frame when I had acting workshops with my peers in Melbourne, Australia, in the 1990s.

In a group full of actors, I often became the main person critiquing the other actor's work when we would play our recorded scenes back on television from a handy-cam camcorder and from VHS cassettes. This was, of course, well before mobile/cell phones.

If an actor had an audition, they would bring their audition scripts to the workshop. My peers started to book work with my direction from these workshops. I soon started to realise what worked and what didn't work. What looked good and what didn't look good.

I'll digress for a moment. Like all my peers, I really wanted to get a gig on the Australian television show *Blue Heelers*. It was my dream.

After I auditioned for the show twice and didn't get a call back, I asked my agent to ask the casting directors why I wasn't making an impact in my auditions.

The casting directors' reply was, via my agent, and I paraphrase, "Paul just doesn't look or sound like a person who would live in a country town. In addition, Paul does this swivel thing in the chair that is effeminate. We don't care if he is gay, but he can't come across as gay on screen – he does a bit, and they're no effeminate men who live in county towns in Australia."

An aside: This was the 1990s!

So, at this time, I went and bought a camera and looked for the swivel in the chair thing and my effeminate disposition. I did see it.

After watching actors in the frame in *The Sullivans* television show in 1979, along with acting workshops with my peers, this was my next stage of analyzing what actors are doing in the frame.

Generally speaking, especially today – casting directors and directors are never going to admit this – but actors, sometimes you are not going to get a job simply because you look gay, or because you have some *manner or ways of behaviour*, for want of a better phrase, that are not suitable for the style of the show or the part that you are going for.

This line of thinking basically applies for anything that you do in the frame, that the audience, via the camera, doesn't like or doesn't want. A casting director or director will generally not tell you this to your face, but these are the facts.

When I moved to Sydney in 1998, I studied screen acting more. I worked a lot with actor Mark McCann – a working actor with 40 IMDB credits. I found myself analyzing and coaching him. Improving his performances.

Then, when I moved to Los Angeles in 2000, it wasn't long before I was doing it even more. Eventually, my school AIDA opened in June of 2002 on Santa Monica Boulevard in Hollywood. I'd hit the big league – as a Hollywood acting teacher! I clearly recall, students kept telling me, even then, phrases like, "Wow, you are unbelievably perceptive about what we are doing in the frame and with our on-camera work overall."

At this time, I started to create terminology for acting on camera. Such as: the V for the frame, passing the baton, subtext on screen, facial expressions, nuances of human behaviour, the power of listening and risk taking, etcetera. I introduced the concept of physiognomy and started to search for actors' work on screen in film and television that personified what I was teaching.

As the years rolled on with my school, I moved to Manhattan, New York, and started a new branch of my school AIDA in April of 2004. I began to create even more on-camera terminology, skills and activities. Then

I opened more branches with AIDA, and I taught on-camera classes in San Francisco and Chicago.

I would introduce actors to their manner, their behaviour, their speed of movement, where their eyes were going. I introduced the importance of the different camera shots and how everything was dependent on the type of shot that you were in.

Meaning, your speed of movement, how far and wide you could look in the frame or off to the side of the frame and where to look and not look. All of this was an evolving thing based on the genre, the style of the show and the camera shots.

Actors started to book work almost immediately after I started teaching them.

And so, we come to you. What do you do in the frame as an actor? Do you have any idea what to do in the frame? Are you aware of your own manner or ways of behaviour? Do you move fast or slow in life? Are you animated in life? If so, with both your head and face or just your face? Are you animated with your body? All these things must be taken into consideration when acting in the frame.

You know, I must digress for just a moment to make two important points.

When I teach on-camera classes or workshops at other acting schools, be it, in Australia, the USA or Japan, including schools that call themselves, "on-camera" or "on-screen schools", well, I continually see actors who have not been spoken to, and given exercises and education, on what to do and what not to do, like I am going to do in this book.

With these other schools, and I am generalizing, I clearly see, many, sometimes even most of the actors in the class, dramatically acting all over the place and overacting in the frame. When I stop them and tell them what they are doing wrong, or letting them know that they are too big, they usually say things to me like, "Wow, no one has said that to me.

Why am I four or five months into a year program and the teachers are letting me get away with that?"

At these points in time, I bite my lip and continue to teach, as it is not my school. Fortunately, at my school AIDA and in my classes, I do tell actors everything and do teach them all the skills about performing on camera.

In support of this, comments like the one here that I am about to say below are common. A young Australian male, early twenties, said to me in February 2023, after his second class on Skype with me, "I have just learnt more from you about acting in sixty minutes than I learnt in a whole year doing that on camera course at ____" (let's just leave out the name of the other school).

The camera shots

The most important and powerful shots that an actor must learn to perform in are:

- ¾ shot. The camera is from the knees up to just above the head
- Mid-shot. Belly button up, to just above the head
- MCU (medium close-up). Chest or breastbone up, to just above the head
- Close-up. Shoulders up, to just above the head
- Extreme close-up. There are many variables with this shot, because it could be any shot of parts of the face, but generally speaking, the camera frame includes the area from just above the eyes to just below the lips

The more watchable and believable you are in these camera shots, the more you will work, it is that simple.

The general rule for auditioning is:

- Commercial auditions most often record the actor in a ¾ camera shot
- Film and television auditions most often record the actors work in a mid-shot or medium close-up shot
- Self-tapes are generally mid-shot or medium close-up shots

When the work has been produced and aired or screened, comedy is generally full coverage of the set (meaning the whole performance space without the lights or things that clearly show that it is a set), two-person or more, full-body and ¾ shots.

Drama utilizes all the shots. Especially the mid-shot and the close-ups.

The editor

As a part of acting on screen, I would like all actors to think, what will an editor be looking for in my work? What would an editor like to see? I say this because an editor's job is to cut the story together and put the best compilation of the actor's work in the finished product of the telling of the story.

Consequently, if you, the actor, present yourself so extremely well in the frame, you give yourself a better chance of having more of your work in the finished product. Please never forget this.

More of you in the finished product turns into being seen more in the production, meaning seen more on television or in the movie theatres. This usually leads to more opportunities, more work and ultimately more chance of a career in the film and television business.

Performing in the V

If I was to choose a single training exercise that has had the most impact with all my students when performing in front of the camera, it is my creation of the V. What I like to call, Performing in the V.

To help you understand the concept of the V, I would like you to think of the letter V. You are the letter V. If you put your arms out in front of you, your arms are the two lengths of the letter V, your body is the back of the letter V.

I created the V in 2002 while teaching on camera through my school AIDA in the States. The creation of the V was most likely influenced by my theatre training and performing, where I was always told by directors to act to the back of the theatre. To act out towards the audience, so they could hear and see me clearly and to not act to the wings or to the stage floor or up towards the lights on the ceiling of the theatre.

The wings are the two sides of a stage, proscenium arch stage or any other type of stage, where parts of the set are placed and this is also where the actors' entrances and exits generally occur. If you look there, you are turning your head sideways and an audience is seeing you in profile. Also, an actor's face cannot be seen clearly if they look towards the stage floor or the ceiling.

Your voice is going in that direction too. An actor's voice cannot reach the back of the theatre too well if their face is looking towards the floor or up to the stage ceiling.

So, to perform in the V, I ask the actor to stand and put their arms out in front of them, hence making the letter V with their body. I then ask them to alter how wide they put their arms out in front of them, based on the most important camera shots:

- If a ¾ shot, I ask the actor to stand on the mark and put their arms out approximately 2 metres (about 6 and a half feet) apart
- If a mid-shot, I ask the actor to stand on the mark and put their arms out, approximately 1 metre (just over 3 feet) apart
- If a medium close-up, I ask the actor to stand on the mark and put their arms out approximately three-quarters of a metre (about 2 and a half feet) apart
- If a close-up, I ask the actor to stand on the mark and put their arms out approximately half a metre (about 1 and a half feet) apart
- If an extreme close-up, I ask the actor to stand on the mark and put their two thumbs on their cheeks and have their hands approximately one-quarter of a metre (about 10 inches) apart

As already said, the mark or *standing on the mark* means standing where the casting director asks you to stand and it usually is where they have put tape or something similar on the floor for you to stand on.

I ask the actor to hold their arms still. Then the actor must move their head and their face within their arm widths. If they move their head or face out of their arm widths, they are moving their head and face outside of their V.

I then do exercises with all the actors in all these shots. I give them text of saying *blah, blah, blah,* simply so the actor doesn't need to focus on what they are saying, but focus on moving their head and face, from side to side, horizontally, within their arm widths. In other words, within their V.

Once they do this well, I give the actor a script and ask them to perform their dialogue while looking within the V.

What influences how far the actor puts their arms out in the V? It depends on the camera shot. The wider the shot, the wider the actor can look and move their upper body, head and face. The closer the shot, the less the actor can look and move their upper body, head and face.

I also talk to the actor about the speed with which they should move their head, face and eyes. The closer the camera comes in, the slower they must move and the less they must move.

In an extreme close-up, for example, with fingers on their cheeks, the general extreme close-up shot has the camera lens just above the forehead of the actor at the top of the frame and just below the bottom lip at the bottom of the frame. In this shot the actor does not move their body at all. They do not move their head at all. They simply move their eyes from side to side, when applicable, but, and importantly, slowly in the frame.

These exercises are the start of teaching an actor how to learn to perform within the frame.

In closing on this exercise, once an actor can do this well, and adhere to it when they perform for me in class or in their self-tapes for casting jobs, I then say, now you know the general rule, try to follow it, but, if your head and face are in *profile* in front of the camera for a while, it will be okay.

This is because having your head and face in profile, for let's say, a little bit at the start of the scene, will give you variety when performing in the frame. But, as an overall rule, try to look within the V most of the time. Especially for your auditions.

When it is a self-tape, you set the camera shot either where you want it to be or where you are asked to put it by the casting director. If it is from the casting director, it is usually in the brief (the information) that they have given you.

When you go for an audition in person, you simply ask, "What is my frame today?" or "How am I being framed?" When the casting director tells you, you adjust your performance accordingly. In fact, most of my actors say this if the casting director or director asks them, "Why do you want to know what frame you are in?" My students say, "Because I will adjust my performance accordingly."

When on set, if you can, ask the director of photography what your frame is.

Over the years, dozens of students have told me that following this general rule of performing in the V has profoundly changed their performances on camera.

I still get email messages every year from former students, some from many years ago, saying things like this: "Hi Paul, so I just shot a film and the director said to me, wow you know how to perform in the frame. You do it so well. I replied to them saying, that's my Aussie acting coach Paul Parker in my head, reminding me of the power of performing in the V. thanks Paul."

An aside: If you Google me and my school AIDA, you will see on YouTube a recording of a class from Hollywood where over twenty actors in a class are with me practising performing in the V.

Looking sideways

There are many things that actors do on camera that are contrived. Actors do these things simply to look their best in front of the screen and to improve their on-screen time in the editing room.

But there are also some things that we do in front of the camera that are a copy of what we do in real life. Here is an example of one. Looking sideways. Looking off in the general direction where we think the person or a place or a thing is, is common in human behaviour. For example:

Person:
"Ahh yes, I'm going to go see Betty" – we look off in the direction where we think Betty is now or where she lives.

Place:
"I'll meet you in San Francisco tomorrow" – we look off in the direction where we think San Francisco is in relation to where we are now.

Thing:
"If you don't do as I ask, I'll go get my diary and prove to you what was said" – we look off in the direction of where we think the diary is.

Nearly all of the best working actors in the world have taught themselves to look sideways when they want to look away when in front of the camera: especially in the medium close-up, the close-up or the extreme close-up shots. They have learnt this, as opposed to always looking off camera, out of frame, or looking down or up.

Whether it is to think, as a reaction to what is said to them, or because they mention a person, place or thing, and look off in reference to where that person or place or thing is, they have learnt the importance and the power of looking sideways when performing on screen.

How much they look sideways, as opposed to up or down or off screen, is dependent on the actor. But the best actors, the most successful actors, have learnt that looking sideways helps keep their face, most importantly, their eyes and their mouth, within the frame; especially in the medium close-up, the close-up and extreme close-up camera shots.

This is another skill the actor needs to learn. Like all things that I talk about in this book, I teach the actor how to do this through exercises, viewings and reminders.

Try to keep your eyes and mouth in the frame as much as possible, in all the shots, in all the takes, and this will lead to more screen time, more work, more chances of making it big in the world of film and television acting.

As a general rule, when you mention another person who is not in the scene or a place or a thing, look sideways, but keep your eyes in the frame in the shot. How do you know how far you can move your face and eyes and keep yourself in the shot?

Well, if it is a self-tape, you know what the camera shot is because you set the camera and you are going to adhere to the V. In an audition you know what the camera shot is because you asked the casting director before you started the scene. On set, you ask the director of photography, the DOP, "What is my frame please?"

In fact, your best friend, the person you should try and become best mates with, with open communication when on set, is the camera person. Sometimes, like with soap operas or recorded live shows, because you are indoors in a studio, you cannot get that opportunity to get to know your DOP, but in film, and in a lot of television, you generally can.

Your look, your manner, the sound of your voice

Verbal communication

I would like you to think about animation films and television for a moment. Yep, cartoons.

What animation films do you like? Specifically what voices do you like to listen to in films or television shows?

Let's look at a couple of films.

Toy Story:

Did you like the voice of the character *Buzz Lightyear*? Did you like the voice of the character *Woody the Sheriff*? Did you like the voice of the character *Bo Peep*?

I'm sure you did. Well, what if I was to tell you the actor with the voice of *Buzz Lightyear* was a series regular on television for many years. At one point in time, that person, that actor, that voice, was in one of the most popular television shows of an era: in a TV show called *Home Improvement*. That's actor Tim Allen with 55 IMDB credits.

Woody the Sheriff's voice was done by one of the most famous Everyman actors that there is working today (more on *Everyman* in another chapter). That's actor Tom Hanks with 96 IMDB credits.

Bo Peep, that's actor Annie Potts with a whopping 110 IMDB credits.

The Lion King:

Did you like character *Simba's* voice? That's Matthew Broderick with 85 IMDB credits. *Shenzi the Hyena*, that's Whoopi Goldberg with 205 IMDB credits.

How popular are the *Sing* 1 & 2 animation movies? Reese Witherspoon's voice as *Rosita* is not only very enjoyable to hear; her singing is fantastic too. Reese Witherspoon has 68 IMDB credits as of September 2023.

Then there's non-animation:

Star Wars:
Did you like *Darth Vader's* voice in *Star Wars*? That's James Earl Jones with 188 IMDB credits.

The Elephant Man:
Did you like the Elephant Man's voice in *The Elephant Man*? That's John Hurt, with a whopping 213 IMDB credits.

Actors do get cast because of the quality and likeability of their voices. An audience wants to listen to their voice. We can't see them, for a lot of them are in animation, and yet, we love their voices, we want to hear their voices.

If you have never thought about the importance of your voice, please now do so. The quality of your voice will absolutely affect your acting career.

In my first book I talk about voice extensively and give vocal exercises, and link your voice with breath, and with technique.

Non-verbal communication

I would now like you to think about films and television that you like. We can't control what anyone else will think; people will remember what they want to remember and will watch what they want to watch.

Who do you like to watch? What movie stars or leading or recurring actors do you want to watch or look at? Specifically, what is it about their face or their body that you like?

Let's look at a couple of films.

Thelma & Louise:
Most people that I mention this film to, especially women, don't talk about the character J.D., the Cowboy, in this film. They generally say: "Brad Pitt. Gorgeous, a great body", etcetera. The movie was shot over

thirty years ago now, and this actor, Brad Pitt, has 87 IMDB credits. People just want to watch him.

Gone with the Wind:

People talk about Clark Gable with 82 IMDB credits. People just want to watch him too.

Then there's Harrison Ford in *Star Wars* and *Raiders of the Lost Ark* – 87 IMDB credits. People just want to watch him too.

I could go on and on. Some people are just popular because of what they look like and what they do with their faces and bodies in the frame, on screen.

I'll digress for a moment. Watchability is one reason actors get cosmetic surgery, especially in the USA, as said already. They want to be more watchable. They want to be watched. They know their looks and their body will influence their careers. So, they get liposuction, collagen in their upper lip, breasts, peck, bum and chest implants. They constantly work out in the gym, too.

Your face and your body are going to influence your career. This is why a generalization like *she is so pretty* is going to influence your career. The prettier you are in life, generally, the prettier you are going to look on screen.

I remember meeting Ewan McGregor and Josh Hartnett in person after a Golden Globes one night at a Paramount Pictures party event, in the Beverly Hilton Hotel in Los Angeles, and I thought to myself, wow, they look so pretty, so handsome.

Simply, without you even knowing, your career is going to be influenced not only by your skills, but by your face, your body and your voice.

Not everyone is going to make it; sorry to say. Before there's any training, your career is going to be influenced by the likeability of your face, your body and your voice.

Do I want to watch you? Do I believe you?

As mentioned, *working in front of the camera* falls into one of the categories of, Do I want to watch you? The higher the number out of ten, the more we are going to employ you. It's that simple.

Do I believe you? That's where I come in. Your training will improve your believability on screen.

The eyes and mouth and lips and use of your voice

An audience doesn't generally notice, but once the camera comes to a mid-shot or to a closer shot, the audience members are watching the eyes and the mouth.

Once we get to act in a mid-shot or a closer shot, the number one thing we look at on the screen is the eyes.

The number two thing we look at on the screen is the lips. In class I jokingly like to call lips the 'Angelina Jolies' because she has such luscious lips and they simply look so good on the screen.

The number three thing that we are aware of on the screen relates to the voice: the tone, the volume, the pitch, the pacing and the pausing of the voice.

Actors must consequently learn to act through the eyes and with the tone of the voice that comes through and out of their mouth; especially in the most important camera shots listed already. They can also use their lips to great effect too.

The eyes

As said, the most important thing an actor must learn to do when acting on camera is to learn how to act with their eyes. What is going on in their minds should be displayed though the eyes. Although many thousands of actors do this, it is no better personified than by actor Al Pacino.

It's vital for your eyes to let the audience know, through the camera lens, what is going on – or what is going on that is not being said – and how you feel that links to the very essence of your character. The very essence of your vulnerabilities, your strengths, your power, your subtext, your insecurities, your deceits, your loves and your hates, all the things you are trying to do with your character. All these things should be expressed through your eyes.

This is far easier said than done, of course.

To help you act through the eyes I ask you to try this exercise. Stand in front of the mirror, in a close-up shot, and try to put the following looks in your eyes. If your face joins in expressing the following words, a little, that is okay, but try to do it with your eyes.

Practise these words:

- Love
- Hate
- Jealousy
- Studious
- Confused
- Insecure
- Powerful
- Lazy
- Tired
- Angry
- Lust
- Annoyed
- Grumpy
- Lying
- Furious
- Shocked
- Repulsed
- Innocent

Well done. That's a good start. No matter what you are saying, if you can show in your eyes the feelings conveyed by the words listed above, it will serve you well in most scenes.

The mouth and lips

I don't profess or promote cosmetic surgery of any kind. But I know what an audience looks at, and what a camera likes, when the camera starts to come closer in on the actor. Do you have nice lips? Do you have a prominent or appealing upper lip?

On set, a productions make-up artist often draws upper lip pencil lines on the actors' face. (Television studios do the same with presenters appearing on screen.) Sometimes they even fill these lines in with lipstick to help the actor look better when on screen. This is because filling in-between the drawn make-up pencil lines will help it look like the actor has a nice lush upper lip.

Believe it or not, having good lips, especially your upper lip, is a definite advantage to the screen actor. Especially for women.

A lot of American actors, living in Los Angeles in particular, know or have knowledge of the importance of their lips on screen as collagen fattens their lips or lip.

This is one of the reasons why many actors put collagen in their upper lips. They do this to help themselves look better, more attractive, more alluring and more watchable on screen.

They do this to improve their percentage in the *do we want to watch* you category. For these people, and I'm generalizing, they think the more lip the better. The more lip the more they will work.

Please think of actors Angelina Jolie and Julia Roberts now. These two women naturally have very good-looking upper lips. Apparently, I'm told, actor Vince Vaughn put collagen in his upper lip before the film *Wedding Crashers*. Many actors simply copy what other actors are doing.

African Americans and Asians have an advantage over Caucasians in this area. A generalization I know, but true, as they generally have prominent good-looking upper lips.

The use of your voice

Actors must learn how to use the tone of the voice that comes through and out of their mouth.

An experienced stage actor has such an advantage over an inexperienced stage actor in this area because they have learnt how to use their voice for effect, such as the best use of tone and flavour and pitch, and how to always be heard. Then the stage actor's biggest challenge is learning how to bring down the volume and not to over use their use of tones and expressions when on screen. For some, their diction needs relaxing, too, as a beautifully spoken voice for theatre is not so essential for film and television.

The biggest challenge for the non-theatre actor is to develop the power and importance of their voice on screen. This is in the area of tone. I like to call the tone, *the flavour*, as this is the screen actor's second most important asset behind the looks in the eyes and on the face.

As the camera comes closer, we, the audience, are watching the actor's eyes and, most importantly, the mouth as they speak. An actor doesn't need to be loud – the microphone is nearby, just out of shot. An actor needs to learn to use their tone in variable ways, all to help them get screen time.

The more we like your voice, the more we will want to listen to it. As said, I talk extensively about the voice and the breath supporting the voice in Book One. I suggest you read it. I suggest you develop your awareness of tone, pitch, pacing, pausing and volume, and play around with text in these areas.

Listening

I say to actors, acting begins with two words – breath and listening. Where do you breathe to and from in your body, and how well do you listen?

Listening is one of the best ways to notice the differences between a professional actor and an amateur actor. Professional actors at the highest levels *really* listen. Amateur actors wait for their cue. What do you do?

And if you are listening, are you listening well enough? There is an expression in Australia that says *listen like a hawk*, as hawks, like most animals, have very good listening skills. Much stronger than humans.

Actors must listen like a hawk. They must do so because the camera will show us if they are not. The camera will show us if they are only listening a little or stepping in and out and/or pretending or acting that they are listening.

Actors not listening well enough manifest into things not sounding and looking right when an actor responds to another actor on screen. On stage, you can possibly get away with it. On camera, once we move to a mid-shot or closer, you cannot.

For example, we hear in the tone of the responding actor's voice, or we see in the look on their face and in their eyes, that they didn't pick up on the way the previous line was said to them. For example, they didn't hear the angst or desperation or hurt in the other character's voice and consequently, didn't respond accordingly.

Or, because they weren't listening closely enough, they didn't hear in the tone of the voice the invitation to come closer or react in a certain way, to the line that was delivered from the other character.

And as already said, we see how well the actor is listening in many ways, most especially through their eyes.

There are many different kinds of listening. There is listening for what you want in a scene. There is listening for the sounds that are coming out at you from others. There is listening for subtle changes in tone, pitch, volume and pausing. There is listening when being in a state of anticipation. There is listening *acting* because you have to pretend that you do not know the lines that are coming out at you, and there is listening to your own voice and sounds.

Try to do as many of these as possible. Most importantly, simply listen. If you do, and you are in front of a camera, you will see that your eyes boggle or dance or move slightly.

Not everybody's eyes dance or boggle or move a little when they are listening; but most people's do. The camera and in turn the audience subconsciously love this.

An aside: US actor Anne Heche has *eyes that boggle and dance* more than any other actors' eyes that I have seen on screen. UK actor Sally Hawkins comes a close second.

I have exercises that I do with actors to help them concentrate and listen.

Firstly, I talk to them about their diet. I encourage them to not drink caffeine or sugar or power uplifting drinks prior to class or at an audition or a job. As all these drinks can affect an actor's concentration and listening skills.

Then I ask actors to let me know if they have any mental health issues and/or if they are on any medication.

For example, ADD – Attention Deficit Disorder, also called ADHD – Attention Deficit Hyperactivity Disorder – could affect the actor's ability to listen and have a clear mind if they are not on some sort of medication.

I write down and do research on medications and how they can affect the human being. That's because some medications affect concentration, mood and even tiredness. Some medications make it harder for people to sleep at night.

I talk about the importance of listening and then spend time with the actor in class asking them to close their eyes and listen to the sounds inside the room and then outside the room and I ask them to then decipher the sounds.

In short, if you don't listen really well, I believe you won't work that much; certainly not in the bigger roles.

Below are a few exercises that you can do to help you improve your listening:

- Sit or stand still. Close your eyes and listen to the sounds in the room. Listen to the sounds outside the room. Try to identify and distinguish between the sounds.
- When spoken to, repeat some things that were said to you back to the other person.
- After you have finished a conversation and walked away from the person you were talking to, think, "What did that person just say to me?"

Anticipation

Anticipation is a wonderful state to be in as an actor. Life is a kind of improvisation, isn't it? This is because, generally, we do not know what will be said or done to us.

We are, consequently, constantly in a state of anticipation. Our face, eyes, ears, our whole attention, are generally all focused on the person who is talking to us. We have a look of anticipation on our face, a look of, we are anticipating what is going to be said to us.

Try to put yourself in this state of mind as much as you can as an actor. You can practise being in a state of anticipation by listening and by doing this exercise: when looking at someone talking to you, just as they start talking, quickly say to yourself, "What are they going to say or do next?"

This will help your listening and help you be much more spontaneous with your responses. You will be much more *in the moment* both verbally and non-verbally and consequently improve your listening by having your face in a state of anticipation, and therefore be much more watchable as an actor. The camera loves seeing it. Watch the magical Sally Hawkins arrange her face and body in anticipation time and time again.

Letting it land

In life, did you hear what was said to you? We hope you did. We live a life of improvisation. Generally, we don't know what is going to be said to us next. Hence, when acting, it is absolutely vital that when people say things to you, you hear it too. You let it affect you and then you respond according to how your character would in a scene.

I call this *letting it land*. This may sound simple, but a lot of actors do not do this enough or well enough. If you run with the concept that the number one thing that we watch when watching actors in a camera mid-shot, or any other close-up shot, is *the eyes*, then we need to see you being affected *in the eyes*.

I ask you to consider this: say you were to go to the hairdressers and spend $150 on your hair and then go home to your partner, best friend or parent, and hear them say, "What the hell have you done with your hair, it looks terrible!", but you like it. How would their reaction affect you?

Well, the same goes for acting. Some actors tend to generally only respond to extreme, dramatic circumstances such as: I am going to hit you; I have cancer; I have AIDS; or I slept with your partner.

In life, we are constantly moved and touched and emotionally affected, and we generally respond accordingly to what is said to us.

Therefore, the good actor must respond in a scene based on her character and the story in the same way. *Letting it land* will help this.

In addition, the use and sound of the voice and the use of body language are also signs that need to be acknowledged and responded to.

For example, in life if you are talking to someone and they raise their voice, you generally raise your voice too. If the tone of their voice becomes comforting and soft, yours does too. If they lean over and put their elbow on the table while talking to you over a cup of coffee, well after a short period of time, you are most likely going to do the same thing. You will mirror them.

Unfortunately, these verbal and non-verbal actions, or ways of behaviour, are often missed by some actors. They are usually missed because the actor is not listening well enough and not letting what is said to them *land on them* in the scene.

In support of this, I would like to add, and please excuse me for the generalization again, but lots of actors are prone to looking at the floor and anywhere else but at the other person when performing in a scene.

If you are one of those actors who looks at the floor or the ceiling a lot, what you have to do is *let it land*. You have to make the choice to do the following: hear it, take it in, be observant in all ways and respond verbally and non-verbally to what is given to you.

Here are the key elements to help you achieve this goal:

- Look at the other actor (or reader, or casting director) in the eyes before the scene begins. Observe their body language and the way they are looking at you
- Listen like a hawk
- Go for your want or opinion or attitude. Your want is your subtext, and at the same time as going for it, you need to be ready to also be affected by what the person says and does to you
- Begin the scene *with* the other person and be affected by everything that is said to you and that is done to you through their body language and the tone, flavour, pitch and volume of their voice

In closing, this does not mean take thirty seconds to respond to every line. Actors have to earn a pause in a scene. Wherever there is a scene where you can drive a truck through the pause, the scene is too slow. But if you pay special attention with your eyes and ears, you'll be off to a good start and, most likely, respond naturally and accordingly. Let it land.

Surprises

The concept of surprises was introduced to me by Australian television director Richard Sarell in the 1990s. It's an important tool that helps make actors become more watchable on screen.

The best way to explain surprises is to ask you to think about watching reality television for a moment. One of the reasons reality television is so popular is that the audience is drawn into watching it without even really knowing why. They are drawn into watching it because the non-actors that are cast in these shows are constantly receiving news – often bad news – and responding to it with a variety of facial expressions.

For example:

- The chef doesn't like your recipe and as a consequence you could get eliminated from the show and not achieve what you set out to do – that of winning the prize money
- You don't do the activity well, you come last, and as a consequence you could get kicked off the island
- You don't get enough friends while doing what they want you to do and as a consequence you could get voted off the show
- You see another woman go up and kiss the Bachelor, in front of you and five other ladies, and as a consequence you won't get the Bachelor's heart

A contestant's or non-actor's reactions to these events in reality television shows often begin with them showing surprise on their face. The surprise is not good news for them and their goal on the show. Hence, they play what I call a *Bad Surprise*. They blush, are mouth agape, they freeze their body for a second, or they swallow or gulp, etcetera.

Well, the audience loves it. They love seeing people have a reaction. Whether it is good or bad news.

An aside: most of the people on these reality television shows have signed contracts agreeing to do what the producers want them to do. Then the producers raise the stakes for the contestants by having extravagant rewards for winning the shows, such as a lot of money or prizes. Then they get them to do things that others don't know about, such as *"Go and kiss him in front of all the other girls"*. This is why their reactions are real. The producers don't need actors.

We also see surprises in all forms of on-screen acting with actors as well. But of course, the actors know where the surprises are and know they are coming. Hence, producers need actors who can pretend (act) that they didn't know what surprise is coming. This is one of the reasons why acting is not easy – actors have to pretend they are hearing something for the first time.

In soap operas, for example, when there is infidelity between characters or some other dramatic news, the audience wants to see how the other character will respond. The audience wants to see the look on *their* faces.

Surprises are consequently profoundly watchable and the more of them you play as an actor (yes, you choose to play them), the more of them you play, the more watchable you will become, and you will help bring the camera in, closer in, on you.

Remember your audience is subconsciously thinking, *Do I want to watch you?* Well, you have just helped them subconsciously say "yes" to that question by continually playing surprises.

That's especially so if your character receives bad news. I say this because bad surprises are more internal than good surprises.

Below is a list of surprises. Try them, practise them in front of the mirror, get someone in your home to call ones out from the list and try to play them, simply by holding the breath, or swallowing or stiffening the body.

Or, you choose the surprise from the list below and ask someone to give you bad news, such as, "I just ran over your dog with my car", and you suspend disbelief and play the bad surprise.

Chapter 1: Acting on Camera | 65

Then put the surprises on your scripts. I suggest you actually write the letter S *(for surprise)* then *G (good)* or *B (bad)* above the line that is about to be said to you by the other characters. Then try to play them in the scene.

A warning, though: in performance, including an audition performance, let the preparation go, don't try to control the scene and have your mind thinking, *I'm waiting for this line to play this surprise.* If you remember to do it, then great. If not, oh well, next time.

Here's the list and introduction that I give my students:

In life we play good, bad and sometimes neutral surprises. An actor playing surprises is more watchable. Bad surprises are particularly watchable because the camera is attracted to the subtext – the things happening internally with the characters.

Sometimes we play surprises on things we have said ourselves. We play them when we have a realization after what we just said, or, we surprise ourselves by what we have just said.

Good surprises are easy to play. The human being is animated and excited and generally speaks louder and has an animated face when playing a good surprise to news or something that has just happened. Bad surprises are much more internal and often not so easy to see. The camera, however, especially in the close-up shots, does see the bad surprises and loves them!

Below are some *Bad Surprise* options:

Non-verbal

- Hold your breath
- Stiffen the body
- Blush
- Head and/or upper body leans back
- Head and/or upper body leans forward
- Scratch of the head or face
- Turn the head away

- Turn your face like you have been slapped on the cheek
- Roll the eyes
- Immediately drop your upper status/change in posture
- Have a long pause before replying
- Have an exhaled look
- Reach up and put your hands above your head
- Stare
- Have a shocked look on your face
- Have a look of disbelief of hearing the bad news in your eyes
- Stop (or freeze) what you were doing
- Swallow
- Have a look of hurt
- Have mouth agape
- Lift an eyebrow (e.g. The Rock – Dwayne Johnson)

Verbal

- Stutter a line
- Cough
- Mutter
- Change the tone or volume or pitch of the voice
- Immediately drop your status with sound, e.g. Oh!
- Sigh
- Make an exhaled sound, e.g. Ahhhh! Or Whatttttt!
- Have a long pause before verbally replying
- Have a sad reply
- Gasp
- Raise your voice
- Make a surprised sound

Remember to try and incorporate the surprises into the scene and your work naturally.

I also talk more about surprises in the next chapter.

Relax

In support of my point made in the introduction, many actors panic when they get in front of the camera. So many become self-conscious. They stop listening because they are thinking and second guessing themselves with questions like these:

- How do I look?
- Am I doing well?
- What's my next line?
- I've got to look gorgeous or handsome or sexy
- Do they like my work?
- Do they like my choices?

As a consequence, they are:

- In their head
- Pushing
- Not listening or not listening well enough
- Not trusting
- Overacting

Actors need to know that the camera sees everything. The camera sees your manner, your ways of behaving. It also sees tension that you are carrying or that is manifesting in different ways.

For example, many actors develop eye twitches, their hands or arms or feet or legs shake, they can't breathe, they get dry in the mouth – all in the name of trying to act on screen and book a job that will go on television or in a film.

All of this I can confirm from personal experience as well as over twenty-five years of teaching actors how to act for the screen.

Learning Point Number One:

- Yes, there are many skills that you can learn and exercises that you can do in regards to acting on camera
- In regards to how you move and the expressions that you have on your face, you need to know what the camera likes and doesn't like
- You need to learn about the importance of the face, particularly the eyes, and the tone of the voice
- In drama, remember the underplay, be more internal with your acting
- Teach yourself how to perform in the most important camera shots
- Relax. There's no point being self-conscious

Chapter 2: Audio excerpts from classes

Audio excerpt 1 - Wants and characters

This chapter comprises a transcript of recordings of an *On Camera* class at my acting school, AIDA, in Hollywood, Los Angeles. To give you context, I am standing in front of a laminated wall chart titled "Acting On Camera 1". This chart lists all the things the actors will work on that month. I then go through each thing, one at a time, during the classes.

There are seven things on this chart in "On Camera 1", and they are not necessarily for beginners. I call it foundation stuff from an On Camera 1 class with my school and I want you to learn about this stuff.

Some of it, tonight we've already worked on. I am going to introduce it to you, and I'm going to get you to write down some specific stuff, because obviously I don't have a lovely big wall chart for you all to take home.

The first thing I want to introduce to you is **Wants**. *After we did our warm-up exercise, we worked on wants. What I would like you to do is write down in your own books, when you work on wants. I want you to choose a want that is separate from the text, hard to achieve, and off or to the other person.*

Tonight, you actually improvised going for your wants and we can absolutely be verbal and non-verbal in our pursuit. In tonight's exercise, you were both verbal and non-verbal and you were improvising, right? You talked for a little bit and then you (the other person) talked for a little bit.

Well, we can do the same with text. When we have text, they talk a little bit with the text, you talk a little bit with the text; unless it's a monologue.

So, wants are separate from the text. If you are doing a scene, and the scene is all about love, you would be best to not choose love. If you read it and you think, my character wants love, then don't choose love.

You know why? Because you are so much more watchable if you choose something else that's not in the text. So, if it looks like the text is all about love, but an actor, let's say, (actor's name) chooses "manipulate", and he goes for manipulate, I can tell you she will be more watchable on that screen than if she went for love. Love is what this scene is all about. So don't choose it.

Why is that? Well, the actor has something else going on at the same time in the scene. This will cause her to take more risks, deliver lines in a different way and surprise the other person that she is working off. She may even surprise herself.

Is this important? Acting coaches tell actors all the time to not always play the obvious, don't always make the obvious choice – this way of thinking that I am talking about here helps you not do this.

Where do you see subtext personified the best? In feature film! Why? Simply because the actors have more time to create a character, more time to have multiple things going on that link to the plot, or their characters journey, and because they are often in a close-up camera shot personifying the nuances of human behaviour.

Film scripts are generally better written than television scripts too.

The main reason I ask actors to play wants is to give their characters something to do. This is simply because, in life, us human beings are generally always doing things that we want or have to do on a day-to-day basis.

As an audience we simply look at someone and decide if we want to watch them and if we believe them. And so, in addition, an actor who plays subtext well is manipulating an audience's brain on a subconscious level into watching them. This is because our brain is initially thinking, "I want to watch this character but I don't know why". But subconsciously, the audience are being drawn into what is under the surface. What is under the surface is often the character's subtext.

An aside: some actors simply have heavy looks naturally on their faces and this helps draw us into wanting to watch them. Think Russell Crowe, Al Pacino, Robert De Niro. They're doing a lot of great things, but their ability to look moody, certainly helps draw us in as viewers.

In feature film we also see what I call the nuances of human behaviour. Nuances such as: blushing; such as ... have you ever seen this ... you receive some bad news, then someone gives you bad news and you do this ... you turn your head as though you have been hit in the face with it? You could say that this is a nuance of human behaviour. You are generally more likely to see this stuff, and real emotion, in film, although you do see it on television too.

So, we see the little nuances of human behaviour best in film. If we can choose a want separate from the text, I can tell you that you are much more watchable as actors as well.

We play with wants in many different ways and that is the first thing ... that's what "separate from the text" means. It means, here's the text, but I'm going to choose another want. "Hard to achieve" means exploring and not wanting to nail it, and "off or to the other person" means going for it off or to the other actor. This is because we either want something from them or we want to do something to them.

Playing Wants separate from the text will help you be watchable on screen.

Guess what I'm going to do tonight? I'm going to give you all a Wants sheet. So, you are all going to have an AIDA Wants sheet, and you are all going to have a scene. I have the scenes sitting over there. They are loaded with subtext for you to choose interesting, intriguing, separate from the text, wants.

As long as you are doing something, whether you want it from them or are going to do it to them. It will make you more proactive in the scene. You've been working on wants in lots of different ways. I know that some people were worried about their approach or how they went for their wants. So, wants are something that you will often be working on, in different sorts of ways for the purpose of having subtext.

We are going to be watching scenes from this feature film, A Few Good Men, *tonight in class. We are going to be watching the actors. We will watch and then discuss the scenes from the film. We will begin with looking at characterization.*

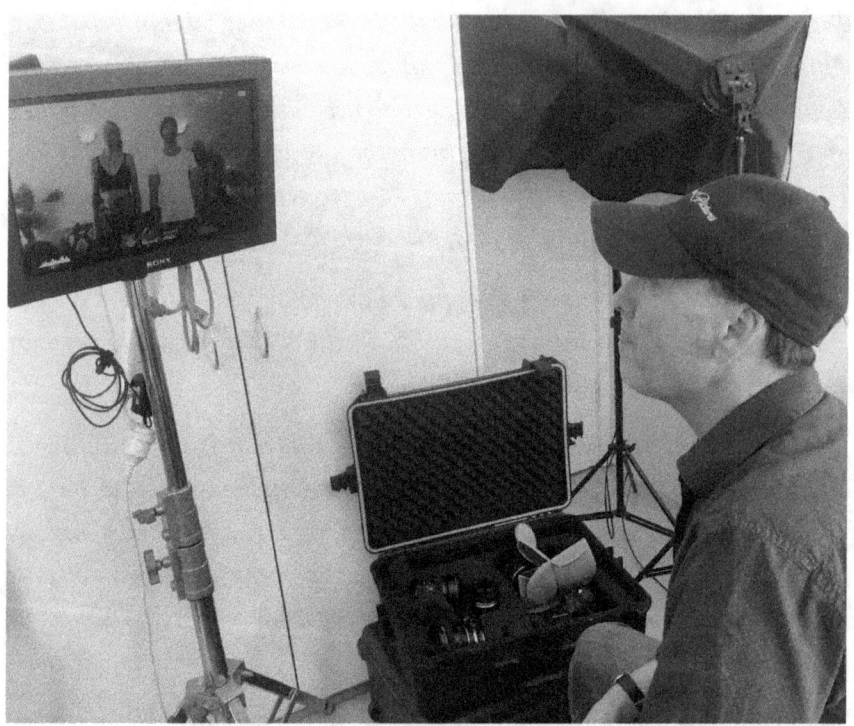

Above: Paul on set, on location, directing actors in 2020.

Characters: are really good; especially in film. Casting directors love actors who create characters. If you look at some of the actors who have won or been nominated for Academy Awards and/or Golden Globes, say for example, in 2022 Benedict Cumberbatch was nominated for The Power of the Dog; *in 2018 Sally Hawkins was nominated for* The Shape of Water; *in 2007 Forest Whitaker for* The Last King of Scotland; *and in 2006 it was Philip Seymour Hoffman's character in* Capote. *And who saw* The Family Stone? *Sarah Jessica's characterization was fantastic, of that uptight girl; well, she was nominated for a Golden Globe in 2006.*

So just look at all the actors who get nominated for Golden Globes or Academy Awards. They are mainly character performances. I see this year after year with the Golden Globes and the Academy Awards. Actors creating characters and winning awards.

Film is loaded with characters. For you guys in class to create a character and take it to an audition is a smart thing to do. It is also invaluable actor training and development.

Now, when our work is on camera, it's often subtle. The actor has to develop the ability to control their face. We talked about looking sideways, as opposed to up and down, especially at the audition for the camera and so the audience can see those eyes working.

Well, some people have been drawing out surprises here tonight in class. That is terrific, because you are going to see all of that and more in these scenes here, as we start to watch them.

Let's watch the first scene that I want to show you from the film A Few Good Men. Let's analyze the acting.

(I play a scene from the feature film *A Few Good Men*.)

My first question is, do you think this actor, Noah Wyle, in this courtroom scene, do you think he's comfortable or uncomfortable in this location?

Raise your hands if you think he's uncomfortable. Nearly all of you raised your hands. Why do you say he's uncomfortable? Tell me how you know that. Let's watch the scene again.

(We watch the same scene again from A Few Good Men.)

What did he just do? He leaned into the microphone. What does leaning into the microphone mean? It could imply, he's not experienced with speaking into microphones; he's in unfamiliar territory and/or he is nervous. Agree?

Now I don't have the script, and I haven't spoken to the director, I'd love to, but I can't ask him now; but I'm intrigued: was it the decision of the actor to lean in toward the microphone? Well, I reckon it was. But we won't know *until we look at the script or talk to the actor or the director. But right here, he leans directly into the microphone. Which implies that something else is going on.*

The people who said, he is nervous, well, there's a non-verbal risk here by the actor, implying he is in unfamiliar circumstances. He's leaning straight into the microphone. It could mean, "I'm unfamiliar with microphones" or "I'm nervous". Let's watch some more of the scene.

(We watch more of the same scene.)

What did he just do? First, he gave a little bit of it, then he made it bigger; he swallowed. In fact, just before he swallowed, he made a little bit of a grunt. And the camera wasn't even on him. Did you hear that? What's he doing there? We've got this guy swallowing. Who was it in the class who said, he's catching himself, unsure of what he just said?

I can already share with you that this character is low status. This Noah Wyle character is not confident, and I can show you many other ways how and why he is personifying that he is not confident.

Wait until you see the Kiefer Sutherland scene. He's the exact opposite to this, this character here. Kiefer Sutherland's character is of a confident man in the courtroom.

Let's continue... He's looking sideways. Now we have colloquial language coming in ... surprise ... still going ... see how he's holding his breath at the start of the shot? ... surprise ... surprise ... The actor is playing bad surprises. He is listening very well and playing surprises.

In addition, what's that awful generalization in North America about people from the South? A bit slow, not as smart, right? Obviously, it's an awful generalization. But what accent is he acting in? A Southern accent.

So, here's something very interesting, something else that helps determine your status. Playing bad surprises. The more often you play bad surprises, the more you lower your status. We obviously have the text supporting this actor. "Yes sir, no sir, yes sir, no sir", he is saying. Look at his posture – his posture is timid. He's twiddling with his fingers. He's leaning forward into the microphone. He's using colloquial language. He does not know what is going on with the books. He does not realize what the two lawyers are doing.

You put all of these things that he is doing together and you get a character in unfamiliar surroundings, not sure what to say. He wants to do the right thing obviously, but he is not sure that he is saying the right thing. His body language is absolutely saying, – yes sir, no sir ... He is under oath!

So, I have to ask – what is his want? What is his subtext? (Actors write their answers down.) *Okay, as a class you have decided on acceptance or trust and this is an actor who is working all the time. He's very subtle with his choices.*

We are dealing with character here, in the making. All the little things, not the one thing, but all the little things that we've been talking about, you put them all together, you get the basis of a character.

As actors, you always want to think, what is the actor doing, and what is the actor saying. Is he using the tone of his voice in a specific way? Is he changing his accent? Is he raising the volume? How is his posture? What is he doing with his body? As well as forming character this actor is also risk taking.

(An aside: Please read the sections on Risk taking and Surprises and the discussion in this section on Wants for further details.)

Just like you guys, around here going for wants in class, you are using your body. The same thing is going on here in the film.

Many actors play subtext, and casting directors know this. Subtext makes you more watchable on camera, as does playing surprises. We all love characters too. We like those moments on screen. Get better at doing all of these things.

Now that I have introduced the importance of character creating, this chart on the wall (a different chart) is called - Creating Characters. With this chart I can draw your attention to a wide range of ways in which you can create characters. This is behavioural stuff with all these chosen things listed on this chart, and as we put them all together, we get the character.

An aside: This character chart I am referring to is included later in this book.

Audio excerpt 2 – *Colours, surprises and risks*

I would like to continue talking about skills that you can develop to help you be watchable on screen. I will do this here through the narrative of another transcription from an on-camera class in Hollywood.

Colours are, in particular, fun to work with. Think – what do they mean to you? What does the colour brown mean to you? What does the colour green mean to you? Does red make you think of power and intensity and anger? For me, red means let's raise the power, let's raise the intensity.

We introduced colours tonight, red raises the stakes. Red is a colour that I used to use as an actor when I was acting, and some of the acting teachers and directors in Australia will add it to the want that an actor is working with.

Red makes you want to raise the stakes, so if you haven't gotten the colours down, you should really do so. Brown is generally muddy, very earthy and hard to see through. Green is envy, white is holy, blue is calm or cool, red is anger or love or passion or excitement or power or intensity.

I find red the best colour to work with because it always gives you that shot in the arm to raise the stakes for the character. So, what I was doing with a lot of the actors last week in class was, I was adding red to the actors wants to help them raise the stakes in the scene.

Facial expressions: Most of the time, people who regularly frown or constantly raise their eyebrows are doing it subconsciously and are not aware of it in life.

I want you to be able to control these actions and have an awareness of your own facial expressions. Not so that you are an actor who doesn't move their face at all (like some Hollywood actors who get Botox), but so you know that you are aware of what you are doing when you raise your eyebrows, etcetera.

When we have an awareness of and are in control of such things, like raising the eyebrows and other things of that nature, like our lines on the forehead or looking sideways as opposed to up and down, we help draw the camera in towards us. Like in a close-up. This is because our facial expressions are easier to watch in the frame if our face is not too animated.

Now, I'll never tell anyone to get Botox, but it is a good thing if you can have some sense on being able to control your facial expressions; especially the frown and the eyebrow lift.

You ideally want to get to a point where you control when to do it. For example, Jack Nicholson lifts his eyebrow at the peak, the Aristotelean arc of his character, think axe through the door in the film The Shining and the 'You can't handle the truth' speech in A Few Good Men.

One way to combat an active forehead is to place two strips of low adhesive Scotch tape on your forehead; so, you are aware of it when you move your eyebrows. This will also help with frowning.

Then of course, if you wish, there is a product called Frownies in Los Angeles that you can buy and wear on your forehead to help reduce and control wrinkles while you sleep at night too.

But the tape works just fine. Don't use gaffer tape. Simply use a sticky tape from a newsagent or office supplies store or supermarket.

So, in class, I might suggest tape for some of you to wear on your forehead. My aim for you is to be able to control your frowning and eyebrow lifting; all to help you draw the camera in on you.

In addition, in being able to control the eyebrows, you also want to be able to start looking sideways when you look away from the other actors' eyes. This is because when you look up, you'll find that it usually won't end up in the final cut of the scene. The audience, via the camera, does not like seeing the whites of the eyes.

You might get away with looking down for a short time before they edit to something else, but try to get into the habit of looking sideways.

Who is seeing this when you're watching television nowadays? Seeing the actors consistently looking sideways. It's terrific. If you see it, you're more than likely to do it. All the best actors do it, and of course I am generalizing, but many, many do it.

You might get away with looking down, like actors Benicio del Toro or David Caruso used to do from the television show CSI Miami who, like some others, do, do it a lot of the time. But what you want to do as actors, until you become a big star, is to put your best foot forward. That's what it's all about; putting your best foot forward and booking the work.

Of course the bigger the movie star you are, the more it doesn't matter, to some extent, whether you look down or not, and of course looking down is also good for deception if your want is to deceive. So, I'm not telling you not to do it; just to have an awareness of when you do lower the eyes. Preferably, keep the eyes up and out in the direction of the camera.

And try not to look up. Keeping your eyes from touching the floor or the ceiling is absolutely an on-camera skill. When we think back to us being a young child, we often look up to the right when recalling something. If you can teach yourself to look sideways to the left or right in life (as opposed to up), then it will help you with your work on camera. Try it. Work on it. You will get more close-ups, more screen time and bigger parts by working on your facial expressions.

This is all a part of what I call physiognomy. Physiognomy for actors is the ability to teach yourself where to look and how to look in the frame.

Betty Davis, an American movie star of the 1940s, is quoted as saying, "Save your best work for the close-up." I believe being able to control your facial expressions is a part of helping you achieve this.

In closing, I am not going to even talk about cosmetic surgery in any form, which I know is very prevalent in some cities, especially in Los Angeles. I believe it's totally up to each individual to make their own choices.

Passing the baton: This is the give and take between two actors. Like the exchange of energy. Sometimes it's physical like the passing of a book.

Listening is the key. As we listen, we are open to everything. A change of status is often apparent when we pass the baton in the scene. A good indicator that the actor is actively listening is seeing the bobbing movement of the eyes. Many times, the director of photography will zoom in once he sees the eyes bobbing back and forth. Listen and pass the baton.

Peak in the scene: *means what is the most important line. Along with this and the colours, this will also help the actor raise the stakes. Knowing the peak in the scene will help you understand the scene.*

When you have a scene that is complicated, it will help you play it by answering the question: what is the most important line? This may change the way you think about that scene. For example, if by finding the peak in the scene causes you to think of the scene in a whole new light, it may also catch your interest to think and discover other parts of the scene as well.

Casting directors like actors who are smart and know what's going on in the scene. Be one! How do you become better at comprehension after you have left school? Read. Read and then analyze and discuss stories or themes or concepts with family and friends.

Surprises: *We hear it and then we decide whether it is good or bad. We decide if we are going to change our want and then we respond. This takes about half a second to a second to do and then we play a good or bad surprise. There are good surprises and bad surprises. Good surprises are often bigger, and when we play bad surprises, we often hold our breath.*

Who in class has been seeing surprises on film and television? I see them all the time and, of course, the bad surprises are often better to watch than the good surprises. If you watch, let's say, old action-packed shows like CSI Miami, or 24, they're happening all the time because the show is written that way.

What I mean by this is, the stakes are high enough for the actors as they keep receiving bad news, they then play bad surprises to this news. On the show 24, from many years ago, there are bad surprises approximately every fifteen seconds for the actors, and the actors need to respond to them. Why? They make you so much more watchable. We hear it, we decide if it's good or bad, we decide if it's going to make us change our wants, and then we respond.

If we get our want like someone did here in class last week, then you might want to go for something else if you got it. But remember, the aim is not to get your want, but to explore all the different options when you go for it. That is much more watchable.

Who doesn't like those moments where the actor plays bad surprises? Here's the thing, it makes you so much more watchable at that moment. If a woman says she got pregnant, you see how you (the other person) react to that news, and it makes you so much more watchable. Drama. Again, if you watch the TV show 24, if you watch any of these cop shows, the drama is like boom-boom-boom-boom-boom-boom-boom. One drama after the other. One dilemma after the other.

Poor Jack Bauer's daughter, in the first four seasons of 24. Something was happening to her every five minutes. Someone was trying to kill her, rape her, everything. Every five to ten minutes. Jack Bauer's saving the world, he dies, they bring him back to life. These shows are full of drama and full of surprises. The actor plays the surprises, the audience are entertained and absorb them, great viewing.

Playing bad surprises is very captivating. If you are doing a scene and a woman says she has gotten pregnant and it was bad news to the man. What is so watchable is seeing how the man responds to the news. Smart actors, while always adhering to the story, often play a bad surprise because, in the scene, they didn't like hearing the news.

Risks: Everybody loves an actor who takes risks. Risks come in two categories: verbal and non-verbal. If you go for your wants and actually explore them, rather than trying to nail the want or the scene, you are more likely to take risks.

So, right from the word go, I am helping you, encouraging you, and also training you directly and indirectly to be a risk-taking actor. Producers, casting directors and teachers love actors who take risks.

I've sat at an Academy Award function in Beverly Hills, and a producer, a serious heavyweight producer in Hollywood was taking questions behind a huge table. He says, "I love actors that take risks." Someone then shouts out, "What's a risk?" He paused. He couldn't answer the question.

We teach them at AIDA. Changing the tone, changing the volume, or changing your accent, are all examples of verbal risks. Invading the other actors' space, taking their hand, touching them in some way, responding with the side of your face, or turning your body language away from them are all examples of non-verbal risks.

Just like the subtle little things that form character, the subtle little things that we do in life are risks.

Some actors at an audition will just stand there with the sides (script) and not do a thing with their body. This is a serious pet peeve that many casting directors have with actors. The actor will just stand there with the script, do nothing at all and then wonder why they didn't book the job.

Some actors do nothing at the start of the scene and wait for the casting director to say something. Do something. I suggest you tap into your senses and link one or more of them in with the senses from the location that your scene is set in. If the scenes whereabouts is not given to you, then make it up.

Tapping into sense memory is what I like to call it, but here in America you already do something similar called, "the moment before", where you create a moment before the scene starts. I suggest you tap into one of the five senses utilizing the location, people and activity present from the scene, as it has more substance.

In case you don't know, generally speaking, most casting directors will give you a bland read because they know that good actors make choices and go for subtext. They don't want to put you off track. You are there to shine, not them.

If the casting director gives you this great performance with a strong want, they could really mess up what you have prepared to do for the audition. They, often, get paid big bucks, and their status as a casting director will rise *if they have great actors that they can call in if the producers need them to cast their projects.*

That's how casting directors get big in Los Angeles, the Debra Zanes and Mali Finns of this world (who are fantastic big league casting directors), are up there because of their ability to call up creative actors to come in and help them cast the job. So, if they give this really strong read against you, they can really mess up all of the preparation that you have done. They want you to look good and then, in turn, they look good at their job. It is as simple as that.

We've got a risk chart that lists all the non-verbal and verbal risks and you will work on them in class, in scenes, on camera, and off camera.

Indirectly, right here through wants, I am introducing risk taking to you by getting you to explore and try different things verbally and non-verbally. On that note, I've read everything off the chart, so let's step into the space and act in front of the camera.

Above: Paul, on set, on location directing actors in the frame.

*Audio excerpt 3 - **Nuances of human behaviour***

I hope you've been intrigued and motivated with a whole pile of things about acting on camera. I hope that this is the start that makes you look at camera acting differently and with an educational eye.

Did you know that when I was a working actor and I wanted to learn new things, I would watch reality television, and I'd watch interviews with football coaches, the news, interviews with the public, in fact anything in which I could see what the general public do naturally because they are human beings living their lives and we are seeing them on the screen.

Here's one great bit of advice that I can give you right now. Like in real life, if we were having an interaction and I'm going to talk but you're still talking, and I'm always on the verge of trying to say something but I don't or can't, well, you watch real people do that in television media interviews a lot.

So why can't you do it in your acting? Right? So that's one thing that I would do as an actor is watch reality TV. You can even watch the reactions of the people on a television show like Sixty Minutes or a show from many years ago called Jerry Springer to see what people on the show naturally do; and copy it.

If you watch that stuff and you watch the news, people being interviewed, like, your football team and watch them interview your coach, or like when they interview basketball players or AFL players or cricketers or baseball players.

The sports players are not actors, but if you watch them being interviewed after games, and watch the things that they naturally do ... take note of them. Take note of their mannerisms, their gestures, their vocal changes. Think to yourself, "I'm going to take that and put it into my work."

I call those things magic moments. A magic moment is that little behavioural and/or audible moment in life, seen in life or on camera that shows **nuances of natural human behaviour**. I repeat, magic moments show a little piece of human behaviour which might just get you that call back.

I don't want to give you too much and make you forget everything we have learned here tonight, but I'm showing you what comes in future classes from the on-camera classes taken from the curriculum. You want to be as real as possible, so take information from anywhere. I repeat, you can take what Russell Crowe does and you can take what Julia Roberts does, etcetera.

If it can help you with your acting, then I say do it. It is possible to think that every actor steals from other actors, especially the smart actors. You want to watch these movie stars and ask yourself, why are they so good?

To me, these actors are great: Denzel Washington and Morgan Freeman. Tremendous actors. CCH Pounder from the television show The Shield and the Avatar films. Does anyone watch her? I've met her three times, she's a dynamite actor.

There are also actors from around the globe who are fantastic. Zhing Zhou from Memoirs of a Geisha and Crouching Tiger Hidden Dragon; she is wonderful. How about the Japanese girl in Babel? The girl who played the deaf-mute character, Rinko Kikuchi, a fantastic actress.

So, you can take from anywhere and everywhere, and I implore you to watch other actors and try to find their subtext (take a guess), and watch their facial expressions. I hope as actors, that this past month has inspired you to never look at film and TV the same way.

This is your business, this is your occupation, and you will get better faster if you see human behaviour and good acting in film and TV. Not just here in class, but see it when you pay your money at a cinema, and see it at home when you're watching television shows, including oldies but goodies like 24, Game of Thrones, Breaking Bad – or whatever it is that you watch.

How the actor looks on camera and how skilful they are on camera, will determine their career and their chances of working on camera. But to the viewer at home or in the movie theatre, (and this also includes casting directors, directors and producers), well, it is an external decision made by these people, who are influenced profoundly by how you look on camera and how you sound on camera and by what you do on camera and even by how you help tell the story – all on camera.

The audience, subconsciously or consciously, say to themselves, "Do I want to watch that actor?" "Do I believe that actor?"

Audiences tell television stations who they like and who they spend their money on at the movie theatres watching who they like. Partners and friends of casting directors, producers and directors also tell their partner who they like to watch. All of this, in turn, influences your chances, your popularity and your career.

However, it is the internal work of the actor that really gives you the great – or the booking or the buyable – external look on camera.

It is the internal work such as the things I have talked about and some that are listed below that matter most.

- *Knowing how to adjust your performance based on the shot*
- *Knowing how to use your face and body on camera for effect*
- *Your knowledge of the scene, interpreting it, understanding the scene, including its journey in the whole film or episode*
- *Your ability to create characters*
- *Your listening ability*
- *Your ability to pass the baton*
- *Your ability to play surprises*
- *Your ability to play wants or subtext*
- *Your ability to take risks, etcetera*
- *In the audition, your script reading ability*

The more you act, the more you practise your skills, the better you will become when acting on the screen.

Learning Point Number Two:

- You have now heard me talk about more skills that you can develop through excerpts taken from group on-camera acting classes in Hollywood
- This chapter's exercises will help you develop techniques that help you be watchable on camera
- Teach yourself to analyze actors' work on screen
- Develop techniques that help you be watchable on camera. Then practise the listed acting skills

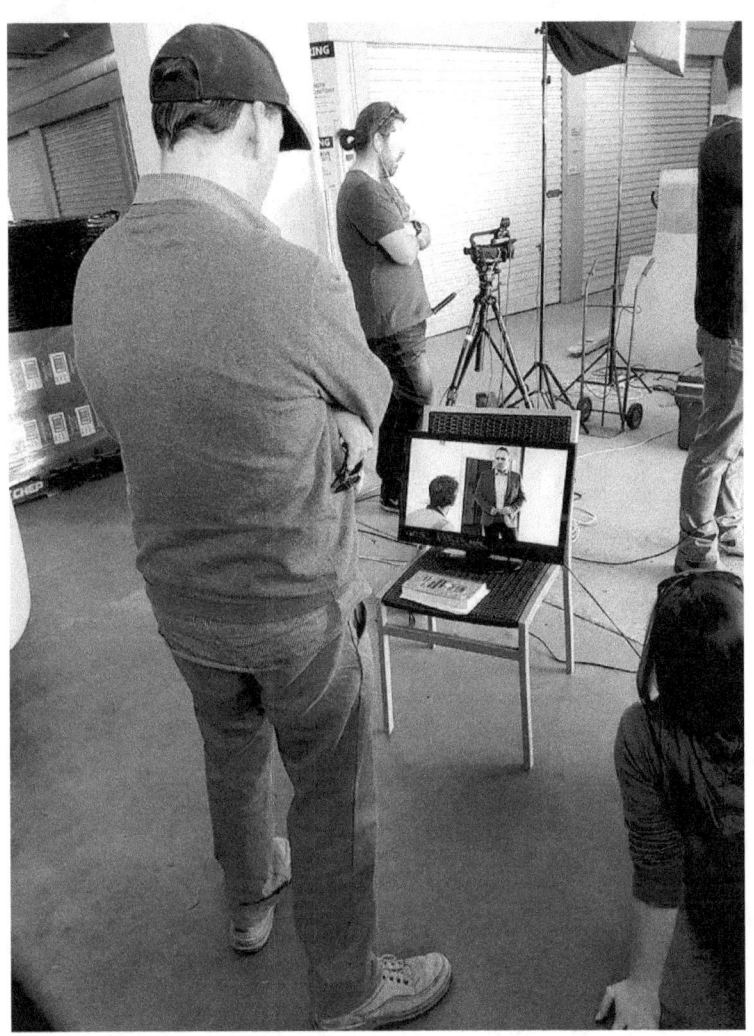

Above: Paul on set directing one of his films in 2018.

Chapter 3: Self-tape Audition

I spoke in detail about audition preparation and training in my first book, where a whole chapter is dedicated to the topic. I would now like to talk about self-tape auditioning.

Life is changing for us all, all the time. Since the worldwide pandemic and Covid-19, more and more actors' auditions are now self-tapes. With Covid, which is under a lot more control at the time of the writing of this book, often the first audition is a self-tape and the call back is in person. This is especially true for larger roles such as recurring or series regular or leads roles.

A self-tape audition is when you record yourself performing a scene (scenes are called "sides" in the States), and then you email it on to the appropriate people, either as an attachment or through an uploading file agency, to your agent, or to the casting people directly.

This is done, usually, by first uploading your audition scene to one of the following:

- Dropbox
- Vimeo
- We Transfer
- Unlisted on YouTube
- Google Drive
- Or, any other such online platform

Sometimes you email submit directly to the client.

There will be some small overlap from Book One in this section as some important things will need to be re-stated to help support the points that I want to make.

I would like you to think this: "What is going to separate me from the other people auditioning for the same part?" "What is going to separate my character and performance from everyone else's?"

I want you to think this way because a lot of actors play safe and a lot of actors are afraid to take a risk. In addition, a lot of actors simply make meek or weak decisions.

Here is a structural list of things to think about when preparing to perform; this includes when you prepare to audition. All of my actors work on these in class with me:

- Know where you are
- Have a start that tries to emulate where you are and be doing this at the start of the performance as we always come from somewhere. A simple movement or turn into frame is sometimes enough
- Know who are you talking to
- Place the person you are talking to in the frame – the V
- Look straight ahead for most of the scene in the V, preferably not down or up
- Know how wide you can look on either side of the camera light or the camera dot
- Be so committed that you will make us listen to you
- Be so committed that you will make us want to watch you. This is done by commitment, trust, passion, energy and a creative character delivering the lines that you connect with
- Always suspend disbelief – you are that character and I want you to think that what is happening to you, really is happening to you
- This character scene performance has to mean something to you when you talk
- Show some vulnerability
- The first line is the most important line you will say

- Take a risk. See the risk-taking list that is included in this book
- Unless directed to, please don't act down the barrel of the camera

Also, remember:

- Your training
- What you are saying
- Breath and breath and voice
- Your technique foundation work
- Your listening
- Be moved/affected by what is done or said to you

At the start of this book, I spoke about actors often wanting a career too much. They want it too much that it affects their mind, in particular, their concentration. This often leads actors to trying too hard when they audition.

Sometimes, we actually do better work when we stop trying. This is because we let go. We take the pressure off ourselves, and our subconscious mind allows us to actually personify things that we have learnt already.

An example of this I've seen many, many times, over many years, is when I have prepped students for showreels or auditions. If a colleague is used for the showreel or audition scene, the colleague often does better work than the actor whose reel or audition that it is.

This is because there is not as much pressure on the colleague and they don't care as much because it is not their showreel or audition.

Therefore, teach yourself to relax, let go, trust and play. These are easy words for me write, of course, but often hard for actors to do.

Actors do often do one or two of the words mentioned above, *relax, let go, trust, play,* but not all of them. This is where I come in. My job in preparing an actor for an audition is to teach them how to relax, to let go of what they have prepared, trust their work, and believe their choices are good enough. I also teach them how to play.

We have to remember that everybody cannot win. Everybody cannot be a movie star. Unfortunately, everybody cannot achieve all of their goals. But we can all try. Learn to relax, let go, trust and play.

Don't try to nail it. Don't try to do it right. As mentioned in Book One, as an actor, you want to explore and not try to nail a scene or a script. Because if you do there is an element of sitting on your own shoulder and watching your work as you try to nail it. If you are saying you nailed it, you were consciously aware that you did this. Consequently, by doing so, you are not a hundred per cent committed in your mind to your character and their journey. Your mind is distracted.

Remember acting is performing art, so explore, play, try to achieve your subtext, but don't worry if you don't. It is the thought of going on a journey and the exploration that will help make you watchable and help you take risks. That along with your skills on how to perform in the different camera shots.

When you have the job or at the start of an audition

When on set or when doing an audition, generally, always try and move a little at the start of the scene – at the call of action. This ensures that when the director says action, you are slightly moving in the frame.

Believe it or not, it is more watchable and easier to edit with this going on too. Move slowly, consider:

- Just a turn of the head, or lift of the head, or a turn of the shoulder
- Slowly slide sideways into frame at the start of the scene

Looking natural

Can you look natural with your acting? Because you need to.

One of the benefits of coaching online nowadays is the actor is on camera for their whole lesson. That allows me to watch their natural behaviour. I watch them breathe. I watch what they do with their head, their face, their eyes and their bodies.

So, when I audition prep them for a role, I can clearly see how relaxed the actor is by what they do with their body, their face, their breathing and their voice. And, of course, I can see if they are really listening well. This is all because I have a history to go on. A history of seeing how they behave when they are relaxed in an acting class with me.

Learning to perform in a relaxed state, as if we are simply living our lives, is an art and a skill, and this helps set apart the working actors from the non-working actors. It all begins with breath and breath and voice connection and then moves into learning the art of relaxing, letting go, trusting and playing.

Left brain and right brain

In regards to our thinking, our brains have two different sides. Below I discuss the left brain/right brain theory because the way actors' brains are wired could be influencing their chances of success in their auditions.

The left brain/right brain theory

"The theory is that people are either left-brained or right-brained, meaning that one side of their brain is dominant. If you're mostly analytical and methodical in your thinking, you're said to be left-brained.

The left side of the brain is responsible for controlling the right side of the body. It also performs tasks that have to do with logic, such as in science and mathematics.

On the other hand, the right hemisphere (right side of the brain) coordinates the left side of the body, and performs tasks that have do with creativity and the arts.

More than 160,000 Americans used our brain test. The results showed that 37 percent of Americans are left-brained, while only 29 percent are right-brained. In 34 percent of participants, the two hemispheres exert equal influence on decision-making. Oct 29, 2013."

I found the above information shared on Pinterest. I suggest you Google left brain/right brain and read about it.

What are you? You should try to find out whether you are left-brain dominated or right-brain dominated. The reason I say this is because it might help you understand yourself with your acting. Especially when you audition.

If you are left-brained you will have to work harder to let go and play and not analyze.

If you are right-brain dominated, you might find that you need to do more scene study and character preparation, meaning more theory preparation. I have included exercises on creating characters and back story to character, and internal and external exercises on helping actors develop characters later in this book.

Relax

Drama classes at secondary schools often start by doing exercises to teach the performer to relax.

Clichéd snippets or re-enactments of performers learning to relax are seen in many mock and ad-hoc scenarios, in film and television shows where they are laughing at, or taking the piss (as we say in Australia) out of, actors learning to relax in their acting and drama classes.

But, these relaxation exercises have real substance to them, as actors do need to learn to relax. The camera shows us if they are not relaxed.

I find I am constantly working and trying different ways to get my actors to relax when they are performing in class or doing an audition preparation.

Let go

By relaxing, as a human being, we are more likely to let go.

Take a look at a professional sports person for example. They are, generally speaking, very relaxed when they play the sport at the highest level. One of the main jobs of the sporting coach is to teach the players to relax, let go and trust their abilities.

I find I am constantly working and trying different ways to get my actors to let go when they are performing in class or doing an audition preparation.

Trust

Nothing improves an actor's confidence more than booking work. When the actor is paid to act, their inner confidence sky rockets. Until this happens, the actor must trust themselves. They must trust their talent. Trust their preparation and trust their teacher or audition coach. They must also learn to trust themselves to remember their lines and trust their choices. So many actors do not trust their choices.

I find I am constantly working and trying different ways to get my actors to trust when they are performing in class or doing an audition preparation.

Play

If we are relaxed, we let go, we don't try to control and we trust ourselves and our preparation, then we are in a very good position to play. Playing is so important for the actor. Life is an improvisation, it is not scripted, actors need to have freedom when they perform and this comes in the area of play. Another term that basically means the same as play, is risk taking.

I find I am constantly working and trying different ways to get my actors to play when they are performing in class or doing an audition preparation.

Teacher provocation to students

The more you think about something, the more you will create it. The more you put energy into something, like making things, or, acting, producing, directing, etcetera, the more you will become this.

So, talk to people about acting and auditioning. Read about acting and auditioning. And act, as much as you can. Learn the art of acting and letting go. Learn how to let go. Don't think, "I have to do it right. I have to follow all the guidelines to a T."

Remember, if you do copy everyone else or make clichéd characters, you are doing the cliché. Put your hand up if you became an actor to do the scene like everyone else? Put your hand up if you became an actor to copy everyone else that goes before you in a class? Many actors do this. They just copy other people and/or choose the cliché, the expected option. Don't do it. Unless you are told you must do it like this.

Soap opera for television is an exception. For soap opera don't do too much preparation. For actors performing soap opera, be as natural as possible, without any in-depth characterization or risk taking.

Actor Ray Meagher has been on the Australian television TV serial *Home & Away* since 1988. This show is the closest thing we have to soap opera in Australia. When interviewed on a gardening/variety entertainment TV show around 2021, called *Better Homes & Gardens*, Meagher was asked by the TV presenter, "How much of you Ray is in your character Alf on the show?" Meagher responded, "About 85 per cent." Be you if you go for a soap opera audition. Be you as much as you can.

When you do your self-tape

What if you could move in the frame like you are moving to music? What if you could move in the frame like you were creating a piece of art? Because you can. Because you are creating art – performing art. I suggest you play classical music in the background as a warm up and when you are starting to create a character.

When you are preparing and/or doing your self-tape for an audition, make sure you adhere to the list below when in the frame. At least until you know how to do those things consistently. Once you know how to honour this general rule, then you can relax, let it go, be in profile sometimes or look down occasionally.

- Perform in the V – remember it, use it to help you make impact and then, as said, let it go; ignore it but know you can use it when and where for effect
- Know your angles/profiles in the frame
- Be aware of your depth in the frame
- Be aware of your movement in the frame
- Be aware of your speed of movement in the frame

If you can, try to give the viewer three to five different movements in the frame, say, from the back of the frame, in profile, up into a mid-shot or medium close-up. You can practise all the things above as a part of your preparation for the self-tape audition that you will send off to the casting director.

Your self-tape set up studio

- Try to have a real studio – if you can
- Make sure you have a blank wall behind you or a backdrop of some sort of material, with no patterns, writing or drawings on it
- A white or blue coloured wall is good for the background
- Preferably set up a studio with light, camera and microphone
- If using a mobile phone, have it positioned horizontally. Make sure you do not hold it
- Make sure you have very good lighting and sound quality
- Don't fully dress in costume for the occupation of the part. Be subtle. For example, if auditioning for a nurse, you don't need to wear a nurse's uniform
- Naturally the casting directors need to see your face, so, generally, do not wear a hat or sunglasses
- Colours to wear: blue and green or grey unless you are Black. If you are Black, lemon and orange are good
- Consider having the slate as a separate recording at the end
- Feel free to computer type your name, role and agent on the screen or do a slate (see below for an explanation of "slating"). Unless directed not to or directed another way to give this information

- Ask yourself, "How am I going to stand out today?"
- Follow the direction and/or information given to you
- Try to have the reader (the person reading opposite you) in the same room
- Try not to hold the script. Learn the lines
- Eliminate any distractions
- Put tape on the floor. I suggest you outline your whole performance area. You could even put different coloured tape on the floor to indicate the following camera shots, in terms of your distance from the camera: the three-quarter shot, mid-shot, medium close-up and close-up shots
- Where necessary, do a still shot of your head and body
- Eye line – if the instructional brief says, "Look down the camera", do so, if not, don't ever do it consciously; unless it is your slate
- As opposed to sitting, unless necessary, it is better if you stand for the self-tape
- Do multiple takes
- Do a practice and email it to yourself so you can see the sound and video quality
- If the given information/brief doesn't say how many takes you can send, send them two different performances of the same scene
- Get your tapes in on time
- Send script via We Transfer, Vimeo or Unlisted on YouTube

In closing on this topic, make sure your headshot and resume are up to date and look like you. If you have a few different versions, send the one most suitable for the part. You could even draw attention to your reel or profile with your reel on such avenues as Actors Access in the USA or Showcast in Australia, or your website, etcetera.

Concerns from some students

Below is a list of concerns from some of my students. All things listed have been encountered by these students. I have taken out their names. Some are American, some Australian, some Japanese. In all cases, their comments and questions are things they struggled with and which we worked with, one by one, in class:

- Where to start in the frame
- Letting go and playing
- Listening
- Less is often more – a simple reaction is very powerful
- Finding the balance between too big and too small
- Learn to know where the camera is, then ignoring it
- Tight lips. Realizing I need loosening exercises
- Multiple takes – enjoying the process versus saying "mucking up"
- Making impact from the word go
- Never doing the same thing for two or three minutes
- Having a change in a scene
- "When you have to be pretending to dismantle a bomb or dance. I had a friend do an audition where she was an alien and had to pretend that she was wearing dancing shoes that were controlling her. So I'd love to know what to do when there is a big caricature-type scene"
- Emotions seen being believable
- Relaxing
- Trusting
- Worried about doing the right thing. What is the right thing?
- Standing out of frame
- Not using the frame as told by the casting director
- What is interesting to watch?
- Learning not to push
- Learning to use the frame, so I don't look frozen
- Showing emotion – emotionally connecting
- Talking about creating characters
- What is moving too much?
- Moving fast is a concern
- Trying to be memorable and stand out
- Trying to get their attention

- My slate – is it a professional, unique one?
- Being off book
- Fitting in all the homework in twenty-four hours
- Did I do enough?
- Try to be objective when I send it to myself to view
- Trying to play, explore, enjoy, get out of my head
- Creating space to move around. Framing, impacting – we're working on it
- Learning to be the director too
- Creating my art
- Being still
- Taking risks
- Connecting with the text, especially when it's trite or poorly written
- Letting go and having fun with it
- Trying to make a personal connection through the camera while performing in a vacuum with a remote or invisible reader
- Knowing how big to be in the shot
- Knowing how to find the right energy and volume in the shots
- Being believable – trusting
- Being vulnerable, including being emotional on cue

Slating

Slating is simply stating your name and agent and the details that they ask, in the brief, about you. Such as your height, weight, age, etcetera. This is done and placed at the start or at the end of your audition performance.

Do a boring slate. As boring as it can be. Then do a lively, friendly slate. Watch the two, then delete the boring one. Know the difference. Your slate should always have energy and life and show genuine interest in the project that you are auditioning for.

Mime and props

You decide if you will use a prop and if you will mime. Some actors are good at these tasks, some are terrible, and some are just okay.

Props – if they are there near you, you don't necessarily have to use them. If you do use them, make sure you know how to use them and, most importantly, do not make them the focus of the scene.

The worst-case scenario of working with a prop goes like this: actors wave the prop around and illustrate with it as they talk. When this happens, the prop, and the actor waving or playing with the prop, dominates the scene. It looks so awful when actors do this.

Mime. To mime or not too mime, that is the question? Are you good at miming? Practise and see how it looks. Be on the phone, eating a slice of pizza, drinking a coffee, chewing gum – anything. Whatever you do, commit to it.

The worst-case scenario of poor miming goes like this: you are holding a drink and you drink out of it, then when you need to illustrate with your body that the person or something is happening – over there, you gesture with the same hand and arm, totally ignoring that you were just miming holding a drink in that hand. It looks so awful when actors do that.

Risk taking

As introduced in Chapter 2, "Audio excerpts from classes", risk taking needs to be discussed again in this book as it is the key to helping yourself stand out in an audition and on set. Risk taking comes in two categories: Verbal and Non-verbal communication.

I have included this list below for you to see the types of risks people can take. Basically, anything that you do, that is not in the script, could be a risk. It doesn't mean do anything. It means, do things that you think are preferably applicable or seem to fit in well or nicely with what is going on with your character.

Verbal risks

- Drunk
- Raising your volume
- Changing your tone

- Changing the sound of your voice
- Change your accent
- Changing the pace
- Playing with the use of breath
- Play the wants!
- Laugh
- Sigh
- Gasp
- Be hysterical
- Stutter or stammer through the line – e.g. as seen by actors: Hugh Grant, Helen Hunt, Rob Morrow
- Whispering
- Groaning
- Whistling
- Saying their name
- Singing a line
- Repeating the line
- Emphasis on a certain line
- Play opposite the script
- Playing surprises
- Being emotional
- Impersonation, e.g. Groucho Marx

Non-verbal risks

- Drunk
- Had a headache
- Physical greeting – high five
- Limp
- Kiss the partner
- Use of kung fu
- Touch the partner
- Laugh
- Sigh
- Trying to get something out of your eyes

- Touching yourself in some way
- Play the wants! Going for them!
- Distract someone for effect
- Caress
- Cry
- Hug
- Lean on the other person
- Change direction of eyes, head and body
- Gritting teeth as you talk
- Use body in opposite to dialogue
- Follow/copy the other actor's movements
- Smelling someone
- Shivering

Risk taking helps you explore the text, the relationship between you and the other characters and the use of your body and voice. Just as importantly, risk taking aids or supports your exploration of your subtext, that of what you actually want in the scene.

Risk taking will help you become more watchable because your performances will be unpredictable. An audience doesn't know this, they simply think unconsciously whether they want to watch you or not and whether or not they believe you.

A note on this: It is important to think of risks and even rehearse risks while rehearsing a scene. But when it is time to *perform live or in the take*, let it go. See if you can still do it, see if it still comes up. Try not to focus all your time in your mind thinking, "Oh, when she does this, I'll do that", in the scene.

In addition, by putting yourself in a position to take a risk, always listen like a hawk and interact. Move and be influenced by what the other person or people are doing and saying to you.

This is so important, as some actors get so caught up with what they're doing sometimes, that they don't let themselves be influenced by the little nuances of human behaviour from others. Such as: a change of tone towards you on a certain line. Be alert. Listen. Take risks. Interact.

This is also why improvisation is so good for the actor as it teaches them to be affected, as in life, by what comes at you both physically and verbally. Doing improvisation will definitely help your risk taking.

Learning Point Number Three:

- The self-tape actor prepares their room where they will record their self-tape as professionally as possible
- Self-taping has made auditioning easier for the actor as you can record seventy-five takes if you wanted to and then send them the best one or two
- The smart actor works on verbal and non-verbal risks in class and at home to build their confidence. Then starts putting the risks into their audition work and their professional work
- The self-tape actor creates a story, a piece of art in the frame; knowing all the parameters of the frame

Chapter 4: Detailed scene study

"*Scene study*" is such a generally used phrase. What does scene study mean to you? In the wording, it simply means the studying of scenes. But how do you study scenes?

I would like to begin this chapter by asking you a couple of questions.

How are your English comprehension skills? How is your imagination? How do you break a script down to work out what is going on in the scene? And then, when you do perform, how do you let your scene study decisions that you made, go, and simply influence your performance, but not dominate your performance? And, how are your risk-taking skills?

You see when performing, the actor must always be open to change in the moment.

In my school's ongoing training in the USA and even today across the world, what scene study means to me is a thorough examination of the scene. Especially in regards to what is going on in the scene and what character choices you can make in a scene. For me, it is also identifying the genre/style of the show that you are auditioning for. As well as determining what category of scene it is. Meaning, is it a romance scene, an action scene, an information giving scene, the set-up to plot scene, the main plot scene, the climax scene? Then letting go and performing that scene.

In Los Angeles, from my experience dating back to 2000, and from hearing from other actors, as well as my students, including right up until today in 2023, scene study to them means picking up, looking at, and then performing as many scenes as possible.

For many in the USA, it also means turning up to a class, being given a scene, a scene partner, and then having ten to fifteen minutes to practise with that partner, then sitting back down and waiting their turn to perform the scene with their partner alongside ten to twenty other pairs of actors; and, in both these scenarios, not doing too much evaluation.

This type of scene study training, such as working on *as many scenes as quickly as possible, and having ten to fifteen minutes to practise and make choices,* is very good for learning how to cold read and sometimes good enough for acting scenes for television soap opera. Please read Chapter 15 on cold reading to support this point.

However, I recommend that you don't follow the trend of simply picking up scenes, making quick decisions and then performing. As said, this type of training does have a purpose, but I suggest you develop profound methods of scene study and then adapt your process based on the genre and style and the time that you have to prepare before your audition.

Scene study is much more than making a choice on what's going on in the scene and then making a choice on how to adapt or create a character for a scene. In scene study we should learn how to break down a script to explore its meanings and its characters' subtext. Whether on camera or on stage, the actor should work on a few different things to help them to understand what is going on in the scene and then make decisions and try to achieve these things when performing the scene. In short, to help the actor give a great performance.

Being a qualified literature and language linguistics major from University, my training in this area is quite profound. Yours doesn't need to be profound. It just needs to be analytical, clever and imaginative. I believe scene study should incorporate all the back story associated with what's going on in the scene and how it all relates to its world, and the back story with what's going on with your character and your character's relation to her world.

For example, below are questions that I believe the actor should ask themselves. Answer those questions, and then use the other scene study questions in this chapter that I ask you to consider to support you during your creation.

Scene study should cover the following

- What is the genre of the show on the said script?
- What is the style of the show on the said script?
- What category of scene is it? Meaning, what sort of scene is it – is it the climax? An action scene? A romantic scene? An information-giving scene? These components, and more, are all important parts of a script's story. This is very important for you to know and decide upon in your preparation because knowing how to perform an action scene is very different to knowing how to perform a romantic scene
- What is the scene about?
- What does your character want?
- You could do the non-impulse work (described in Book One)
- You could do sensory work on the location of the scene (exploring the five senses)
- You could ask yourself what are the overall thoughts of the play/script/scene (see below for details)
- You could and should create a character
- You could do the character background charts – internal and external in Chapter 5 of this book
- You could put the character on camera and simply do things as that character. (Doing things as that character is common theatre production preparation and acting training school preparation for creating characters.)

What you do is use your creative mind to make some decisions. Then improvise and use your imagination to discover some other things. During this process, exploration should be the key.

All of the topic areas above are to help the actor explore the possibilities of the scene and the journey for their character in the scene.

After you have received the scene, I suggest you start by turning the script or audition scene over and write answers on the back to the following questions:

- What is this scene about?
- What is my character doing?
- What initial thoughts do I have?

The reason I ask actors to immediately answer the questions above is because some actors forget their initial thoughts. Their initial impulse. You can change your thoughts later if you wish, but writing these initial thoughts down is a very good starting point.

Then break the scene into sections. You do this by simply drawing a line across the page where you think the story/topic changes and then give that section a heading; just a few words, like "Tom & Mary greet one another on a train".

Then move through the script to the next time you have drawn a line across the page and follow the same format of writing a heading on all subsequent headings.

Here is an example from a script of mine. I decided when to put the line in highlighting each section. The sentence heading at the start of each section is written in bold italics.

FILM / TELEVISION SCRIPT
TO BE OR NOT TO BE

INT   LOUNGE ROOM OF HOME   DAY

Dawn approaches Dusty, who is distant

> DAWN
> Why are you going?

> DUSTY
> What?

> DAWN
> Why are you going away?

> DUSTY
> I need a cleansing. A spiritual cleansing. You know that. When did you decide to go away?

> DAWN
> The other day. (*Beat*)

Dawn probes deeper, Dusty stays distant

> How long have we been going out?

> DUSTY
> 9 months

> DAWN
> Well don't you think it's time to sort some things out?

> DUSTY
> Yeah, that's why I'm going to the mountains, to relax, think and sort some things out.

Dawn tries harder to get Dusty to reveal the truth. Dusty blocks Dawn

> DAWN
> You want to control me don't you?

> DUSTY
> No

> DAWN
> Yes you do

> DUSTY
> No I don't

I then suggest you share the scene with family and friends and get their views on the scene too. You don't have to go with their view, but by getting alternative views, it helps you form an opinion, an understanding, to help you make your choices.

Then answer the questions that are under the Scene Study Character charts that are in the next chapter of this book. They begin with you asking the questions: Who am I? Where have I been? Etcetera. And the Internal and External chart questions.

Then answer the following questions:

- What decisions will you make in regards to what is going on?
- What decisions will you make that are different from others?
- Have you experienced in life the things happening to your character in the scene? If so, can you recall them and use them?

If not, can you think of a similar time or ask someone else if they have?
- Based on what happens in the scene, how would your character feel?
- How can you show that and/or say that? When and where in the script can you show that?
- What is the occupation of your character? How can you show that? How will that change what you do?

Make sure the stakes are high for your character.

Character thoughts of the play - script - scene

Even if you only have a scene, as opposed to a whole script or play, please answer these questions. You can make up the answers if you have to.

- **What is the main statement of the play/script/scene?**
(In one sentence summarize the play, script or scene.)

- **What are the playwright's intentions?**
(Sometimes playwrights or writers write through allegory. The playwright has a story, something that happened to them, or a particularly strong view of a social or political issue and they share it through their play. If you don't know what the story is, take a guess and/or make it up based on what you do know that's been given to you in the scene or sides.)

- **What is the political and social content of the play?**
(What is happening within the play?) The playwright links the social and political issues in the script to real life within the play. For example, in Lord of the Rings teamwork is important to achieve a goal and it's important to not give into temptation or do evil doings.

- **What is the political and social context of the play?**
(What is happening outside of the play?) What are the similarities between the issues in the scene/play and events happening <u>outside</u> the play in the world today or during that time period? For example, in

Lord of the Rings – friendship, temptation, pressure of responsibility, leadership (say, in a workplace), teamwork, intention, good vs. evil.

- **What is the main action of the play/script/scene? The super objective?**
(the bigger picture/ philosophical view) For example, Lord of the Rings – goodness will prevail!

- **What is the spinal objective of the play/script/scene?**
(What storylines/plots are there? Are they entwined?) What thread do you think is running through the whole scene? For example, Lord of the Rings – The ring: Which concludes with: I'm going to drop this ring into the volcano (in New Zealand 😊)

Have a discussion with someone and use examples on each section from above to help you understand what is going on.

Setting yourself up to be in the top group of actors

Many actors do do a lot of prepatory scene study work, but unfortunately, their work choices carry into their performance and they try to control what they are doing all the time while they are performing.

In this sense, they are stepping out of their work and not focusing on what should be happening. For example, not being in the moment and responding both verbally and non-verbally to what is being said or done to them and how it is being said and done to them.

An aside: I'm guessing that in reference to *Making decisions and carrying the decisions strongly into performance,* some acting schools know this. So they introduce no acting methods, no classical training in some modern schools. I've often thought, I'll give these schools some latitude, perhaps these schools do that because they don't want the actor to be in their head? Because they may not know how to get the actor out of their own head. They don't know how to teach an actor to let go, trust, relax and play in performance. These are just thoughts.

In reference to teaching no acting methods, or having no classical training in some modern schools, this type of acting training is also simpler to teach. I'm generalizing, but many of these acting schools also employ *actors* to teach the students. Actors who are or have been successsful themselves, and they pay them to teach the young aspiring actors at their school.

Many of these successful actors, or, so-called *experts in the industry*, generally have no teaching training at all. As said in Book One, would you let a non-dentist give you a filling? Would you let a non-mechanic service your car? If the answer is no, then why do you choose to be taught by a non-teacher?

However and consequently, the best actors in the world do spend time studying a script and do create characters and then do let go when performing.

This is what sets the movie stars and the series regular actors apart from the pack. It is their ability to prepare and then let go in performance. As said, deliberately, many times by me, you need to learn to do this too.

However, if you simply follow the modern teachings of some modern acting schools that I am aware of, even today, in the USA and Australia, and to a lesser extent in Japan, it is hit or miss as to whether or not you will work. Most of you won't work. But, you will pay the bills and mortgages of the people running these acting schools.

To be really specific about your scene study preparation work, okay you've made your decisions, and so do you now carry those decisions into the performance? What you have to learn to do is find the balance. Do the preparation work and then learn to let go of all your decisions and see what evolves with your character in the moment. See what comes up as the scene goes along.

This takes talent. This takes hard work. This takes patience and skill. This also takes trust and self-confidence. This also encourages you to go into a space where you have to let go.

You do think about your prepatory work prior to the call of action on set, or let's say, in the foyer outside for an audition, but, then you let go of it all when you start performing and you must be moved and affected by what happens to you verbally and non-verbally, in the moment, when you perform the scene.

How do you let go as an actor in performance? How do you let go of the back story stuff?

To answer the question above, try addressing and if necessary, dealing with these three things:

1. As life is an improvisation in that we don't know what's going to happen moment to moment (unless we try to control people all day when we talk to them), we need to let go in the performance. So say to yourself, "Let's see what happens." See where the scene goes. See where it takes me.

2. Ask yourself, do you like to control? Ask yourself how much do I try to control things in my everyday life? How much do I try to control during the performing of a scene? I suggest you surrender your need to control. Surrender your need to have the scene go the way you want it to. If necessary, try to stop yourself in both categories.

3. If you have a critic in your head, learn to tame the critic. The critic in your head or on your shoulders may have a desire to control and to put you down. Talk to your critic. You need to tame it. You need to stop it during the reading or a performance.

It is good for you to also acknowledge that the critic can also motivate you, guide you, encourage you to think and do things in certain ways. So talk to the critic. Tame the critic. Set the guidelines, say to the critic during class or at practice at home, if the critic speaks up, "Be quiet!". You can even do this out aloud.

During performance of any sort, don't say "Be quiet" out aloud, but say in your mind, "Go away. Come back at the end and I'll let you say whatever you want."

Activities to help you use your imagination

1. **Focus and concentration exercise.** I like to walk students through an exercise where they are in a tunnel confronted with spiders, rats, etcetera. I then give them a task to do by themselves, while they are still in the tunnel

2. **Suspend disbelief.** You might be surprised to know that many, many actors cannot do this with strong conviction. You need to do this. You need to suspend disbelief where you simply believe a hundred per cent that what is happening to your character is happening to you

3. **Improvise** that you are at different locations. Such as, you are in a spaceship and interacting with aliens. Or, pretend that you are in love. I would like you to chat to someone about being in love and then perhaps having that relationship end

I would also like you to think about making a different choice. A strong choice. Do not make the obvious choice unless you are auditioning for the genre of soap opera for television or for a commercial, or if the casting brief says, "You must do it like this …"

Otherwise, I encourage you to think, how can I give this a new twist? Then write three ways you can do the scene differently and play with those in preparation.

Finally, what are your rituals? Create a list of things that you intend to do in your scene study preparation.

I hope these guidelines can help you. In finishing this chapter on scene study, if you get the whole script or play, you make your decisions on the whole script. But, most of the time, you only get a few pages. You simply have to make it up.

Trust that you can make it up. Use your imagination, do all the things listed in this chapter and make it up. Try to remember you can't be scolded for your creative decisions if you have not read the whole play or feature film script or television episode.

Scene study is about creating back story to scene and character. It is a time of exploration. It is not just a time of picking up a new scene and making an immediate choice and then performing the scene within an hour.

Unless you have to audition quickly for television or if you are on a television station set and working as a series regular or in a recurring role; otherwise take your time and explore. I say this because, when on a television set, you will need to learn lines and scenes very quickly.

For the most part, I suggest you don't rush into making a quick decision, especially when working on scenes for theatre and film.

Please also remember, with soap opera preparation, we don't need to create complex characters or have complicated things going on in the scenes because soap operas are written in such a way that what is happening is all that needs to be said and then replied to. I could say more on this, but it would all relate to the style of drama that soap opera is. This book is about acting not an analysis of the soap opera style of writing.

Learning Point Number Four:

- Scene Study the Australian way is about developing different ways to analyze the scene
- The best literature in the world is ambiguous. Meaning, it can be interpreted in different ways. Remember this
- Read, read, read and try to improve your English comprehension skills
- Don't be lazy and make a quick, easy and often clichéd decision about what is going on in a scene. Unless it is for TV soap opera, don't do this, be smart
- Always make decisions about who you are and where you are and what is going on – all according to the genre and style of what you are doing
- Create, then let it go in performance. Trust that your choices will come through your work. And if they don't, don't worry for now

*Above: Paul performing in the lead role with actor Amanda Forti in the theatre play Fur Better or Worse at Gasworks Theatre in South Melbourne, Victoria, Australia, in 1997. Paul played a **character** who lived a life where he spoke to his puppet-like cat, called Felix, as if the puppet was alive and they both fell in love with a girl who lived nearby. The play was written by Colin Donald.*

Below: Paul performing in the lead role in Life What A Front! In the Adelaide Fringe Festival in Adelaide, Australia, in 1998. In this play Paul played a **character** *that talked about the different masks/the different faces people walk around with from day to day.*

Chapter 5: Create Characters

Some young actors utter the following words to me: "Why should I create characters?"

Developing characters is very important. Actors should know how to create characters and simply create them, continuously.

Actors who have performed in theatre generally know about the importance of characters, but often TV/film actors do not. Soap opera actors generally don't even play characters; they, most often, simply play themselves or various parts of themselves.

Over the years, hundreds of students of mine have told me that some acting teachers simply say: "Just learn the lines, make no decisions and go out and do the scene." This is such a provocative statement to me and one that I firmly do not agree with.

Please allow me to digress for a moment. In 2002 – when I founded and started teaching my school in the States – I wrote the curriculum, initially comprising twelve levels. Four subjects per level. In Level One, I immediately created a month of classes called Creating Characters from Nothing and actors either loved or were ambivalent about this course over many years.

Some actors did not want to do character-creating classes. Some actors simply wanted to learn lines quickly and then perform. Over the years I have said to these actors that this is lazy. This is a lazy way to think and behave.

American actors, for example, would reply to me by saying things like, "Our history is continually doing cold reading and scene study classes where we are given scripts and make a quick decision and then perform under pressure."

I acknowledge this with the student but believe that this is not the way to go. When I addressed this topic with one of my Skype students, this is what she said to me. I quote: "You are very perceptive, that's why I like you as an acting teacher. I did struggle with creating a character even though I wrote a pretty good monologue for my character I didn't feel connected to it. I found myself working on other career related things than on my character. That's how I ended up getting myself to some open calls, so it wasn't all bad. Why did that happen? I honestly don't know. Maybe I'm not as interested in creating characters as I thought I was."

What I love about teaching this *Creating Characters from Nothing* subject class, that I still teach today is that casting directors, especially in Australia, are now talking a lot about the importance of actors developing characters, and many, many actors around the world are now listening.

A very important part of working as an actor is learning to create characters. I sometimes incorporate developing character work in with my scene study classes. In Book One, I wrote a list of things to do to help you create characters. I would now like to elaborate on this list and give your much more information on creating characters.

Character definition (from Wikipedia)

I would like to give a dictionary definition of character because many actors do not realize the importance of character and they often don't really know how to create a character. This is how Wikipedia defines "character":

"One of the attributes or features that make up and distinguish an individual ... The complex of mental and ethical traits marking and often individualizing a person, group, or nation: the character of the American people ... a person marked by notable or conspicuous traits quite a character b: one of the persons of a drama or novel c: the personality or part which an actor recreates an actress who can create a character convincing d:

characterization especially in drama or fiction ... in character: in accord with a person's usual qualities or traits behaving in character."

Memorable character performances

Can you think, please: what are your most memorable characters on stage or screen?

My most memorable character performance on stage is watching Sir Michael Gambon playing the caretaker in the West End of London production of the same name (written by Harold Pinter), and Antony Sher, playing Richard III, with the Royal Shakespeare Company. On screen, my most memorable character performances include the following. Note, in some cases, the names of the films that they have been excellent in, have been listed too:

- Daniel Day-Lewis – in basically anything that he does
- Stanley Tucci – in basically anything that he does
- Meryl Streep – in basically anything that she does
- Al Pacino – in basically anything that he does
- Humphrey Bogart and Ingrid Bergman – Casablanca
- Sally Hawkins – film Happy Go Lucky and basically anything that she does
- Denzel Washington – in basically anything that he does
- Gary Oldman – Darkest Hour
- Christoph Waltz – Inglourious Basterds
- Forest Whitaker – The Last King of Scotland
- Philip Seymour Hoffman – Capote

Here is a list of a few character actors that I love on screen

Female character actors

- Sally Hawkins
- Krysten Ritter
- Cate Blanchett
- Carey Mulligan
- Meryl Streep
- Allison Janney
- Melanie Lynskey
- CCH Pounder
- Jodie Comer
- Toni Collette

Male character actors

- Daniel Day-Lewis
- Philip Seymour Hoffman
- Stanley Tucci
- Denzel Washington
- Tom Hanks
- Guy Pearce
- Damon Herriman

When I work with actors on this characters' subject class called *Creating Characters from Nothing*, I work in six different ways:

- From words – from adjectives
- From observation
- From props and costumes and make-up and hair style
- From using visual images
- From technique charts I have created that derive from classical theatre/acting teachers. Such as, Grotowski, Laban, Brecht, Stanislavski

- From my Australian Techniques

When actors think they have their character ready to perform, I put the actor/character in a spotlight interview.

I turn a spotlight, theatre light or floodlight on a space on the floor and the actor enters it as their character. I, and members of the class, ask the actor questions about their character. Basically, the audience can ask them anything and the actor has to respond as the character. The audience takes note of both the verbal and non-verbal communication.

Actors love this exercise and it helps them suspend disbelief, create new things and think about their character, on the spot, under pressure as they are in front of the audience and the teacher.

Creating characters: Comments from students

When creating characters in my classes, my students have commented about what they'd like to achieve:

- I would like to walk away with a process for approaching characterization of scripts for screen; examining the expressive skills – voice, movement, gesture and facial expression in regard to characterization
- Have greater confidence in how to approach creating a character from text for the screen
- Develop realistic, relatable and authentic characters
- Know how to refine the back story of a character
- Have a well laid out step by step process to create a character which addresses both the internal aspects (what the character is going through mentally, emotionally) and external ones (props/clothes/physical trademarks and characteristics) and then bringing that onto camera without messing up the frame and not worrying about camera/frame technicalities, ensuring the character is truly different and my own self is not projected on the character
- Non-verbal movements and the extent to which I can break the "V"/basic rules and move my eyes around within the frame

- When to use them, how big and when to go big or reduce
- Knowing other types of characters to I can be aware to expand my range. Ways to create characters – techniques
- Improving "acting", being more natural and authentic in a relaxed way, as well as expressing and accessing parts of myself that go beyond what I believe my capacity and range of emotions are. I also struggle sometimes with being grounded and still, so it would be nice to work on how to be still on camera yet still captivating, as I sometimes get stuck in the mindset that more is better (e.g. bigger reactions and movement, louder voice), but I'm learning that sometimes less is more
- The opportunity of playing challenging characters for me, and remembering what I can do if I just let go
- Creating a character from something well-known or a character that has very strict requirements and how to make it my own. Making a stereotype interesting. Making a character from scratch without any input or starting ideas. Standing out as a support character or a character with only a few lines. How to people-watch actively and the types of things to pay attention to (e.g. how they walk, where their eyes look when talking to someone, their little tics, etc.). How to play characters from a different era, e.g. the 1800s, where to look when creating those types of characters
- Making one's actions and objectives believable
- Staying in character and not choosing to be something for the sake of creating a character, but choosing something interesting that makes it stand out, while staying true to what the author intends

Can you relate to some of these comments? I cannot address each point above in full detail, but this section will give you things to think about and exercises to do, to help you in most of these areas where these points are raised. I listed them, because, as said in Book One, lots of actors have the same concerns when learning to act and book work.

Character background charts

In working intensely on developing characters with actors, I find it's very useful for them to create a chart on which they can ask questions about a character and then fill the answers in. This helps an actor start to think about developing a character's background.

I first make the connection between them as human beings and the theory of developing characters.

So, I ask actors to ask themselves the following questions: how do I generally feel that day? What did I do just before going into class? Why am I here? What is the weather like? The season? The day of the week? The time? Where am I? Who am I? Where have I been? What place am I in now? What time and date is it? What am I going to do here? What do I want? How will I get it? What must I overcome? Who else is here? What are the sensory realities of the place I am in?

The source of the above questions originated from Russian acting teacher Stanislavski. Lindy Davies adapted them. I did too.

Then I ask the actor to answer these questions for the character they are developing and about to perform.

All of this helps the actor develop and understand a sense of history of a human being's life and a fictional character's life. Answering these questions and remembering that we all have these things going on in us at all times, gives us that sense of our past history.

A sense of history that influences us. This is what I would like you to do for the characters that you play and put into practice. I suggest you create both a character's internal and external world.

A character's internal world

- What is the character's need, desire, want, objective, or other internal stimulus?
- What is their social background?
- What are their ethical values?

- What are their physical peculiarities and/or ways of thinking?
- What are their psychological peculiarities and/or ways of thinking?

CHARACTER BACKGROUND CHART – INTERNAL
Filling in these charts will help you development your characters.
I have put some information in the charts to assist you with the understanding of the questions.

INTERNAL (need, desire, want, or other internal stimulus)	INTERNAL Social Background	INTERNAL Ethical Values	INTERNAL *Physical Peculiarities *both phys. and psych can link in	INTERNAL *Psych. Peculiarities *both phys. and psych can link in
Want off the AIDA want sheet	Religion, where the character comes from, family, status /class	Learned behavior through family/ surroundings, values, religious values... i.e., they value marriage, love. What is their code of ethics I.e., they don't kill, they abide by Government and society rules, etcetera	Age, Habits i.e. biting fingernails, lips, and twirling hair. Twitches, Facial features, body features, peculiar expressions, physicality from an accident or birth defect i.e. limp... Psychological damage could change physicality I.e., being yelled at or abused as a child could affect posture and/or the use of body	Speech impediments, psychological damage, personality traits, disorders, thoughts and ideas. A physicality could make one insecure or shy... You do things or say things that could be peculiar and could stem from your thought patterns

A character's external world

- What is the character's social environment?
- What is their physical environment?
- What are the relationships and or attitudes towards other characters?
- What are the specific given circumstances?

CHARACTER BACKGROUND CHART – EXTERNAL

EXTERNAL Social Environment	EXTERNAL Physical Environment (setting)	EXTERNAL Relationships and/or attitudes towards other characters	EXTERNAL Specific Given Circumstances
Social Class of the environment, I.e., Beverly Hills or Sth. Central? What's going on in the place, the majority political view of environment I.e., Conservative vs. Liberal Environment, Time Period I.e., modern day vs. Elizabethan What can you see there? What does the general neighborhood look like? Hotels? I.e., city, state, building	People in the space, season, location description of room and things in it, date, sensory realities	Make a decision about who the character is with and how you fell about them. Age? Why you like/dislike them? How long have you known them? How do you know them, etcetera?	Most important things you want to note that are given from the scene. List them here. i.e., they are married, one has a broken arm, etcetera

Chapter 5: Create Characters | 129

Sensory reality

Thinking of the five senses of sight, smell, sound, taste and touch will help you with the moment before the scene starts. I ask actors to think, what did my character just do? Where are they? How can you establish that? I like to walk actors through the five senses. Take them on a journey that incorporates the five senses one at a time.

I like to take them on a journey into imagining they are in different places – e.g. in a shopping centre like the Beverly Center in Los Angeles, or a beach somewhere, in the desert, a government office, etcetera – and ask them the following questions: What does your character hear? Please react to it. What do they smell? React to it. What can they touch? React to it. What can they see? React to it. What can they taste? React to it.

Character archetypes

In the world of character choices, it is good for you to think about character archetypes. Some people say there are 16 character archetypes. Others say there are 14 or 7, while some people say there are only 6 character archetypes.

Archetypes are basically characters displaying inherent truths in nature. Each character archetype below represents a small piece of ourselves. Which ones do you identify with?

- The hero
- The shadow
- The sidekick
- The villain
- The lover
- The mentor
- The mother
- The Everyman
- The damsel
- The trickster
- The guardian
- The herald

- The outlaw
- The revolutionary
- The ruler

The reason I have listed the archetypes here is because it is a really good idea for you to think of this list when you are working on developing your character for your audition. Are you the *guardian*? Like a teacher. Are you the outlaw, like a criminal in a TV drama? Are you the lover, like the young heart throb in a soap opera?

I suggest you could also think which ones out of this list of character archetypes am I generally, as an actor?

You then target your headshot and your reel towards those archetypes to help you get work. The industry calls this *knowing your type* or *knowing your brand*.

Character types

To begin with, let's look at one that is not normally known or spoken of, but exists everywhere. Everyman – the dictionary description says, "an ordinary or typical human being". Think: males: Mark Ruffalo, Stanley Tucci, Philip Seymour Hoffman, Tom Hanks. And females: Meryl Streep, Helen Hunt, Scarlett Johansson, Amy Adams, CCH Pounder.

This article from Screen Rant lists ten Everyman actors: https://screenrant.com/everyman-actors-hollywood/

Below is a list of character types that I like to work with. Which ones can you relate to? Which ones do you get called into audition for?

- Everyman
- Executive/business person/lawyer – professional business look
- Professional athlete/pro tennis player – athletic look
- Personal trainer, physical therapist, surfer
- High society girl/debutante
- Girl next door/mom, boy next door/dad, best friend

- A specific look for your hobby – for example roller-skater, stamp collector
- Sexy vixen/assassin, femme fatale, mistress
- Police cop/detective, uniform
- Computer programmer
- Nurse, doctor, orderly, X-ray person
- Secretary, intern, personal assistant
- Artistic type, like director, writer, photographer, painter, actor, musician, bohemian
- Publicist, teacher, agent, therapist
- Blue collar, factory and trade worker
- Can't get it together character, drunk person, "hot mess" (e.g. Kramer from Seinfeld)
- Homeless, addict, mental disability
- Feisty sidekick, organizer, spiritual type, e.g. actress Gloria Foster playing The Oracle in Matrix; Danny De Vito
- Refugee – lost, confused, looking for a place to belong
- Villain, terrorist, drug dealer, assassin

An aside: Ask your family and friends what types of characters they think you are most like, and what types of characters you could play. Their perspective will, most often, result in better choices than the ones you choose yourself.

Next, think: comedy or drama? Or, both? What are you best at? You should focus on this and the character types chosen should reflect on your type/brand: in your headshot, showreel, the characters you choose to market yourself as.

To help you with character creation, here is a list where you can watch a few simulated occupations being brought to life

Nurses
https://www.youtube.com/watch?v=ffcrgAZbfN0
Corporate Entrepeneurships
https://www.youtube.com/watch?v=e1rEHiuDtuc
People talking about how to act like certain occupations
Police Person
https://www.youtube.com/watch?v=dVYigRXLleg
first 2 min then to 8.55 for 30 seconds
Girl Next Door
https://www.youtube.com/watch?v=GLGxB-Fb60I
Lawyer
https://www.youtube.com/watch?v=3NcDB1F5zGw
or
https://www.youtube.com/watch?v=n9qO4O4ihbQ
or
https://www.youtube.com/watch?v=W2JllRVumCY
Actors playing these occupations
Female Detectives in Television
https://www.youtube.com/watch?v=mf8GmDSRaXU
Ten Detectives in Film
https://www.youtube.com/watch?v=hUsVrQNDhNo
Finally, Elizebethan characters. A touch of fun.
https://www.youtube.com/watch?v=TmQKihNpsHk

This list is just to get you started. Do Google and YouTube searches yourself.

Getting applicable scripts to play and rehearse with

- Go through the scripts on your computer
- Look for scripts you have stored somewhere or from other actors in class
- With suggestions from film/TV shows, find them and transcribe or print the scripts
- Research on YouTube/Google
- Write your own or get someone to write them for you

Give yourself some homework by preparing the scene based on the above. Then do an activity like: use a method from my Character Development charts. Go get props and costumes if you wish. Say to yourself, "Bit by bit, I will improvise focusing on verbal and non-verbal communication, all to help me develop characters."

Note the language you use when you improvise as the language has to reflect or relate to the character you choose. The non-verbal communication with the body has to reflect the posture, the attitude and status of that character to some degree. Then perform screens with the character that you have created. Focus on the development of these characters.

Some options for creating characters
Use of body

- Gait (a person's manner of walking)
- Mannerisms (the way you use your body)
- Affectation (behaviour, speech, or writing that is pretentious and designed to impress). Think of the character Capote played by Philip Seymour Hoffman in the film Capote
- Posture (how you stand or sit)
- Affected by: age, war, pregnancy, emotions/thoughts, occupation, missing limb

Imitation

- Copying, imitating someone as best you can
- Drawing attention to what you're doing

Here are a few more ways to help you create characters

- Your observations in life
- Seeing people in their occupations
- Writing down three physical characteristics of your character's occupation. Then three verbal characteristics. Then improvise with that. Then move to music to help you
- Finish off by putting yourself in a spotlight interview and have a friend interview you, where you respond as the character

Some concluding thoughts on creating characters

As actors, one thing you are continually doing is trying to emulate human beings in life.

So, think, what do we human beings do in life? How do we interact? How do we behave? Am I, as a human being, paying attention to the people, the type of characters, that I am meeting on a day-to-day basis? Am I paying attention to what people are wanting from me, especially without them saying it?

For example, when people, including strangers, *talk* to you, as well as simply listening to comprehend and reply to that person, you could be reading their body language and listening to how they are saying what they are saying to you. Pay attention to their tone, volume, pitch, intensity of their voice, etcetera.

Most of us do this subconsciously anyway. That's where your instincts come from. For example, when you say to someone "I don't like that person" or "I feel a bit unsure about that person", well, it is often your instincts that have influenced this point of view.

So why not make your subconscious thoughts be conscious ones? Australian actress Ruth Cracknell was such an avid human being watcher and would take note of character behaviour from women that she met, or saw, and store this in the back of her head for future female characters.

Hopefully, you are most likely noting what people are doing non-verbally when in your presence too. This could be a look in their eyes, or something they do with their body. This could also include the distance they are from you and if this is changing.

You could also take note of the pauses in their discourse. What is existing or could be existing in the pauses? The time in which no one speaks. Don't forget this – as this is human-to-human interaction. Your job is to mimic this as an actor.

I encourage you to please heighten your awareness and observations of people, so you become acutely aware of them. Your decision, your gut feeling, on whether or not you like someone or not, your impulse, is based on this interaction. Actors often forget this. Don't. Use it.

As described in Book One, the non-impulse exercise where you sit opposite another actor and think deeply about all the different options of what you are about to say and what the other person says to you, is a terrific reawakening of what we do, quickly in life, but slowed down in the exercise; so, consider exploring this exercise.

If necessary, slow down your thinking process. It will make you a better actor and help you not act. Which of course is paradoxical as we are acting, but we must give the illusion that we are not.

One final note on this. This makes me think of the late and great English writer Harold Pinter. Pinter wrote his plays with the pauses written into the script for the actors to follow. Explore the possibilities in the silence. Explore all you can, then think about what you are about to say and how it could be said and then speak.

As already said, what sort of characters or occupations do people generally say that you naturally look like? For example, do they think you look like a killer? Or a young mum? A tradie? Or a nurse? I ask this, as I suggest you start creating characters based on what people think you look like. When you get strong at this, branch off into creating characters that you don't naturally look like as well, but characters that you want to play or practise creating, as a part of expanding your acting skills.

Your look

In closing on creating characters, I see many actors make the mistake that I made – that of, not knowing their type, their brand.

As an actor, I used to think I could play anything. In hindsight, I think my headshots looked plain and did not match the type of characters and occupations that casting directors brought me in to audition for.

My headshots were either a clean-shaven and smiling shot or a dramatic look with a three-day beard growth. At one period of time, this included the collar turned up on a leather jacket. I was often thinking that I was the latest heart throb. In hindsight, I don't think I targeted myself very well.

What characters are best suited to you? Have you ever thought, "What is my type?" Have you ever thought, "Does my headshot refect a character that I can play?" Or is it just a nice photo?

Your headshot should look like one of the characters that you can play. If you are a beginner or have low credits, as a developing actor, you should especially think of creating characters that suit your look.

Your type of character

Do you have a showreel? Does the showreel have you playing characters that are similar to the type of characters that you are most likely going to be cast as? I recommend you target your choices to your type. I do this with actors and their showreels. I direct them on their *brand*, their type, to help them get their careers going.

It is show business after all. Knowing your brand and marketing yourself with that brand falls into the business category of show business.

Learning Point Number Five:

- Never underestimate the importance of creating characters
- The actors who create interesting and believable characters win awards around the world
- Life is full of interesting characters – take from them
- Enjoy the process and learn to create characters
- Be bold and daring with your character creation and see where it takes you
- Use the charts and the lists that I have included in this chapter to help you create characters
- Know your brand (your look) and create characters that suit your brand

Chapter 6: Differences between Australian and American acting training, Part 1

I teach around the world, particularly in the USA and Australia. Probably a thousand actors have asked me what is the difference between Australian and North American (USA) acting training? What are the differences in the classes? In the training of the actor to perform in front of the camera? What are the differences in the people?

This chapter compares acting training in the United States and Australia. It is based on my long experience of living and teaching in both countries.

I want to put forward a hypothesis about Australian and American psyche, culture, thinking and behaving, based on extensive experience in Australia and the United States. Experiences that also include what many, many, many students have said to me.

Please allow me a bit of latitude as I walk you down a path of acting training history, a path of entertainment industry infrastructure, a path of creative craft of mass production and of mass marketing. A craft that has longevity and has had a profound influence on film and television making from the United States of America. Production that is also seen from all around the world.

I will then like to try to link all this information into a hypothesis concerning Australian acting training versus, or including, American acting training. Culminating with some points to consider between the two countries in their ways of thinking, their ways of approaching the work and in performing the work. This includes performing on screen.

What are the differences between Australian acting training and American acting training?

Let me begin to answer that question by saying, I'm grateful, America, for your in-depth entertainment industry, especially for film and television and especially in Los Angeles.

I grew up watching American television shows. Still today, the dominant television drama that I watch are US TV dramas. It is the best! The majority of films that I watch are US-made too. I do love French, Belgian, British, Australian and Japanese films – in fact, I will watch a film from anywhere in the world – but American films dominate my viewings.

One of the reasons this is made easy for me, and probably all Australians, is because America has a dominance over the movie theatres in Australia. I think American companies own all of the big movie theatres in Australia.

Me settling into living and working in America

How did I join the entertainment industry profession, the *team* of *other* teachers in the States and influence actor training in America? How did I offer advice to a country, where its actors and the industry are known throughout the world as having *Hollywood* and *Broadway*? How did I offer advice to a country that has a rich history of film and television production and so many famous film and television actors? I humbly state, I just did and still do. My resume of actors' booked work speaks for itself. This grows monthly and will continue to do so.

All actors at my school AIDA in the States have learnt what I called Australian techniques, and I am still teaching Australian techniques worldwide on Skype and Zoom and in person when I tour today.

Consequently, I humbly state that I know I can improve American actors' work because, for one important thing, I really speak from the heart. I give Americans truth, justice and the Australian way of candour with my teachings. I teach with love and with wisdom, wisdom from both my education and my experience. I teach techniques. I also have an astute eye and ear. I teach my Australian way.

An aside: As explained in my first book, I teach *other* international acting theorists as well as what I developed and called Australian techniques. So as a teacher, I would like to remind the reader that I don't just focus on teaching Americans – *Australian* techniques.

I have taught, most likely, over two thousand American actors. I have asked them to broaden their minds and consider Australian actor training, and grow. If you are an American reading this book, I hope you will consider it too.

Culture – sub-culture – psyche

I would like to give three definitions from Wikipedia here, simply to help us in this chapter.

Culture definition: *"the ideas, customs, and social behaviour of a particular people or society"* and *"The arts and other manifestations of human intellectual achievement regarded collectively"*.

Sub-culture definition: *"a cultural group within a larger culture, often having beliefs or interests at variance with those of the larger culture"*.

Psyche definition: *"the human soul, mind, or spirit"* and *"in psychology, your psyche is your mind and your deepest feelings and attitudes"*.

I first visited America from Australia in 1988 as a tourist. I went to Disneyland, Universal Studios and Hollywood.

I arrived in America for the first time as a professional performing artist/teacher, to live, in September of 2000.

To begin with, from my experiences, Americans were wonderful at accepting this foreigner onto their soil. In the States, people would often say to me, "I love your accent and you Aussies are really nice. We love you guys!"

I was introduced to the black and white and Hispanic/Latino cultures. It wasn't too long before I realized that, not only were there many immigrants in Los Angeles, but there was also a *Thai Town, Little Tokyo, Little Armenia* and many other sections of Los Angeles, all named after a particular culture.

Of course, there is also the profound Spanish and Mexican influences too. In addition, when I moved to and started teaching in New York I was experiencing Manhattan which has a *Little Italy* and a *China Town* and, in particular, a massive Puerto Rican influence. This multiculturalism was terrific to see.

I grew up knowing that Australians Errol Flynn, Rod Taylor and Olivia Newton John had come to America and were successful. To see all of these different cultures existing in the one city, and in some other parts of the one country, made me feel like anything was possible in the good old US of A.

For the most part, on the surface, I noticed Americans embracing new concepts and opportunities from everywhere. From my life experiences, Australians didn't do this as much.

In terms of culture, I experienced some similarities between Australians and Americans. For example, in both the States and Australia they often call *it* for what it is – meaning they call things for what they are. Especially in New York.

US openness

Millions of people worldwide want to go and live in the USA. Even in 2023, they see the USA as a country of freedom. A land of self-expression. A land of financial and business growth. And it is all these things. In some ways it is a brilliant country and a brilliant place to be.

With multiculturalism evident in America, I am sure this made it easier for me to be accepted. Accepted in theory and in practice, both as a personal acting coach and as the artistic director of AIDA.

Over my time of *living in* America, I taught probably over two thousand actors, and a fair share of actors from South America, England, Europe, Asia and, of course, Australia, on US soil.

There's a terrific openness by many people in the USA. Americans allow other cultures to settle in their country, and then they allow themselves to be taught by somebody from another culture.

This openness, this welcoming, this desire to learn from other parts of the world was and still is seen and experienced today. It is extremely pleasing and flattering to see, and many people from the States have this. Thank you.

Australia is also very open to doing this. But I do wonder if the USA gets enough credit for this acceptance. I know that America does have an immigrant background dating back a few hundred years, but it is very nice to experience it first-hand.

Differences between Australian and American actor training – a hypothesis

I would like to discuss now what it is about Australia and Australian acting training that did help American actors through my school. This could help actors reading this book and help other actors in the future.

I will also try and address why Australian actors could find it easier to act well, as a general rule, than American actors.

I would like to preface what I am about to discuss here by saying that I can only talk about my experiences as a human being living in America, touring and teaching in America and my experiences as an actor and a teacher; teaching through my school in the USA, and when I now tour to the USA to teach and my online classes. I add, I also pay attention to what actors have told me over the years.

Brad Pitt or Julia Roberts did not walk through my doors prior to making it big. However, I am very comfortable with the training received, the work done and the improvement made by the likes of Jeannetta Arnette, Gerald Webb, Tarnue Massaquoi, Preston Jones, Naama Kates, Elina Madison, Cyanne McClairian, Nicole Dionne and a couple of thousand others who have walked through my doors and then got better. With many, many, hundreds of them booking work along the way. They still do book work.

Why Aussies?

It takes an Australian fourteen to fifteen hours in a plane to get to the USA. Longer if they fly to New York. Then to work, an Australian has to apply for visas to stay and work there. They must produce lots of paper work, they sometimes financially and emotionally struggle and then they pay a lot of money to immigration lawyers to get a Green Card or working papers. Then they have to try and get representation and auditions and work.

Australians are away from their culture, their way of being, especially their family and friends. Australia has no Hollywood or Broadway. An Australian comes from a population of 25 million versus 330 million in the States; and yet there is an Australian actor as a series regular in many American television shows and in *so many* movies. And a very long history of this now.

Most Australian actors in the USA are acting in the lead roles or as series regulars and doing American accents. Thousands of British actors are also in the USA and are very successful too.

That's right, for the most part, the Aussies and Brits are acting with different accents. This is not so easy to do and takes training and constant diligence and time to learn.

An aside: Some people in the States might be surprised to know that Christian Bale and Gerard Butler are English and that Anthony LaPaglia and Naomi Watts are Australian.

Aussies and Brits consistently booking lead roles in America must piss off quite a few American actors. Some Americans must ask themselves, "Why are there so many Australians and Brits in American roles? Doing US accents. Why is this so?" Well, this is one of the main reasons that I am presenting this hypothesis.

When I arrived in America and started teaching, I came across one other Australian acting teacher. When I left, after living in the States for nearly eleven years, many acting schools had Australians working for them.

It is absolutely amazing as to why so many Aussies are doing so very well in America. There is nothing in the water. So, what is it? Let's continue this hypothesis.

Some possible differences between the cultures

To begin with, from my experiences, my teachings and from talking to American students over many years (*here is a generalization coming*), generally speaking, Australian training seems to me to be more internal than US training. Perhaps Australian training is also more diverse than US training.

In addition, the psyche of an Australian is far different from the psyche of an American, and this, I believe does affect the training, the preparation taken and the work.

Australians are, generally, more polite and far more humble than Americans. Perhaps the Australian acting teachers are more honest in their feedback to actors in training too. Let's hypothesize on these points.

You know, as I am writing this, I feel I have to step lightly. As I am not out to belittle American, South American or any other type of actor training from anywhere throughout the world and/or put Australian actor training on a pedestal.

I am just stating my experiences, my thoughts, a hypothesis, and trying to identify the differences to help educate and assist the US actor and of course gain a better understanding of my teachings, as well as how best I can train Americans even better with my teachings. I always strive for excellence from myself.

Internal training?

I am well aware of the abundance of technique schools and classes in America.

The two biggest places for actors in the States are:

A. Los Angeles – which is mostly known for its cold reading, scene study classes and casting director workshops, and,

B. New York – which is known predominately for its musical theatre and Broadway shows, and its classes on acting, singing and dancing. I've lived in both cities for many years.

The city of angels

In Los Angeles, the actor is open to cold reading and scene study classes and casting director workshops everywhere.

In these classes or workshops, for the most part, the actor is paired up and given scenes from scripts, as they arrive at the class. Then they work on the scenes with their partner in the hallway, or outside away from the teacher or the person taking the class.

After the actors perform in these *cold reading, scene study classes and casting director workshops*, they may get a few words said to them by the person taking the class, maybe not, maybe they get to do the scene again, maybe not, maybe they get put on camera, maybe not.

The comments below are based on personal experience and on me paraphrasing, or quoting, American actors who have told me that these comments are common when in front of, in particular, Los Angeles casting directors. I have also heard these comments myself when I have invited casting directors into my school in America and they have talked to the students.

Quite interestingly, my students have told me what their former acting teachers have said to them as feedback. Those comments are most often identical to this list below too.

US actors generally get the following feedback:

- I really liked your choice. Well done. Thank you
- Can you do it again – just like that
- Thank you!
- You didn't take a risk. I like to see risks. Thank you for showing me your work though. Who is next?
- That's not what is going on in the scene ... you should have done it like this...
- Wow, look at your hair, it is so nice in this headshot of you
- I see on your resume that you worked on ... what was that like?
- Do you get called in for thirty-somethings? Cause I think you could play younger?
- What is the origin of your last name?
- Are you in SAG?
- You know I think you're going to get your big break when you are older
- I need more. Give me more
- You are just not standing out enough

As said, if it is an acting or cold reading or scene study class, I have personally experienced and been told by hundreds of American students, that they often get the same comments as written above.

Sometimes the actors get verbally abused or put down. They get told what they did was wrong. They also sometimes get told that's why they are where they are as actors, and they get told how they should have interpreted the script.

Then they sit and watch fifteen to twenty other pairs of actors get up and do their scene for three to four hours; then they all go home. And they pay money for this privilege.

If they are lucky, these actors are learning how to: better cold read, how to take, what American actors call *minor adjustments* (although they often don't get any), how to take and hopefully *handle abuse*, and also from what I've been told, and what I have personally experienced myself, *not that much else*.

Yet, actors flock to these classes. Actors spend their hard-earned money in these classes in America. Particularly in Los Angeles.

But what if they are not good enough actors yet? What if their skills need work? What if they don't know how to interpret a script well – such as the plot line and its changes – and all this under pressure? What if they don't know how to create a character? Or create a character quickly? Or how to connect with the text so they look believable? Or know how to cry on cue? Or even how to cold read? What if they have no technique to assist them?

The list could go on and on with what *ifs* as to why they don't book work, but yet, they will flock to a US *named* or sometimes *not known* teacher's class or workshop, including a casting directors' workshop, like sheep; because they think that this is what they have to do.

I can understand why a casting director wouldn't talk too much about actor training, as it is not their job to. But a bit more feedback would be nice, instead of just hearing the clichés mentioned, wouldn't it?

Acting schools that run their classes and workshops the same way as described above, in my humble opinion, have no excuse. As stated in Book One, they should be training their actors, not simply out to take the actors' money. Because that is what they are doing – they're making money.

Most of the people teaching actors in America and Australia and Japan are not even qualified teachers. They are called *Industry experts*. Sometimes self-proclaimed *Industry experts*.

An aside: Some Australian schools and classes are now in America and doing the same thing. Also, some Australian schools are starting to follow the American ways of running classes in Australia.

I suggest you thoroughly check the background of every person that you are considering being taught by or the schools you are considering studying at. Is the person or are the people teaching at that school trained teachers? And if so, in what fields? They should be a drama and/or a performing or actor training trained teacher. Sadly, I know many are not.

Check out people's IMDB credits too. As many are contrived. Has the person teaching you added every single music video and all other types of corporate videos done to their IMDB page to help get their tally of credits up?

Check out their work. Watch the actor on stage or screen and see if they are or were any good when performing.

What do they teach? Often ask, what is the origin of this work? As many teachers or people called industry experts are simply stealing things from other teachers. For example, dozens of students have told me of teachers taking and teaching what I teach and not acknowledging the source – meaning me.

Finally, and most importantly, ask yourself, are they a good teacher? What am I learning from that teacher? Please always ask yourself, what am I learning from that teacher or person who is teaching me?

Whatever kind of class the actor is in, whether it be a cold reading class or a scene study class or whatever they want to call it, surely the teacher should try to improve the actor's work? The actor's craft? The actor's skills? A lot of these *so-called teachers* do not do this. Some have told me to my face, they are there for one thing only, the money. I believe this is very sad.

Back to thinking about teaching in Los Angeles. Could then, this way of thinking, this behaviour and these experiences, have a direct correlation to the training that the actors receive in Los Angeles? I'm sure it does. I know it does. Please now think of my definition of the words culture, sub-culture and psyche as this is the culture Los Angeles actors are living in.

Above: The AIDA theatre on Santa Monica Boulevard in Hollywood, LA 90038, in 2010.

New York, New York

I lived in Manhattan, New York, for approximately four years. I then travelled there for work with my school AIDA for four more years. I returned and taught there in 2014, 2016, 2018 and 2019. I also ongoingly teach actors who live in New York, online.

In New York, the city produces and performs musical theatre everywhere and it is indeed *showy*. Meaning it is all about pizzazz and glamour. Just think of the musical *42nd Street*. Actors sing, dance and kick and *ham it up* for audiences from all around the world to see.

America has a rich and successful history of this on Broadway, New York. Most actors working professionally in New York can either, or are in training to, sing, act and dance as best as they can.

Light *showy* entertainment is a part of show business and I see it as entertainment in the realms of *variety entertainment*. Variety entertainment that grew from vaudeville on the east coast states of America.

An aside: For all the times I taught in Manhattan over many years, while I was teaching acting in one room, through the walls I could hear piano keys being pressed and an actor singing the *"nor nor nor nor, nor nor nor, not nor"* notes through one wall and the constant tapping and sliding of dance shoes from another adjacent room.

I am going to use a not quite apt expression here, for want of a better phrase, I am calling it *shallow variety musical theatre*. Please think musical theatre and not dramatic theatre, as musical theatre is what dominates Broadway, and Broadway has a history of it. I am not a fan of it.

Could then, this type of product, that is produced in New York, have a direct correlation to the training that the actors receive to get them into these productions? I'm sure it does.

Please now think of the topics, and their examples under the headings of: culture, sub-culture and psyche. Because really this is the only reason

I am talking about the showy types of performances on the east coast. Yes, I am sure there are correlations. This then clearly is the accepted *way to learn and to perform* for many actors on the east coast of America and is therefore food for thought.

So, the point that I am making here is that, in some cases, we don't have depth in the training work in New York, because the performances are rooted in *showy* musical theatre.

An aside: Let's contradict that point straight away by saying that in New York, in particular, from my experiences, actors seem to have much more love for theatre, much more interest in education and training and much more diverse training than in Los Angeles.

But to summarize:

In New York, New York, let's at least consider that there is some correlation between *showy musical theatre* work and actors having a lack of substance and depth in their training, which influences their decision making, their preparation and their performances.

In Los Angeles, generally speaking, actors have a tendency to flock to a cold read or scene study class, or a casting director workshop, where they are not generally taught acting *per se*; the students' focus is often on getting accredited names on their resumes, as if it is one of the most important things to an American actor.

As pointed out, they are often getting taught by non-qualified acting coaches, deemed "industry experts" and sometimes failed actors, who can't act.

As discussed in Book One, actors are also often taught by untrained teachers and older actors who simply got work because they were pretty or charismatic when they were younger.

Australia

There are strong correlations between the actor who is trained really well and who then performs in strong theatre and then moves across into work in film and television.

Australian productions put on *showy* musical theatre too. But Australian theatre predominately produces strong, in-depth, meaningful, socially provocative, character and plot-driven theatre. Think Australian playwrights: David Williamson, Michael Gow, Patricia Cornelius and others. Generally speaking, it is the overseas musicals brought into Australia that are showy. Most of these are from America.

This strong Australian dramatic theatre is seen through such companies as the Melbourne Theatre Company, Playbox Theatre Company and the Belvoir and Sydney Theatre Companies, etcetera. Even at small theatres and independent places like La Mama in Melbourne, theatre is often of a very high standard. Generally speaking, many well-trained Australian actors follow this path and perform in strong theatre and then film and television.

In regards to work that is produced on screen: after living and working in the States for so many years, I notice that Australian film and television seems to me to be much slower, much less aggressive, much more focused on the morals and values of its characters' behaviour. It is also much less violent. It has far fewer explosions, car chases and special effects in its productions.

Most of the time Australian actors are creating and playing these characters. Consequently, could this focus on characters' morals and values in Australian productions be one of the reasons Australian actors produce stronger, more rounded, more in-depth, three-dimensional characters than Americans? I believe this is highly probable.

I'm guessing the same could be said for British actors.

I have mixed feelings when watching Australian content, but the acting is generally very strong and the characters and the stories are, often, far more believable than the journeys of its characters in American productions.

I say this only to generally compare the essence of what is mainly produced in Australian and American productions.

In all my years attending classes and workshops as an actor in Australia and in teaching Australian actors, I had never attended a class as an actor, or until around 2015, had not heard from actors attending a class, that was set up just like a Los Angeles cold reading or scene study class.

I now know that they do exist and I have been really surprised to see and witness schools in Australia simply out for just the money and where they don't really train their acting students.

An aside: American acting teachers are also now coming to Australia to teach and also teaching online in Australia.

From *my experience*, generally speaking, certainly prior to 2015, Australian actors always get critiqued and given constructive criticism in acting classes or workshops. They certainly do in mine. As said in Book One, if they achieve the objectives in the lesson plan, they are doing well at achieving objectives. Objectives which are taken from a lesson plan, that is derived from a curriculum. A curriculum whose main purpose is to improve an actor's work. This ensures the actor improves and consequently receives value for money.

From my experiences and from what multiple hundreds of US students have told me, this is often not the case in America. Americans tell me they are often criticized for their choices of the *understanding* of a script or scene and of the personal coaches' *likeability* of their created character. Many students don't even get that.

I have been told this story below from approximately two hundred US actors. One American student who came to me for training at the end of 2022 was consistently told, "You are not enough. You don't give me enough" by her acting teacher. This went on for years.

This actor only wants to perform on screen and I have spent the past ten months trying to pull her back as she is too big. She keeps doing too much in the frame. I also work with her on building her internal confidence and her self-esteem as her confidence as a performer was shattered by her previous American teacher. This is an example of what I mean when I talk about the effects on actors when they are trained by non-qualified teachers and/or poor teachers.

It is important to state that Australia does not have a Broadway or a Hollywood and consequently the Australian cities where actors go to *en masse,* are Sydney and Melbourne. They are the biggest cities in Australia, with populations of around five million in Sydney and four million in Melbourne, as opposed to ten million in Los Angeles County (some people say there are twenty million in Los Angeles County as California has over forty million) and ten million during the day in the very tiny area of Manhattan alone, as of the writing of this book.

An aside: I am sure that the number of actors in a class has something to do with the amount of attention that an actor can receive in a class too. And, as said, there is a massive population difference between Australia and America. One can always give more training to a class of ten as opposed to a class of forty.

The importance of American marketing

Based on the USA's large population and wealth, American production studios have a rich *history* of performance and marketing of their performance products, worldwide.

Such as, with their film and television. America has created an infrastructure to support its industry. Well done, America! We are all grateful for that.

Nowadays, America has the luxury of thousands of self-made production companies and producers too. All trying to make work. In fact, many actors that I know personally, or that I have met socially, market themselves as a producer in America first, and then as an actor second.

Here are a few interesting points to note:

- American actors, producers, directors and writers are so successful worldwide because the USA has an infrastructure in existence supporting them for over one hundred years; especially in Los Angeles. American productions, with their special effects, have consequently simply gotten better and better
- Many countries around the world are heavily influenced by America. Australia is inundated with everything from America, including American politics
- American culture, the psyche, leans itself towards the assertive and the dramatic. Some could say the over-the-top culture that thrives on imagination and exaggeration. This helps makes riveting drama. (Comedy is naturally over the top)
- Aspects of the American culture, such as, people having a gun licence, and being a self-professed, world police nation, assist this too, in the sense that American productions can personify American cultural views through their war movies and their use of weapons
- In addition, the American entertainment industry welcomes actors from all over the world. This openness, can only help make Hollywood and Broadway better. Thank you again, USA

American marketing: The pomp and ceremony

Everyone knows that Americans are masters of marketing. They are indeed, for good or bad, infiltrating the world with their culture, their food, their sport, their clothing, their ways of dressing. Even their language – their syntax. Cultures to begin with, think countries: Australia, Philippines, Japan (Okinawa in particular).

For American actors in class with me, especially those who were just beginning to study in my school, it would, sometimes, take them a while to settle. To do what I wanted them to do, let themselves go and trust that what they were learning was beneficial for them.

I would talk openly to the students about this. Many said they were jaded, tired and physically exhausted as so many acting teachers and schools simply wanted to take their money.

One day an American student suggested to me that I needed the pomp and ceremony to help my school. I needed to spend time talking to the students about my and my staff's achievements and about everything they were going to do, before they even did it.

Really? I thought.

An aside: Over the years, many American teachers tried to get a job working with my school. If I gave them a chance, the American teacher would talk for at least half of the three-hour class. Firstly, about how good they were, and secondly about their philosophy on acting and what actors should and should not do.

I didn't like this. I used to welcome my students with a hug, say g'day to them, introduce the lesson plan topic, then do a warm up and jump into the lesson plan, the acting work that had objectives for them to achieve in each class.

Back to the topic of the pomp and ceremony. For a period of time, we introduced some pomp and ceremony into our bi-monthly free classes. Americans call this auditing. These free classes included things like introducing staff to the audience, talking about teachers' achievements, some name dropping, student bookings, etcetera. And guess what? During these times, our enrolment numbers went up.

I clearly remember I, and my other Aussie staff, feeling very uncomfortable with this pomp and ceremony. We even cringed at times.

This behaviour confirmed to me that American actors needed or wanted the cushioning, the exaggerating, the pomp and ceremony. Because that's what they were used to.

Is there a correlation, then, between wanting the pomp and ceremony, the cushioning, before a student can trust a teacher or a school or a technique? I believe that there possibly is a correlation.

Of course, if so, this is not any American actors' fault. Expecting the pomp and ceremony is simply a culture that Americans are born into.

Human psyche, spirit and mind in your culture

I am not a qualified psychologist or sociologist and so cannot address too much in psychological detail, the cultural differences and diversities of psyche, socialization, ways of thinking and codes of behaviour between Australians and Americans.

But I will try a little because it has to be explored and I think that there is relevance in it. What influences are you born into in your culture?

From what I have seen and experienced, Americans are hand held so much more than Australians in their lives. Especially in their primary and secondary stages of socialization.

An example of being a hand-held society goes like this: I, and all adults, along with the general populace living in America, would watch the television news programs, and be told when to:

- Put the trash out at night
- How to use personal hygiene
- When to take a rain coat or umbrella as you walked out the front door of your house
- Many of life's daily events, such as, how much sleep you should have each night
- How you should take every drug imaginable to help you with your life (often introduced and supported by the anchor newsreader on the nightly news)
- Why you should keep buying products that are advertised on the television (through fear-based advertising)
- When every public holiday was coming and what was expected of you

- How many days it was to Christmas and Thanksgiving and Halloween and what was expected of you
- Who to vote for in elections. Focusing on the deficiencies of the candidates

A lot of it was controlling and even fear-based advertising. For example, and I paraphrase: *"Take this insurance out or this is what will happen to you!"* Then pictures of an illness or terrible state or condition would appear for the viewer to see.

How does this affect an American actor's training and their performance? Well, we can only surmise, can't we?

American actors are generally very good at improvisation, so that can't be it.

Perhaps the American actors need this time, this hand holding, this pomp and ceremony, to get used to something new? Perhaps they also need to be spoon fed? Perhaps the government thinks they need to be spoon fed? Perhaps it is a part of how the government can try to keep control of its people?

The culture that they are born into is relevant here because many are spoon fed on when to do many things and how to do them – by an American. An American voice.

In support of this, with this way of behaviour, you could say, it is a pressure that is put on them by their culture. As a consequence, could they then be less flexible and less likely to let go as an actor? Because they are used to simply following the norm, being hand held a bit and wanting the pomp and ceremony?

Perhaps they also expect other cultures to do exactly what other American teachers and schools do?

That of, *blow their own horns,* and if you don't, then perhaps, they think, *you're probably not worthy* and consequently don't totally let go and have trust in class. As we all know, letting go and trusting are things vital for actors to do to achieve success. This is all food for thought.

An aside: Following the norm is very much the case in Japan too, where people are socialized to not stand out. To fit in with society in nearly all areas. For example, Japan has a Noise Police; neighbours call the police if there is a noise level coming from your home that the neighbour does not like.

Here is an interesting supportive thought, perhaps related, perhaps not. Many, probably over one hundred, American students have proudly said to me that they came to *me and my classes* and chose me as their acting coach, so that they could put my name on their resumes as one of their teachers. I have heard many other actors tell each other to do this, in classes that I have taught as well.

The actors put my name on their resume based on my reputation in America. They, of course, go to other teachers for the same reason, thinking that this is the most important thing to do, that of *having an accredited teacher's name on their resume*. To use an American phrase here, Oh my god! Surely it should be about what they learn from that teacher? How they can get better?

No, sadly, in America, especially in Los Angeles, for many, it often is not. It is about marketing. Marketing your resume with good or credible or known teachers' names on it. This is common attitude and behaviour in Los Angeles, nicknamed the city of angels.

Possible different kinds of focus

I would now like to explore some other cultural and psyche differences between Australians and Americans.

The Australian psyche lends itself to the underplay and to laughter. Scientists have proven that laughter causes the mind to have less stress put onto it. As a consequence, perhaps an Aussie actor's work is freer and less stressful because of this link to our sense of humour, our laughter and because Aussies are growing up in a much quieter, much less populated and less stressful living environment? I do think there is some validity in this. We have 25 million. America has over 330 million.

Below are some of the words to a song, *Statue of Liberty*. The words were written by an Australian rock singer and songwriter, Glenn Shorrock, who lived in the States for a period of time in the early 1970s. I have included some of the words from this song here because it was Shorrock's viewpoint at that time. I believe it was written in 1974. If nothing else, the words in this song are provocative.

For me, two lines are particularly pertinent: *"...this is America, we try a little harder"* and *"We've got our own values, but they're built on the dollar"*. I will come back to these words during this chapter.

America is known worldwide as a culture that focuses more on money than any other country that I know of. I certainly constantly felt, saw and experienced that from living there for over a decade. I still do experience it today.

For example, between 2000 and 2011, every company I had dealings with, including my gas, water and power, phone and cable companies, were always trying to get more money from me. They would, at times, over-charge me.

My phone company would create long distance and overseas phone calls and hence charges to people for calls that I never made and then try to charge me for the calls. I always seemed to be on the phone to them. Hundreds of students have complained to me or to others in class about this too. When I left America in 2011, many of these companies tried to charge me a cancellation of service fee too.

An aside: Many actors have also complained to me about the money that acting schools were charging them.

Perhaps this focus on always wanting to make money has some bizarre connection with the reasons why Americans say take care to one another all the time when they say goodbye?

They know how hard it is to live in the States? They know how aggressive, deceiving and, I have to add, how violent some people can be.

Americans are known for *marketing* more so than any other country that I know. A clichéd sentence I have often heard is, "*If there's anyone who can tell you how good he is or how good a product is, it's someone from the US.*"

Again, I say, I am not out to belittle the USA. I love the USA and American people. I am just hypothesizing here that this culture of *marketing, this focus on money,* I believe, has to affect everyone in some ways. Including the psyche of American actors living in this culture, and in the sub-cultures within cities.

I believe that it is possibly in the way of *show* and in *push* and in *rushing* and in the lack of time that they will spend on creating a character and exploring a story's possibilities; and possibly even in the ways that they are taught.

For example, money is very tight for many actors so they will rush to learn and improve and perform, so they can stop taking classes, because they can't afford to keep taking classes for too long. I have experienced this as teacher for over twenty-five years. Especially from the American actor.

In my view, the American actor puts too much pressure on themselves to succeed, which reflects the society they grew up in, which also puts pressures on them to succeed.

In the next chapter, I'll explore these differences further.

> ## *Learning Point Number Six:*
>
> - If studying in Los Angeles or New York, is your general training, training you the *fast-food* way? Influenced and dominated by either showy musical theatre on the East Coast, and cold reading and scene study classes on the West Coast? And if so, is the content of the training shallow and not rooted in substance?
> - What pressures are you experiencing from living within your own culture?
> - What pressures are happening within your own mind?
> - Do you really need the pomp and ceremony before you can feel at home in an acting class? I propose that you don't
> - Band-aid steps should not be taken. If you feel the main focus of the teacher, school or university is on making money, then consider going somewhere else for your training
> - Consistently ask yourself, what am I learning from this teacher?

Chapter 7: Differences between Australian and American acting training, Part 2

American actors come from a nation of confident talkers, of marketing experts, focused on making money, the people are under a lot of pressure, they are extremely competitive, assertive and sometimes aggressive.

These thought patterns could possibly infiltrate down through their minds and into the ways in which they think and the things that they do. They could think, I'll *show* you how good I am; verbally and non-verbally, as opposed to simply just doing the work. As opposed to simply seeing and exploring the journey of a scene or a play and creating an in-depth character.

Three generalized asides relating to aggression and money:

1. Some acting schools in Los Angeles are known in the industry for their aggression in doing everything possible to maintain the students that they have in class. And when a student leaves their school, they hound them to come back.
2. As a people, I would say Americans are far more aggressive than Australians.
3. Money rules in the USA. So many people outside the country see America as the land where they can make a lot of money, and that

is why millions apply and pay for a chance for a Green Card each year through the US lottery.

With the US lottery, I'm told, 50,000 are chosen each year to live in America by the US Government. Then there are numerous visas that the government has going via visa exchanges with many countries fostering inter-country business relations. This is big business in money indeed.

I am talking about money being the focus and aggression being more dominant in Americans than Australians, because I believe that the type of culture which focuses on money could infiltrate down through the thinking and behaviour and affect the acting schools' teachers' *psyche* or the universities' curriculum to care more about enrolments, money and student numbers, and not necessarily focus on providing the best training and education for their students.

Simply because, in *their* psyche, they live in a country where people think, "We must make money all the time." I have heard some people, many people, use the expression in the States that they feel like they are, "Constantly getting screwed." Or worse.

Many, many actors in LA and New York not only say this all the time, but they are very cynical about many acting schools and coaches too. They tell me so.

Surely focusing on the actor's craft, education and training, and not the money, has to be linked in there somehow, doesn't it? Surely it is vital?

An interesting point: In Australia, two of the biggest acting schools, one in Sydney and one in Melbourne, both have a history of *cutting* or asking actors *to leave* at the end of first and second year. Not all actors get to complete their third year.

Thousands audition to try and get into these schools each year and then many are cut after first and second year. Are these schools focusing predominately on money? On enrolments? Well, if they are still cutting students from years one and two, then I don't think they are.

US psyche experience: narcissism?

At my school *AIDA* in the States, we taught one particular seventeen-year-old American for two years. He was in class, sometimes up to five days a week because he was a Diploma student. He had been acting since he was a little boy and had had American teachers all that time before my school started teaching him. He had and still has great potential as a performer.

It took me, and other staff, a long time to try and get a lot of the show and the *push* out of this actor's work (noting, his youth), and even when I closed the school, he still had bits of show in his work.

I put this down to his beliefs on what he thought acting was, his cultural experiences, the pressures he was under and his previous American teachers. His parents said, and I paraphrase, "You have this amount of time to book work as an actor. If you don't make it by this age, you are going to join the military."

This actor wasn't *overacting* as such, but what he was doing was performing for himself and was not totally absorbed in his character and its journey. For want of a better phrase, I will call it this: there was a narcissistic quality in his work and this was the biggest problem with his acting.

Perhaps propagated by a previous poor teacher or teachers? Possibly influenced by his American culture and pressures and also on what he believes acting really is?

If this actor never really makes it big, he still has a magnificent smile and a gym-fit body and is excellent at marketing himself. These things deemed so very important in the mind of an actor in the Los Angeles market.

I tried hard to make him better, and he did get better. But not to the level that I would have liked. He is married now and has been in the US Marines for many years.

Sometimes I really want to say directly to students: train now, market yourself later. Sadly, lots of American students enter my classes and within a very short period of time, their focus and their influencing, that of what they want me to teach them, shifts into them wanting me to teach them to market themselves. In truth, many are simply not ready to be put out there with reels, agents and headshots.

US psyche experience: social pressure

When discussing differences between the American and Australian psyches, another of my students at AIDA, a mature American female actor, said this to me and I asked her to put it in writing:

"In America there is an element of fear that relates to having to always be the best if you put yourself out there. I think in the collective consciousness, there is a level of fear that may not exist in the same way as in other countries. Having to be the best public speaker or the best singer or the best at anything if you want to put yourself out there can be a daunting task. Describing this as, 'This phenomena', is actually feeling that it is potentially dangerous to try something new without being excellent at it. But how can you be excellent without training and encouragement and trying? You have to walk before you can run."

This student wishes to remain anonymous.

While I fully thank the student and understand this comment, I think it would be good for the teacher, their family, their culture to not pressure the student or the performing artist. If elements of this quote are true, what a shame "they" (Americans), have a reluctance to do something unless it can be or is "perfect". How sad. Americans should not feel a sense of perfection is needed. In fact, this notion of perfection is counter-productive as it takes the creativity and the journey and/or exploration out of an artist's work.

Psyche differences between the USA and Australia

In regards to acting, I believe that there is one fundamental point and difference between the Australian and the American psyches. The Australian is less likely to put the perfection label on their work before, during and after the performance art has taken place.

The American, as described above, and I witness it all the time, could and often is, or feels, pressured to do this.

I see, over and over again, Americans putting the *seeking perfection* label on their work. This is articulated through a large number of American actors often using the phrase, "I nailed it!" when they think they did a good performance or audition.

I think it is also worthy to note that this acting student I quoted above used the word *fear* twice in her comment. Coming from fear is a sure way to instigate a negative experience. And, what is perfection anyway? It is subjective.

I believe there is no such thing as *perfection for the collective consciousness*. In fact, there is no such thing as *perfect*. There's no such thing as doing it where you feel you *nailed it*. As already stated in this book, this is because perfection of anything is subjective.

In teaching Americans, I see way too many of them do not do their preparation or their homework. I see them *try to wing it* and, as a consequence, not produce a very deep level of work; and yet they are supposed to be or aspiring to be professional actors.

Teachers can only *lead the duck to water, we cannot make it drink!* I often see the American actor in LA and New York improvise and as I've proposed, for some, or many, I believe it has roots in their previous habits and training. Much longer *historical training* than I have given them.

I will, more often than not, see the Australian *do* their homework and also have *more creativity* in their work due to their thinking, their commitment and their training.

Based on Australian culture and psyche, the Australian will also generally come from love and not fear and not feel *Oh, I can't do it because I might fail!* The Australian would laugh at themselves if they tried and failed. The American would often be devastated if they tried and failed. I have seen this happen time and time again too.

Tall poppy syndrome

Please don't think I'm putting Australians on a pedestal here through this comparison. The Australian psyche has its negative side too.

The tall poppy syndrome is an Australian belief. Which I believe originated from the fact that Australia was colonized and its original settlers were often convicts, small-time crooks deported from England.

The tall poppy syndrome means that if you big-note yourself, especially to others, other Aussies will criticize and mock you in a playful way. As a consequence, Aussies try not to big-note themselves, they try not to be "tall poppies".

Consequently, as soon as an Aussie actor *big-notes* themselves or verbally announces their achievements, other Aussies will put them down. In other words, *degrade them or what an Australian would say, Put shit on them!*

A tall poppy syndrome example is as follows: a young Australian AFL footballer, an ex–Collingwood player, won the Victorian Football Leagues' best player in the *Reserves* Competition in Victoria. He was rewarded by being put onto the seniors list and played in the opening seniors practice match the following year. When interviewed the day after the game with the seniors, the interviewer mentioned all his achievements and how well he played in the opening practice match game that year.

The first words out of the *player's* mouth in reply were, and I paraphrase, "Yeah well my first two kicks went to the opposition and then it took me a while to get going." He underplayed!

At no time did he say how good he was or how well he was going to go in the seniors that year, and he totally ignored the comments about his achievements. He simply said, when asked about his future goals, "I hope I can get a senior game this year." We all know he played well the day before. We all know he has a great future as a player. But that is what he said.

Does this tall poppy syndrome affect an Australian's approach to their work and the humility they display when they have completed their work? I'm sure it does.

An exaggerated or over-the-top culture

It is sad to say but many countries in the world do not like Americans. From my experience, most Americans don't know this. Many people in many countries in the world, not me, think that Americans are overly dramatic and they are loud and rude and they exaggerate. In addition, they are ignorant, and all have plenty of money.

Let's think of some American linguistic expressions. For example, *Oh my God!* and *You know what…* and *listen…* and *I'm sooo stressed* and *F—you!* and *I'm walking here!* and *Let me tell you something.*

Americans give themselves extravagant names for their job titles too, e.g. *Senior Vice President.*

Americans express their views openly. They are articulate and assertive. Americans openly discuss their political and social views too, including on social media like Facebook.

I believe Americans speak louder than any other culture too. Their actions are often dramatic too.

An aside: Australian satirical television shows *Fast Forward* and *Full Frontal*, in the 1980s and 1990s, were very successful for many years in writing, producing and acting sketches that would often mock US culture, language and behaviour. Eric Bana was one of many Australian actors doing this.

Now you might think, if Americans are very good at exaggerating and being overly dramatic, then why can't their exaggerations produce great acting work? Well, it can. And it does. It can work for some, but not for other actors.

Living in a culture with a heightened state of drama creates great scripts, great television and film viewing for us all to see worldwide.

But, this might, in ways, be counter-productive for many American actors. As I am sure living in the US culture could influence an American actor's acting and the trainings of actors too.

Living in a country of *over the top* and/or *exaggeration* could move some actors into a state of show. Where some are even narcissistic in various ways.

The actor's work is somewhat forced, detached and not grounded. The actor is pushing or doing too much and exaggerating, or being overly dramatic, and with some, this is producing a sense of show. The industry calls this, overacting.

The general public can see this too, but they generally don't know what to call it. They often say things like, *"I don't like that person's work",* or, *"I don't like this production."*

Culturally speaking, people from other countries could think this about an American's work too: if you're an exaggerated over-the-top, dramatic culture of people, then, to use a camping metaphor, other people could try to pull you *down a peg or two* as well.

What is the philosophy behind the teachings?

What is in the general curriculum that is set out to train the actor in America in *cold reading* and *scene study* classes and *casting director* workshops? What are the focuses of the people who teach actors in these classes in LA and NYC? How does this compare to Australian training? Let's explore this topic here.

From what I have introduced in this chapter so far, as *happenings* or *ways of behaviour* on the east and west coasts of America, well, could this then have something to do with a *lower standard* or a *lack of real in-depth* actor training in some or more acting schools and/or universities in the USA? Or is it just different training? I want to explore this.

As mentioned already, this doesn't seem to make too much sense initially for New York actors, as they generally revel in education and training and are often sought out and more respected when they move to California. (Like actors from Chicago.)

But let's at least explore this further. I am generalizing about a city, Los Angeles, that is full of *cold reading or scene study* classes and *casting director workshops*. All classes that, from my experiences, give very little in-depth or acting training feedback to actors.

Plus, also a city, New York, that has a history of producing musical theatre that is often *hammy* or *showy*, because perhaps there is a correlation with the predominant array of *fast-food* classes in Los Angeles and the predominant *product* that is wanted and produced in New York. That of, the quality of acting training classes and subsequent work that is produced in these cities.

If nothing else, it is worth considering – right? That an over-abundance of this type of training in Los Angeles and this type of production produced in New York, which began with an actor's training, could have a direct correlation with some shallow work or work with a lack of depth. Not profound. Not rooted in substance. But light hearted and *external* in nature. Ahh, there's that word – *external*.

Well from *my* teachings and experiences in America, the answer is possibly a yes. I'll explain why.

Prior to my ongoing training, the American students that I have had in my classes, from both coasts, will, for the most part, begin classes with me by having a strong desire to not want to do the preparation and a lot of them think they will do their best work with no preparation. They wanted to fly by the seat of their pants and improvise as much as possible.

An aside: They also constantly want to add their own lines, their own dialogue to the given scripts while they improvised.

Flying by the seat of your pants with improvising, I believe, has strong correlations with the shallow (for want of a better word) common behaviour experienced at a cold reading or improv class in Los Angeles, where *prepare by yourself* or *prepare with your partner* and you might get minor adjustments or you might not; or the shallow common variety entertainment of showy musicals that ham it up in New York theatre where most actors are trained to act, sing and dance.

While acknowledging the contradiction I made earlier concerning the breadth of training that a New York actor seeks, I have included New York actors here because:

- I have made the link with *the product* they generally produce – *musicals*, and not their *desire* to seek training
- I can only comment on my experience teaching them, while they are in my classes and by what they have told me
- I believe other things are probably involved as well, as I'll discuss in this chapter

An aside: The USA is rich in stand-up comedians. Many stand-up comedians in America have become film and television comedy stars and, whether you like their work or not, there is plenty of *showy* elements in stand-up comedy too.

Is it laziness?

Are these actors' *lazy actors in training* then? Some are. Some are not. Are the teachers teaching these actors in these types of classes lazy or unqualified or don't know too much about acting training? I'm sure some are, some are not. It is surely worth taking into consideration, isn't it?

Some American actors have told me, over many years, that they just feel they do a better job when they improvise. For me that means, flying by the seat of their pants at auditions and in class. *Yikes to this,* I would say.

Also, as said, I feel, that there is possibly a correlation between this and their training or lack of it. I often call this, *taking the easy way out.*

An aside: I do want actors to improvise when given direction from a casting director or director, after they have applied technique and made multiple choices in the areas of character, scene study, risk taking, etcetera.

Of course, there are many benefits to improvising with the script and American actors may also book the job because of this, as improvisation often leads to creativity and freedom in performance.

But, for many, and please remember so it doesn't seem I am contradicting myself, improvisation should be a component of the training of the actor. Done mainly to teach the actor to suspend disbelief and to use their imagination. I don't believe it should replace formal training.

In my opinion, focusing on improvising at auditions because of an actor's possible lack of technique and grounded work often leads to the American actor's performances not having the complexities, the subtext, the rooted in character idiosyncrasies, such as, relating to values and morals, and the character's journey of, let's say, the Australian or the British actor.

Generally speaking, it is the Australian or the British actor who is more likely to bring out a lot of their internal *acting chops* and the depth of character to the *characters'* table. I really believe this is so. For example, think of Jodie Comer's character portrayal of Villanelle in the television series *Killing Eve*. It is brilliant.

From my experience, the Australian, the Brit, the European, the South American, the Scandinavian, and to a lesser extent, even often the Asian, will generally do their best work with *technique* and *character* and *back story* in place. As a consequence, they often produce stronger, more complex, more watchable work, than an American actor. This is certainly the case with actors that I train.

An aside: Of course, American actors trained by me do produce very good work too. I have trained thousands of American actors and many, many hundreds of them have booked professional paid work and many have won acting awards too.

Some adapt quickly, some take time. I simply have to get their desire to not be lazy, not be showy or push, and not wanting to do much preparation, and try to get them to not add dialogue with the given script, out of their acting philosophy and behaviour. Once I get these things going, they then start to really improve.

An example from a US television show that we all loved

I would like to say that my DVD shelves are mostly filled with films from the USA and season box sets of television shows such as *Game of Thrones, Breaking Bad, 24, Lost, Prison Break, Battlestar Galactica, The Shield* (by the magnificent writer/producer Shawn Ryan) and *Rectify,* and so on.

In reference to many of the American films and television shows that I watch, it is the story, the often *profoundly dramatized,* often the *unbelievable story or set of circumstances,* and the *quality of the production values,* that keeps me watching; more so than the characters' journey or the actors' work.

I often find, after a series or two of a US drama, the lead characters are often irritating and repetitious in their *book of acting tricks,* such as their repetition of expressions.

For example, although I really like his work, take Kiefer Sutherland in *24* as an example. I would like to draw attention to this actor's performance for a few reasons:

- I loved watching the TV show *24*. It was cutting edge in its day, especially due to the pacing of its editing
- I know people who have met Kiefer Sutherland and they say "he would welcome this sort of constructive criticism"
- I used to refer to this show in my classes in Hollywood for many years

In Kiefer's defence, they shoot so much television so quickly, (I call it the fast food of film making) that the actor often has to keep delving into his bag of tricks and repeating the same expressions because they are shooting so many scenes in the one day.

But I know, if I ever meet Kiefer Sutherland face to face, I will have no qualms in asking him, and here is my example of an American actor playing a character and their performance in a television show, "Did you get a bit lazy with your acting from series three of *24* onwards?"

As I do believe the characters in this television show were most often shallow. Not that watchable. The production seemed more interested in how many car chases or explosions or arguments or fights that the characters would have than the characters' journey dealing with values, morals, feelings and then decisions.

I contrast this with the American television show *Breaking Bad*. It was different from the norm. The characters in this show were complex and detailed, and had an array of personal, internal decisions to make and interesting behaviour going on in their journey. Well done HBO and to the writers and producers of this show.

I should also point out that I am a tough critic. As a teacher of stage and screen acting, I guess I am simply, by occupation, going to be harder to please. I'm also Australian. I want to see characters that are complex, detailed, and have an array of personal, internal decisions and behaviour going on, as a part of their journey. Practise what you teach, right?

Above: Paul teaching in the AIDA theatre in Hollywood.

Exploring the work

As I've stated before, I am trying to find and understand the differences between Australian and American actors and their training methods.

I repeat, I am not out to slander Americans in regards to anything.

Generally speaking, is Australian acting training possibly more *profound* than American actor training? By profound, I mean more detailed, with variable options and rooted in technique.

Also, does Australian acting training possibly spend more time on *the development of the work* and has more *freedom to explore* the work, both in its acting class and in its rehearsal going into performance?

Also, is there a difference between exploring the work, exploring the options and choosing to improvise with the work when performing?

I think Australia is diversified in its training. Australia not only creates and develops its own types of working techniques, but it is also very keen to learn from all other cultures. This has happened certainly in the past fifty years in particular.

I have not experienced British actor training yet (although I lived in England), so I will not comment here on this aspect.

However, Australian actor training more often than not includes: its own creations, and not just what I adapted from my teachings and called *Australian Techniques*, but also: Japanese Kabuki, puppetry, French neutral mask and Italian *Commedia Dell'arte, and* classes on meditation, tai-chi and yoga. As well as international theorists such as Brecht, Grotowski, Laban and Stanislavski. As well as some Michael Chekhov and some others. Plus, movement and fencing and breath and voice classes.

In addition to different techniques, as I discuss in this book, there is also a very strong emphasis on developing character and to explore what is the *journey of that character* in the play or the script or the scene that they are working on.

Often the story and all its complexities are thoroughly discussed, analyzed, plotted out and followed through to the end, generally, in Australian acting training too. Especially in theatre.

Australian actors are trained by me to discuss and make decisions on what is the journey of the script or play? *What is the journey of the character?*

In support of this, Australia is also keen on teaching actors the history of theatre; especially Ancient Greek theatre and Elizabethan theatre, which is often compulsory in Tertiary and Further Education (TAFE) and university studies.

All of this *type of actor training* is in existence, subject to funding, and generally flourishes in Australia. For example, for one year (full time), and over two years (part time), I taught actor training at TAFE through a subject called *Small Companies & Community Theatre*. This was a post-secondary course offered to adult actors. The aim was to train the actors to not only be professional actors, but to develop self-sufficient ways of creating a small company and producing their own theatre.

What these things bring to the acting craft, through all these types of education that I am discussing here is: an *appreciation* and *a richness* in both the origins and the history of actors and actor training and how to get work in theatre, film and television. A *richness* in learning all about acting in as many ways as possible.

My mentor, veteran actor Reg Evans, said to me in Melbourne when I was twenty years old, "If you want to be an actor, you must learn about the history of acting and the history of theatre. This knowledge, this appreciation will serve you best in your career." I followed his advice.

With this knowledge, the actor firstly opens themselves up to these experiences. Then implements them and then eventually decides on a system of acting or performing that works best for them. All to help them book work. In short, tapping into worldwide education and training with a sense of humility and a will of exploration.

Many, I would guess hundreds, of American actors who I have met and many that I have trained, who grew up or have lived for a long time in Los Angeles, do not care and do not want to know about most things that I have just mentioned in the above fourteen paragraphs in this book.

This has been my experience. Many have told me to my face that, "They don't care about the history of acting or theatre, they just want to book work in film and TV."

An aside: I have been told that many universities in the States do teach the history of theatre and diverse techniques with their actor training.

I haven't taught or been a student at a university in the States, so I do not know personally *how* diverse or *how* thorough they are. I don't really know what the teachers are teaching their students. I only know what my students tell me. I don't know if the teachers are qualified teachers or just deemed *industry experts* or simply academic Doctors of Drama or

Doctors of the Arts. People who simply did a thesis study in the area, but are not necessarily trained to teach.

Some are good teachers and some are not. I can only really comment from my experience. I only know what I see, what I have experienced, what I train and what hundreds of American students have said to me.

Unfortunately, I have to say that some actors that I have trained, who have graduated from universities in the States with acting and/or performing arts and theatre/drama degrees, are sometimes poor actors have been very naïve or ignorant in their knowledge of the history of theatre and of acting training methods. I know this because they have told me to my face. They have come to me for training and I have seen it and they have then reinforced it.

To be as specific as I am prepared to be: many students have come to me for training after they have completed an acting four-year university degree, while studying in the area of Southern California. Many have had poor knowledge and poor skills.

In support of this, many past post–secondary school students that I have trained doing a *Diploma* course in my school in the States have said to me, and I paraphrase, "*You assess me too hard. You are really strict and particular with your assessment and grading. You make us work so much.*" I don't believe I am too tough. I have been given the same feedback about students coming to me for on-camera training as well.

I have always wanted, and still do want, to see depth in character, depth in an actor's understanding of the script and the story and the character's journey in that story. I believe we all do. An audience often does too. The people who vote for the best performers at award ceremonies demand it and then reward it when they see it.

When I see it, I acknowledge it. Because then we have an exploration, a journey, a development from both character in performance and story in production. I believe an audience demands this nowadays. As a trained

English teacher, I love to see actors dissect a script for all its possible meanings too.

Hence, again from my experiences, generally speaking, Australian acting training *seems* to me to be more diverse than American training. It appears more internal and perhaps more critical in making the actors make decisions, and hence from my experiences; definitely *more specific* in its creation of characters and its dissecting of the story and their characters' role in the story.

A journey that will uncover or display in some way the characters' morals and values and their emotional journey.

An aside: American actors Stanley Tucci and Meryl Streep are wonderful contradictions to this point just mentioned above, aren't they? I'm sure they're plenty of other American actors in this category too.

As discussed in this book, I teach character creation in many ways. Sometimes simple, easy ways, to show the actor how easy it is to create characters.

I often struggle with knowing (from experience) that many American actors I have trained do not want to or couldn't be bothered wanting to create *in-depth* characters.

In this sense, my sincere apologies to some sensational actors from around the world that create great characters: Daniel Day-Lewis - Stanley Tucci - Cate Blanchett - Sally Hawkins – Meryl Streep – Denzel Washington – and CCH Pounder. I try. By geez, I try.

A country of people under pressure

The pressures within a population. Approximately 330 million people live in the USA versus 25 million people in Australia. I am sure, both sociologists and psychologists write a lot about the pressures of human beings living in large populated countries.

I bring up this topic as generally speaking, there is less pressure in the mind of the Australian actor than in the American actor. Perhaps the

Australian actor's thought patterns are less anxious, with less urgency and pressures on them in the mind to succeed because there is less competition as there are fewer people in their country.

Being under pressure could lead to fear. Perhaps the Australian actor is living in a less *fearful* country of people too? A country with less aggressive people? I propose that these are possibilities. As a consequence, is the Australian actor less likely to perform with a sense of coming from fear?

Australians underplay and self-deprecate

Built into the Australian psyche and culture in all Australians is the tendency to underplay.

What I mean is, the Australian thinks, nobody could pull this *tall poppy* down! That's because she didn't big-note herself in the first place. The Aussie will pull themselves down first.

Here is a lucky paradox for Australian actors. The *tall poppy syndrome* can be seen as a positive for Australian actor training because the Australian psyche, heavily influenced by this syndrome, will, more often than not, underplay, because if they don't, if they overplay, they will be ridiculed by their peers and also by their society in general. Perhaps even by the media.

As a consequence, I believe, this leads to more quiet, internal, centred work by the Australian actor. I'm thinking in dramatic roles here. I believe subconsciously and for some, even consciously, the Australian and the Australian actor could be thinking: If we don't big-note ourselves, we will have a stronger core, a greater sense of who we are and what we are doing. We are more self-aware, internally proud and have inner strength and have more outward real confidence.

In support of this, Aussies appear less reliant to seek the acceptance of others as we live our lives, as we work and explore. Aussies have a history of being convicts (as settlers); we were deemed low life in the past. So as Australians, we don't feel or want to feel that we have a licence to big-note ourselves. Our convict history is not something to be proud of.

I think Australians are grounded and confident. And perhaps they are even on a quest to discover and grow and be acknowledged as a people, acknowledged as a nation.

So, the Australian actor's approach tends to be *cleaner, simpler, freer* and *less showy*. The *Aussie* will underplay and hence be closer to the truth, or what appears to be the truth, as they act.

That's especially so on camera, because the camera wants to be captivated by the underplay, the stuff that is not so obvious to us, the audience. For example, the moodiness, the subtext: think Russell Crowe, Cate Blanchett.

I do believe, all actors, performing drama, should be centred and should underplay, as opposed to being showing or exaggerating.

As an actor who underplays you leave more room for the audience's imagination to ponder, because what is going on is not obvious. It is not instantly given. And it is profoundly watchable, especially in dramatic productions.

Interestingly, most Australian series regulars on American television work in drama. It probably has something to do with the things I am discussing here as well as their training.

Generally, for comedy, and comic acting, the focus of breath and the sound of the voice is much higher up in the body. For example, across the chest and in the shoulders. So, the actor in comedy is ready for fast-paced work and is often moving.

American actors dominate comedic work in film and television productions.

American actors do a lot of improvisation and are generally very good at it – which supports this thought. Aussies are doing brilliantly well at, in particular, dramatic work in the States.

In my first book, I talk about my teachings, in particular classical training, connecting with the text and breath and voice work. These techniques are a profound personification of an actor's preparation prior to the work. British training has this too. I know this because some British training has influenced my Australian techniques.

The world loves Aussies

To reiterate a point that I made in the Introduction: clichés, generalizations and stereotypes exist in our language and in our thinking, because there is validity in them.

As we discuss cultural and psyche differences between the American and the Australian and the American actor training and Australian actor training, I am starting to put some hypotheses together concerning actors from these two countries.

The world loves Australians. Everywhere I go – and I have been to approximately thirty countries – everyone loves Australians.

Could *loving Australians* affect people in the world in wanting to watch and employ Australian actors? I'm sure it does.

Just noting that there are exceptions, of course. As we all know, there are wonderful actors in America, throughout the world and not just in Australia.

Some other possible cultural differences

Honesty, I am flabbergasted with how honest Australians are.

After living in America for nearly eleven years, upon returning home I noticed that I had become protective of my boundaries. In the States I had become much more fearful in thought, and I noted that I became much more introverted the longer that I lived there. I had also developed undertones of anger, building up under the surface, from my time living there.

Upon returning home to Australia to live in 2011, I was amazed by the honesty of Australians, personified in their speech and behaviour.

There are probably dozens of ways I could exemplify this. Just talking to people, often there is no hidden agenda. It is just talking and listening. Open, relaxed communication. We are not talking to make connections, or to see what we can get from each other. I felt and experienced the opposite very strongly when living in the States.

Another example is the culture that we live in. When Australians go to a service station, they put petrol (gas) in their cars and then go inside to pay the bill. But in America, you have to hand money over the counter before you put gas in your car.

I wonder: Do casting directors and producers see things like a relaxed, caring, inquisitive, openness and honesty in an Australian actor's eyes, in their energy and in their work that they love? And then they want to cast that actor? I am sure they do.

Interestingly, casting companies put Australians in so many of *the macho roles* nowadays. Think Gibson, Crowe, Jackman, Worthington, Bana etc. British actors too.

Many casting people say this, and I paraphrase, "If we want a lead macho male, we get an Australian." Which is paradoxical as Aussies are generally more passive, and quieter in comparison to Americans.

The camera loves the brooding man look. Does this have something to do with the brooding, underplayed, quietly spoken face on screen, as opposed to the pushed, aggressive or fearful aggression, or crazed look, pushed on screen by some actors? I'm sure it does.

Eye contact

In the time I lived in the USA, I wish I had a penny for every time someone said to me, something like, *"Wow when you look at me, you really look at me."*

When I ask that person, *"Why do you say that?"* They usually would say, *"People, mainly men, in the US do not look at me or in the eyes as much as you do."*

Direct eye contact is common among Australians. I watch body language like a hawk. I see Americans, especially men, continually looking elsewhere, everywhere, the floor, anywhere, except at you for a prolonged period of time. Yes, I know this is another generalization.

In reference to acting, if you're in a scene and you look everywhere and not in the other actor's eyes, it makes it harder for you to connect with the person that you are talking to. If this is what some are doing as actors, and for many I have taught, it has been, well they're not connecting strongly enough or for long enough.

As a consequence, they will not be making the other person accountable enough in the scene and therefore, perhaps not performing with high enough stakes. Noting the higher the stakes, the more heightened the internal drama.

The "stakes" is a term generally used, and commonly known, to encourage the actor to see their goal in the scene as an actor's rise in intensity. The higher the stakes, the more the actor goes for what they want with importance or intensity.

When acting, try to keep your eyes on the other person as much as you can. Unless your subtext leads to your actions, of course. For example, when we *deceive*, we often don't look at the person we are talking to for too long.

Living your life thinking: No worries, as opposed to I'm so stressed

When I arrived in the States in September 2000, the only people I ever heard saying *"no worries"* were Aussies. There are many thousands of Australians living in America now. And now seemingly everyone in Los Angeles says, *"no worries"*.

What are the connotations of no worries? It means, *"She'll be right mate, don't worry about it, all will be OK."* This is the general laidback attitude of Australians. Don't worry, we will sort it out or I've got it covered. I'll do it. Or, it is not a problem.

Even though many Americans may now say no worries, I wish I had a penny for every American that has said to me, *"I'm soooooo stressed."* I usually say back to them after hearing their stressed story, *"You're not stressed, you're challenged!"*

If we have a positive, laidback mindset and attitude, then theoretically, we will get it done and with very little *hoo-ha*, very little concern or drama, we would say in Australia. Meaning there is very little concern of there being a problem.

Do you say *no worries*? Do you personify what it really means? Or do you say *you're stressed*? And follow that path of thinking?

I suggest, where necessary, you can change the way you think, change the words that you utter.

In support of this topic, I think it is worth bringing up the case study scenario – *You want the truth, you can't handle the truth* – from Book One, because continually saying *I'm so stressed* comes from a psyche of fear.

Remember in this case study, I talked about the Australian actor hugging me and thanking me for me being honest and for being particular with comments about her training, versus the two Americans who complained and left the school. (Leaving the school over this, is not common, by the way.)

Generally speaking, I believe that this is because Australians seem to have no fear. Americans seem to come from fear a lot of the time.

In support of this, as mentioned earlier, people in the States say goodbye to you by saying *"Take care."* After hearing this all the time, this has the implication to me that you have to take care. Why would you need to take care? Of course, we will individually take care in our lives, but why does an American feel they need to say, *"Take care"* so often?

I believe this usage has a root in fear and not in love. I have to say take care because something bad might happen to you – that is the implication. Of course the other implication is, I care about you, so take care.

When saying goodbye, Aussies generally say, *"See you later, mate."* How friendly and low key is that? I cannot encourage you enough to relax, think positive, think that the words that you use are a reflection of your thoughts and your psyche and the culture that you live in. Try to enjoy the journey of being alive and of being an actor.

This will help you as an actor because you will be calmer, more centred and grounded in the moment and as a consequence, you will listen and respond better and, most likely, act better.

You might now be thinking: do the American students that I teach adapt in some ways to my psyche, my ways of thinking and behaving? Do I subtly influence their psyche to help their acting? And the answer to all these questions is absolutely, a capital, YES.

Work ethic

A huge and yet unspoken contemporary trend in the acting industry in Los Angeles is not only the casting of Australians, but the casting of Americans into acting work who are from out of the Los Angeles and New York areas. The *Los Angeles Times* published a story on the castings of many, many multiple actors from outside of LA and New York, in 2010, I believe. It is still happening a lot today.

Why is this happening?

Most profoundly, could it be because of the work ethic of these actors? The work ethic of those from the Southern States of the USA, from Texas or Mississippi, for example, or from other countries like Australia or England. Are those actors, generally, *easier to work with*, compared to the Americans from LA or NYC?

If there is validity in this, perhaps this is because Americans in LA and NYC, in particular, are somewhat spoilt and want *what they want, when they want it* or they will throw a tantrum and yell until they get it. In Australia we would say, *they are taking their cricket bat and going home*. In other words, they're *spitting the dummy*, leaving unhappily because they did not get what they wanted.

In support of this train of thought, managers, agents, directors, casting directors and producers, and even actors, from Los Angeles have told me many stories that so many actors have complained about a required task on a film shoot, a television set, on stage or in rehearsals, with the actor saying, *"I'm not doing that! I'm calling the Union! I'm not staying on set that long. I'm not doing that!"*

In this last comment, I have linked Americans who originally came from outside of LA or NYC, and Australians and British actors as being the preferred actor to book or be given the job. This implies that attitude could have something to do with it. The actor living in LA or NYC might have an attitude problem that is affecting their work and their chances of being cast in work.

What's your attitude like? How is your work ethic? I can share with you, many American producers have gone on record, in all media, stating that they love the work ethic of Australians as both actors and crew members.

I recall reading an article many years ago on Jerry Bruckheimer, (one of the world's biggest film and television producers), and him saying he puts an Aussie actor in every project that he does. He does the same with his crew.

I'm paraphrasing him here, but he said, "If there's a tough film job to be done, with long hours, uncomfortable situations, such as: making a film that is made to look like the sea, where actors will be stuck in water in a water tank and the crew will work really hard and this is all going to be shot in a studio; well, I'll get an Australian crew!" Bruckheimer says that this is because of their work ethic. "No worries, I'll do it", an Aussie would say. What would you say?

A sense of community versus dog eat dog

Australia still has a sense of community.

Every time I return home to Australia, I am amazed and reminded how friendly, caring and supportive of one another Australians are.

"We're straight forward and we'll do what we say," said Australian Prime Minister Julia Gillard in March 2011, while visiting and talking to the media in America.

Australia has a health system called Medicare that cares for its people. People of all ages are eligible, and treatment is either free or heavily subsidized. Australia's Medicare is very different to Americans' Medicare.

In America, if you have money and you can afford private health insurance, then usually you can live and do well in life and business. But, if *you do* not have money, you don't have insurance, you could end up on the streets, with no support whatsoever.

Even if you have a leg missing or a mental or intellectual disability. Even if, for example, you fought for your country, you could, and many do, *die* on the streets.

I believe this state of affairs helps create a psyche in America, of not quite desperation, but certainly of dog eat dog. It says this: you must fight to stay alive and prosper or die on the streets with no public health system and no government or social support for the individual.

In short, if you are poor, you are left to beg or turn to illegal things. I have seen people begging every single day while living in America – begging for food, for shelter, for a drink, for bus money, for help.

An aside: Of course, I have also seen people begging on the streets in Australia too.

I am using this example as a supportive point of generally saying that there is a much greater sense of community and support among the people in Australia than I think there is in America, where it seems much more of a *dog eat dog* world.

I believe that this concept of dog eat dog is heavily influenced by population size. The smaller the population, the more people are connected and supported.

I believe that this can affect your acting. As if in the back of your mind you feel a sense of community, of social and government support, including financially through *Unemployment Benefits* (that you don't have to qualify for), when you cannot work. Your way of being, your psyche, your way of life is not desperate. Not aggressive. You are not alone. You are not left to sink or swim.

As opposed to perhaps thinking that you have to live your life thinking you have to market yourself every minute of every day to survive. Like I believe many actors in the States do.

Please think again now of the quote from the former AIDA student that I mentioned in this chapter when she wrote about focusing on *fear* and trying to be *perfect*. American actors might be thinking that they want to do well all the time, simply so they are not one of the people who end up poor and on the street?

Which is fair enough, because the actor who is tense, uptight, a bit desperate to survive – because they know the consequences if they don't succeed – is less likely to totally let go in performance.

They're afraid. Afraid they may do something wrong or not good enough with their work and, so instead, they monitor their work, they don't let go, they don't totally come from love and be totally open. Instead, they come from fear. Fear of failure.

Well perhaps this too has something to do with the differences between the Australian and the American actor? I think there is validity in it.

If you think there might be some validity in this, and you are an American actor reading this, just work on totally opening up and working on your skills, without thinking that you have to have an outcome in your work: You don't have to be *perfect* or *brilliant* every time you act.

In fact, I believe there is no such thing as perfection. Perfection is subjective. Trying and failing is not the end of the world. You can try again, can't you? Also, we can't all be Pacino or Streep.

Americans don't really talk about the social class system, like England and to a lesser extent Australia does. However, this has to be said, in my years in the entertainment industry, dating back to 1979 professionally, the middle-class actor has a much better chance of getting work and making it than the working-class actor.

It is so much harder to move social class in America than in Australia. Education leads to money and privilege and also the reverse. Money leads to education and privilege, and then assets, and so the working class is up against it, right from the start.

The celebrity vacuum

Sacredizing is when you put someone or something up on a pedestal, above you. You look up to it (whatever it may be) and kind of worship it or them, if it is a person. Psychologists suggest that this is not a good thing for a person to do.

I have travelled to, lived in, and/or visited many countries in the world. But I have never travelled to a country where celebrities are put on a pedestal more so than in America.

For example, if there was a guest celebrity from any nationality at my school in Hollywood between 2002 and 2011, Americans would attend that sessional talk, in mass numbers. More so than in any acting class or anything else that was going on at the school.

America has special valet parking for celebrities and just about everything else that you can think of in life – all for celebrities. Celebrities can basically get away with doing and saying what they want. Their position in US society is hugely exaggerated. These people are only human beings after all, right?

Does this help build anxiety towards the acting craft in America because we have put *star actors up* on a pedestal? A psychologist would probably tell you, *yes possibly it does*, because you have *sacredized* the star actors and their position in society.

From my personal experiences, I know that sacredizing is not good for the psyche. I used to do it. A very smart and respected doctor working with me on performance anxiety in the 1990s told me that sacredizing is not good to do and it will often trigger nerve reactions in your mind, body and life. You will look at that celebrity person and the position that they hold in society and deem them or your goal as unreachable or unachievable. As a consequence, you will not be relaxed when you need to be, such as in a casting audition.

You will be too busy comparing yourself with the celebrity and thinking I'll be a celebrity too if I can book this job.

Try not to ever put people on a pedestal and sacredize them. I did from time to time and it never did me any good. I was often nervous around celebrities and in auditions and I always ended up having feelings and experiences that I didn't want. De-sacredize the person and the experience. Always.

We are the superior culture

I know and will never forget that there are many thousands of really good American actors working in American film and television.

In my circle of life, everyone that I ever meet in America is either or wants to be, in the entertainment industry.

I would like to ask this question. Thinking *en masse,* does the American actor put themselves *enough* into a state of *humility* concerning education provided by foreigners? As a mass, are they clearly open to grow as an actor under the tutelage of someone from overseas?

I am not talking about their attendance in a non-American teacher's class, I am talking about it from the perspective of in their mind, body and soul, in their thoughts.

Sure, I have taught thousands of American actors and many hundreds of them are successful and have booked professional work, but the reason I am asking this question in this book is firstly, I am again trying to find differences between Australian and US actors; and secondly, unfortunately, I want to at least address the topics of superiority, arrogance and theft.

For the entire time of my school, on the ground across America, but predominantly in Los Angeles and New York, actors stole from my school AIDA. They did this by taking and then not paying for classes.

The only nationality of actors that stole from my school in this way were Americans. I am talking about a minority of people that, over the years, probably tallied to around a hundred actors. They took the classes and then took off, like a motorist not paying for petrol(gas) at a petrol station.

I would always be left thinking that this was very sad. When followed up to pay for the classes they had taken, they wouldn't respond to phone calls or emails and were never seen again.

An aside: One American student, an ex-Marine, got back in touch with me years after studying with me in Hollywood and did pay for the classes that he took. To the value of about US$800.

In regards to the theft, my first thoughts were always: If they didn't like the school or the training, why did they stay and study with AIDA for one or two or six or twelve or, in one actor's case, eighteen months? One thing they all had in common was they were all from the USA.

I was often left thinking that I am extremely trustworthy and naïve. Perhaps the reason they stole from the school was due to their *arrogance,* their belief that they were from the *superior culture.*

This feeling was personified dozens of times by the behaviour and by the things some actors would say, or things that I would hear them say, or I was told they said (hearsay).

I often wondered, and would talk to other learned people, about what is ingrained into the American *culture* through their *psyche,* that is influenced by such things as through the primary (from parents, family), and the secondary (from peers and school) levels of socialization. As well as also through their social mores and values and even through the work of the ruling class (people with the power to produce), and the marketing that comes from them, the people with power.

I often wondered what is ingrained in the US culture as to why they would steal? I always came back to the thought of sadness and the topics of arrogance and superiority.

I cannot take it too personally as American acting coaches, casting directors, agents and managers would tell me stories of actors stealing from them, too, by not paying for classes.

This is a huge psychological and sociological topic. I don't know the answer. I cannot propose too much of a theory as to why it is so. I do not want to sound like I am coming from a superior culture myself.

Here are a few more examples on this we are superior topic.

I obtained an American agent's personal contact details. I mailed him my school's company brochure. He sent it back, in the same envelope, with no words, just with a headshot of Tom Cruise clipped to my letter.

Also, many Americans have told me to my face, "We are the best country in the world. We are the best at everything."

I believe, from my own experiences and from talking to other teachers and entertainment industry people, that Americans will often go to an American acting school or class, even if it is poor, and accept what is given to them, even if it is poor, much more so than go to a school and receive education taught by someone from overseas or from a minority culture.

An aside: I generally did not have low numbers at my school that ran for over nine years in Los Angeles and over six years in New York. I closed the school for personal physical health reasons.

Interestingly, though, generally speaking, many people from other nationalities in the world do think that Americans are arrogant and that Americans do think that they are the superior culture.

Could we consider then, that perhaps US culture is manipulating its people in ways to always think that they are the superior culture; so preferably you, me, we, buy American?

For example, on Wednesday January 11th 2023, US President Joe Biden was being interviewed by a television news reader and he said, "We are the greatest country in the world." The interview was seen on television stations in Australia. I hear him say that statement a lot. George Bush Junior used to say it a lot too.

A human being's psyche is manipulated by both subtle and not so subtle influences. Marketing people, for example, follow this line of thought regarding business: *let's influence and infiltrate the psyche of our customers, human beings, to attract custom.*

They do this through the images they show, the sounds they make, the language they use, the actions they portray. Their desired ways of getting you to remember and be emotionally moved and feel the way that they want you to feel; so, you then buy their product.

If we believe that this is so, or that this way of thinking has a lot of truth in it, then it is possible that through American culture such as movies and television – even its commercials – many different ways can illustrate, through its images, actions and words, that American people are coaxed and/or manipulated into thinking that they are the superior culture.

Therefore, it is foreseeable that people thinking that they are from the superior culture, could have an *I'm superior* and/or even, an *attitude* demeanour or an *arrogant* attitude. *They could take something* without asking or without paying for it, be disrespectful, and/or not totally trusting on a deep level, concerning what they are being taught.

American actors reading this book, please now think of your views. Think of your inner beliefs on this topic.

Having taught over two thousand American actors in my time to date, I do wonder how Americans feel, deep down, about almost *anything* from overseas. My feeling is that, deep down, they don't really like it, want it or respect it.

An aside: I can remember in 2001, telling the eighty-year-old, successful businesswoman who I was living with at the time, the things that I didn't like about America and American culture.

Her reply was, *"We are twenty years ahead of you in Australia. What we are experiencing now, you will have in Australia in twenty years' time!"* My thought at the time was, I hope not and there is a bit of arrogance in what you say. However, there is some truth in this. Some of the worst parts of America are infiltrating themselves into Australia, usually associated with American power and money – particularly in the areas of clothing and in the following of sport and in the eating of fast food and beverages.

An Australian accent apart (Americans truly love the Australian and the British accents), there is little else that Americans, *en masse*, prefer from overseas compared to something from their own country.

Having said that, perhaps every country thinks it's the superior culture. Every country evokes a sense of we are the superior culture and hence projects arrogance because of its cultural manipulations, through such avenues as film, television and advertising. Some would say it is simply called patriotism.

Based on my extensive experience, I believe some Americans do not trust foreigners anywhere near as much as I believe they should. I also believe that this is possibly because their psyche is being heavily influenced to think *we are the superior culture*.

An aside: Perhaps relevant, perhaps not, in many American productions: the villain, the character who committed the crime or is about to commit the crime, is very often from overseas and/or speaks with an accent; especially in American films.

I see this time and time again, going back many generations. To help get your mind thinking, start thinking about the *Die Hard* films, six of them, starting in 1988. Then think of the character Ugarte played by Peter Lorre in *Casablanca* from 1942. This villain had done something illegal at the start of this film. In what accent do these villains speak with in these films? From memory, I think many of the villain characters are speaking with German accents. Even the bad guys, the bears, in the animated children's film *Sing 2* from 2021, they have Russian accents. Let your mind wander down this path in history a while.

Chapter 7: Differences between Australian and American acting training, Part 2

As you read this, you might be thinking – *"How does this directly affect actor training then?"*

Well, I believe these cultural differences, including under the heading of *we are the superior culture,* can explain some of the differences between an Australian approaching acting work and an American.

An Australian would, generally speaking, come from a sense of having *world cultural respect or humility* for others when taught by foreigners, as opposed to a sense of having arrogance or a *sense of superiority* over that foreigner.

Noting everyone looks up to and respects most things from America.

As a teacher, I have sometimes been verbally aggressively challenged by American students concerning their desire to change and grow as an actor. Could this have something to do with ingrained thought patterns? That they are thinking that we *are the superior culture?*

I have brought this topic up not to blame anyone, not to say it's *so and so's fault.* Nor to put any culture down by insulting them. I just do hope that American actors try more to have an open mind about the thought, that perhaps other countries could have many things that could be just as good or perhaps even better for them, than what an American produces in America.

I know I had and still do have a lot of success teaching Americans. Most people who came or come to me as students were or are accepting of being taught by someone from overseas. Most, but not all. Of course there are always exceptions to the rule and unfortunately, I have trained some actors who have not put themselves *enough* into a state of *humility* concerning education from *this* foreigner.

For these people in my mind, I felt that they were not clearly open to grow as actors under the tutelage of someone from overseas. Even though actors I have trained have booked many hundreds of paid professional jobs, unfortunately I did experience some actors who seemed and/or acted like their cultural views, experiences and ways of thinking and living were better than mine.

Naturally this arrogant mindset usually holds this minority of actors' work levels back a step from other actors.

Not having the right attitude or being arrogant towards the foreign teacher affects an American's trust levels: they *lack trust*. Could that have some correlation with an American student wanting to go *with what they know* or where the general populace goes to study? Does that same actor believe that *flying by the seat of their pants*, for example, at an audition or in class, is the way to go? As this is what many American actors want to do.

This all goes back to thoughts to me of "we are the superior culture", a sad situation. We can always change and get better, can't we? But we need the right mindset first.

A philosophical viewpoint

Are my teachings in America since 2002 then, simply, an adjunct (meaning, I've been added into the teaching world in the USA but am not an essential part of it) to teaching in a country that does have a superiority belief and consequently will take the bits and pieces from my teachings that it likes, and then move on?

I believe that this is possible. In support of this thought, history tells us that many American acting techniques taught in the USA, Meisner, Strasberg, Hagen, Adler, Morris and Chubbuck, all came from the one *Russian* root of acting – Konstantin Stanislavski.

US acting teachers like Meisner and Strasberg and Hagen and Adler took bits and pieces of Stanislavski and then developed their own techniques; like branches of the mother tree. Morris and Chubbuck and others are often called the new derivatives of that tree.

Interestingly, many of my American students, who are also teachers, have told me that they are teaching their students in secondary schools (high schools in the States) acting and drama based on what I taught them.

The nineteenth-century English poet William Blake talks about life as we enter into it as a state of *Innocence*, we then move into a state of *Experience* and we eventually reach a state of *Higher Innocence*.

I like this poetic revelation. Perhaps there is some relevance and significance here with how an American approaches what they learn from foreigners? We meet it, learn from it, take bits of it, then move on. We consume it. Ahh, that makes some sense. Americans are indeed great consumers. And if so, is that so bad? Probably not.

Mental health issues, illness and drugs

I need to state that in my lifetime of teaching, the number of American students who have openly told me, one or more of the things listed below, was far greater than any other nationality I have taught.

1. They have a mental illness
2. They are on medication for it
3. They are seeing a therapist
4. They have addictions
5. They battle depression and anxiety
6. They are using illegal drugs

I don't want to delve into why this could be the case as, I believe, that opens up a whole political and sociological view on American politics and the way of life in America.

But in relation to teaching, I say to my students, usually to all of them in a class setting, *"If applicable, please tell me what drug you're on?" "Please tell me if you have a mental health issue or illness or a disability?"*

I would ask this so I could be as thorough as I could with my understanding of the students' concerns or disability, and teach them accordingly. Meaning, I would adapt the ways I spoke to them and the speed in which I taught them. I still do this today.

My first wife is American. She is a USA Board Certified Psychiatrist. She helped me by educating me on how a specific drug worked and how best to adapt and teach an individual who was on a certain drug.

In reference to mental illness and drugs, it is widely known in the entertainment industry that many, possibly thousands of American producers, directors, writers and actors take illegal drugs. I know this is a huge generalization, but I have seen it and heard about it personally, and of course, there are many stories about this on the news in the States.

From my reading, not my experience, in this heightened state of the mind on illegal drugs, the human mind and body will let go, go to different places and often be very creative.

Many famous actors are known in America for performing their best work while on illegal drugs on set. I know of a couple of *well-known* Australian actors too.

I have never taken illegal drugs. Of course drug taking is not only synonymous with people in America; it is a worldwide problem.

Naturally, I suggest you do not take illegal drugs and you should be cautious before you take any type of drug. I also suggest that you let your teacher or coach know what mental health issue or illness you might have and/or what medication you are on; as they could/should research it and adapt their teaching of you.

An aside: *Rolling Stone* magazine published an article by Andrew Leonard on 20 November 2015 titled "How LSD Micro dosing became the Hot New Business Trip". According to the article, regular doses of acid have become the creativity enhancer of choice for some professionals.

I am sure mental health issues and taking drugs does affect actors' work and whether they get cast. If you need a medication, that is fine, let your teacher know about it. If you are taking illegal drugs when you perform, it is not a good thing.

This teacher, for one, will never utter your name in one of my classes, calling you a very good actor if you take illegal drugs. That's because actors on drugs are creating and performing their work while in a heightened and illegal state.

Let's lighten things up a little

I'm guessing, there are approximately thousands of successful American actors who have not studied Australian acting teaching methods or with an Australian teacher. There are many and varied answers to why this is the case. Here are a few:

- They train with a good teacher
- They go to a very good University or College
- They have natural talent
- They have the magical *je ne sais quoi*
- They did their own research on acting and techniques and then history of theatre, etcetera
- They have learnt a technique that works for them
- They are just so gorgeous
- They are learning from other foreign teachers
- They live in a country that has the world's largest entertainment industry where there is more opportunity than elsewhere, so they simply get some work, particularly in LA and NYC
- They have family or friends in the industry who help them get work
- They have an incredibly strong desire and they work bloody hard
- They read acting books from around the world
- They have not had the opportunity to study with a teacher from overseas

Me teaching American psyche and cultural differences

Dealing with and teaching the American psyche is a challenge – a challenge I relish. Coming from overseas and having lived in America, I can bring a subjective and objective viewpoint into analyzing the behaviour of Americans and the decisions they make, and even teach non-American actors to personify American attitudes and behaviour.

I think like this because I have to teach actors to do this. I teach foreigners to act this way. To be American in their auditions. As a teacher it is my job to continually learn about America and to learn about what makes an American think and act and what their influences are and why they do behave in certain ways.

There are aspects of the Australian and American psyche and behaviour that I teach willing actors from all parts of the world to try and adopt into their work. This is done in theory and in practice in developing character, subtext and story.

Such as, the generalizations of an Australian psyche: a relaxed, laidback, no fear, explorative, hard worker. A hard worker who has technique, good attitude and is generally honest and a nice person and a good listener too.

Or, the generalizations of an American psyche: an assertive mind and tongue, strong improvisation skills, a driving passion to succeed and for some, an inquisitive nature.

In regards to behaviour: an Australian and a Brit will cut their food up with a fork and knife and then commence eating – continuing to hold both the knife and the fork. An American cuts their food up, then puts down the knife and simply puts the food in their mouth with their fork only.

I do all of this, of course, to make actors better actors as they produce characters from many varied nations. One of my ways of coaching and teaching American actors is to subtly try to reduce or eliminate their elements of *show*, and aim for more truth.

This is done in many ways. For example, by getting actors to get in touch with themselves. Their emotions. Their past experiences. Their blockages. This begins with breath work. My training includes their breath, their voice, their emotions, their truth. Teaching them to be in the moment, where they can link breath, thought, image, and voice together.

If necessary – I say to the actor, please *stop. I don't believe it. Or, what are you doing here? You're showing. You're external, you're telegraphing. What are you trying to do?* I give them tangible direction and then they start again.

I also create activities and exercises for them to do to help eliminate bad habits. Of course, a lot of what I am saying here is already imbedded in my lesson plans and curriculum.

I also like to talk to the actor about how they are thinking. The thoughts that are in their heads. For example, I encourage them to think about acting from the perspective that acting is a performing art. It is not carpentry so you don't need to nail it. (Things don't move if they have been nailed.) An actor needs freedom in their work. I want you to explore. Explore all the possibilities and try not to have a results-based element in your work.

This is very important because why would you choose a role in any type of work – theatre, film, television – in which you know *all* of the outcomes? You will know the journey and discover nothing. It would have no challenge attached to it at all. If there's no journey for the actor to go on, it would just be like *a walk in the park*. A park you know very well. Consequently, you will not be anywhere near as watchable if you choose the option to not explore.

I like to teach, and train teachers that I teach, to teach by developing the *inner awareness,* self–acceptance and confidence from *within* the actor. Sometimes I will push the actor through a barrier, if necessary, as explained in some of the *Student Case Scenarios* described in Book One and in Chapter 17 of this book.

With the breath and voice training, I work on getting all actors to breathe down into as much as their body as possible. That is, have breath connection deep down into the body, using the diaphragm, back and buttocks, and even having them thinking that their legs can have breath filtering down them.

This all helps the actor to obtain a connection with themselves and their text, and when linked in with other Australian techniques, such as the layering system of *Dropping in the Text* as described in Book One, it gives them a foundation, a cornerstone, from which to build.

What I hope is this: that no matter where you were brought up in the world, you develop freedom and non-judgement in your work and *don't* try to nail it. You may not realize it, but most times, we actually do better work when we stop trying. This is because we let go. We take the pressure off ourselves, and our subconscious allows us to actually personify things we have learnt already.

Explore! Explore! Explore!

Acting is a performing art and your ability to explore and discover will help you become a better actor. In return you will be more watchable as an audience likes to watch someone discovering things as they go along.

Try thinking actor and audience before you begin. Think to yourself, we will go on this journey with the audience together. I encourage the actor to explore and discover the journey of the story, the production with the audience as it goes along.

Audiences love this. Especially in theatre where the audience can end up breathing along with the actor on stage as he breathes. Yes, a crazy thought isn't it. But many believe a strong performance on stage by an actor influences an audience to even breathing when the actor breathes. An accomplished theatre actor knows this and taps into this and moves the audience along emotionally with them.

But even with a film or television script you can think of the discoveries as if an audience member might do. This is an art, but feel it, sense it, work with it. Trying to nail each scene will not give you this experience.

If you are open to change, if you believe you can learn from everyone, from anyone, anywhere in the world, then that is a good start, as education is power. Don't just say it, fully commit to it with your mind, body and soul and your wallet or purse.

American actors have done this in my classes, because they have let their ego go. They have changed their thought processes to allow themselves to be trained by a foreigner, someone not born into an American culture. I humbly thank them and continue to do so.

For some actors I say to them: "Say to yourself, I'll flick a switch from now onwards and trust and let go – as you just don't know where you could get to with your commitment, your creativity and your work."

A recap to help all actors.

Let's recap the comparisons hypothesized in this chapter and ask the actor, including from America, some questions:

- How internal is the training that you receive?
- Do you have a teacher who constantly tells you what you are doing is wrong or bad?
- How important to you is it that you get trained by a qualified teacher?
- Do you choose a teacher based on their teachings or their pomp and ceremony?
- Is your training and preparation before performance a lazy one or a thorough one?
- Do you flock to a poor teacher's class or to a teacher who won't say much to you at all, just to get their name on your resume?
- How strong is your focus when doing the work?
- Are you narcissistic or *showy* with your work?
- How can you internalize more?

- Do you know about the history of theatre? Of film?
- Do you learn different acting techniques to find out which one works best for you?
- Are you in tune with yourself as a person?
- Do you pressure yourself to try and achieve perfection every time you act?
- Do you come from love and not fear?
- Do you focus more on marketing or the acting craft?
- Do you look other people in the eyes when you talk to them?
- How is your overall work ethic?
- Are you relaxed or do you go around saying *you are so stressed* all the time?
- If you are on medication, do you know how this may affect your work?
- If you are taking illegal drugs, do you know how this may affect your work?
- Do you honestly give yourself over to the work and its creations?
- Do you consider and/or strongly believe that a teacher from overseas could actually make you a much better actor?

To assist change, I suggest you please consider developing some or more of the following:

- An awareness of how your culture, your cities' sub-culture and your psyche and the pressures of the city that you live in, are influencing your decisions and are those decisions the best ones to make regarding your acting training
- Humility
- Honesty
- Totally letting go
- Use technique
- Trust – in yourself and others
- Have more of an element of play in your work
- Have strong focus

- In drama, be centred and internal and underplay, as opposed to show or exaggerate
- Get in touch with who you are
- Choose a teacher who won't cause you cell damage by abusing you
- Do ongoing breath work into the body, linking breath, thought, image and voice
- Create a thorough character back story
- See your scene study class time as a time of exploration. As opposed to a time of picking up a new scene and making an immediate choice and then performing the scene
- Have subtext
- Do the work without prejudices
- Don't continually judge the work
- Don't continually compare the work
- Don't be lazy
- Don't be narcissistic
- Don't think you come from a superior culture
- Be confident and assertive – but not arrogant
- Come from love and not fear
- Remember the journey is the most important thing
- Develop on-camera skills that have roots in observation on how to perform in front of the camera
- Open yourself to hear the truth and grow from the truth
- Laugh, don't stress
- Remember you are a story teller so help tell the story
- Remember that acting is about the relationships between you and other people you talk to or talk about
- Don't procrastinate or self-sabotage in any way
- Be diligent about homework
- Read, read, read
- Don't blame the teacher if you can't do something or if you don't book work
- Pay for your classes

I work very hard to get all of my actors to do these things and to think like this with their work. Most of my students do, do this.

All I have tried to do in this chapter is to try to put together some cultural and behavioural and psyche differences between two cultures. These thoughts and topics have been mulling around in my mind for a long time.

If you are offended by anything that I have written, please put the book down and pick it up another day and read it again. I am not trying to be arrogant or degrading or put Australia or Australian actors or Australian acting training on a pedestal and saying that it is better training, it is just different.

This is a hypothesis, one that will continually change and grow. As I and many other teachers are still teaching and there will always be teachers.

I make suggestions to American actors because many do ask for them. Many do want to consider changing and adopting new ways of thinking and acting. I trust that you will consider some of these ideas in this hypothesis.

For American actors: An additional checklist

- Be totally open in your mind and psyche to learn from anyone in the world
- Try not to see everything that you do as a marketing or an opportunity to sell yourself
- Try to totally let go and not judge your work
- Try to stay embedded in character development and your character's history and journey for as long as necessary
- Work a few times, not just once, on the same text/scene to develop character and a deep understanding of the text/scene
- Try to never, ever rush into performance
- Unless you have to, try to never read a scene, then immediately make a decision and want to perform it

- Don't be lazy. The foreign actor often works harder and smarter than the American actor
- Educate yourself on all theatre and on the history of theatre, film and television
- Perform the classics and Elizabethan, Edwardian and Victorian scenes from plays
- Don't try to nail it – change your vocabulary to say *I'm going to explore*

For some reason, American actors want to rush into performance all the time. I have to try very hard to slow them down.

Rushing into performance is something that I see clearly as a difference between the American and the Australian, European/British actors that I have trained. Please don't do it.

Improvisation aside (*which Americans love and a lot of them are very good at*), an Australian or European or British actor is much more likely to explore, in my experience, than an American actor.

As discussed already in this book, there are a few reasons for this. Firstly, it is the fact that, especially in Los Angeles, the actors are cold reading and doing something very similar in scene study classes, all the time. In fact, for a lot of them, they think that this is actor training.

Secondly, maybe it has something to do with the world in which we live in. A world in which whatever we want we can have and have it now. For example, we all have cell phones (mobiles), flat TV screens and computers on which we can do just about anything.

Thirdly, perhaps it is within the psyche of the American? As they often feel compelled to compete to succeed in their society. Consequently, they want to make decisions quicker, so they rush into performance to succeed or feel they are *progressing and/or succeeding*, as mentioned in previous chapters of this book.

Please remember the power and the importance of *playing and exploring and the journey*. We're complicated people us human beings. Things can be interpreted in many ways, so why rush into a performance?

One of the reasons you became an actor could be because of this: think of yourself as a little boy or girl playing with the hair brush. Holding it as a microphone as you sing to music or dance in your party dress. You are being admired, complemented on, given positive reinforcement and of course, given attention.

If you can relate to this, well one of the reasons you probably became an actor then was because you loved *playing* and being looked at. Remember that, and remember to play and explore everything. The rewards are priceless. And your work will be richer as a consequence; in more ways than one.

Learning Point Number Seven:

- Most acting performances begin with their training
- Take the pressures of your culture, your society, your people off yourself
- Try not to think you have to be over the top and/or exaggerate where it moves you into a state of show
- Don't be narcissistic with your work
- Consider trying not to think and behave that you come from a superior culture and that you are learning other things just so you can absorb them and change them. Respect the source
- Try to stay calm and play and enjoy the journey. Acting is a craft and it is not easy
- Focus on the work – explore the work, have a strong work ethic – much more so than on your ego or your marketing brand
- Come from love not fear
- Be grounded
- Create characters of depth, of substance
- Create three-dimensional characters. You have values and morals as a human being, so create them for your characters. Use the text as a guide to help you
- Actors who are nice people, humble, respectful, hard workers, and who don't complain all the time and are easy to work with, continue to work
- Explore, explore, explore
- Australian acting training just might make you a much better actor

Chapter 8: Training Japanese actors

There are brilliant actors all around the world. I have been lucky enough to teach Japanese, Chinese and South Koreans. I have been fortunate enough to watch and assess and teach Japanese actors, in particular, with their training and their work in person and on screen since 2013.

I like to think that I can add non-native English-speaking countries into my potpourri of actor training countries and share my teachings of acting.

I firmly believe that we can learn from any nationality, any culture, any body of people. I also believe that I can improve an actor's work no matter where they are from in the world and even if they are performing in a foreign language and I am assessing and guiding them.

I teach with interpreters, and my handouts and my scripts, taken from my curriculum, are transcribed into foreign languages for the students.

Racism and thoughts of superiority (this includes thinking of a sense of superiority on screen) are often underpinned by fear and ignorance. Consequently, I would like to talk about my training of Japanese actors because I believe it will help all readers of this book to learn to have an understanding, some knowledge, an empathy and a humility with people from a non-native English-speaking country; in this case, Japan.

Analyzing and improving Japanese actors' work on screen is a challenge I love.

Between 2002 and 2011, I taught Japanese, South Korean and Chinese actors who had moved to America, in America. I then began teaching

Japanese actors on an ongoing basis, in person in Japan, and also on Skype, from 2013 onwards.

What impresses me the most about Japanese actors is their humbleness, their respect for teachers and their desire to learn.

Generally speaking, a Japanese actor will tell you to your face what they feel their deficiencies are and/or what their cultural deficiencies are too. This actually makes it easy to train an actor because they have humility and respect for teachers and an awareness about their own culture.

Cultural factors

To improve a Japanese actor's work, they have to learn to let go. (This is similar to teaching American actors.) Typically, a Japanese actor is afraid of letting go.

With the American actor, as discussed in the previous chapter, it could be fear because they could be pressured into making choices quickly so they can move on and be successful. As already stated, I believe this is because of the fear and the pressures on them to succeed in their culture, their society.

In the Japanese actor's case, it is fear because they are generally not used to personifying real, honest behaviour in public. This is because Japanese people, in general, do not try to stand out that often.

That is, Japanese culture is very conservative when it comes to behaviour outside the home. In public, Japanese must, and do, adhere to the conservative social mores of their society. They consequently want to do this in acting classes. They feel they must do this at all times.

This way of living has an effect on their psyche and their way of approaching acting because they are under a lot of pressure socially to conform to these ways of behaviour. They respect everyone. They are polite to everyone. They are generally quiet in public. They look down at the ground a lot. They line up at public transport stops and will not push in or get on board a train, ahead of someone else in the queue. They say, "Thank you very much" all the time. Even for the smallest things.

Hence, when they get into an acting class, they are reluctant to display certain behaviour or say certain things, because of how they may be socially judged by their peers.

In their culture they are taught to be passive and quiet. And, as stated, they generally have not had a lot of the experiences in life that they are asked to relate to in their film and television auditions.

This makes starting to teach a Japanese acting class very interesting, as they are all wanting someone else to go first.

Fortunately, in general, once the Japanese actor is encouraged through warm-up activities and my opening statement where I acknowledge and talk about their cultural mores of wanting to conform and stay quiet, they usually do get to a place where they are not only surprising each other, they are surprising themselves. But this takes work and trust in the teacher. It also takes time.

I love the challenge of teaching Japanese actors. Even with their cultural mores and ways of behaviour. Behaviour that is, kind of, encased withing itself, within their society; they eventually, generally push through this boundary and freely take risks.

After the work they may drop their head, bow, tell one another how good the work was, give polite positive constructive criticism to one another, and of course continue to be socially *correct* (for want of a better word).

A couple of other interesting points about Japanese actors. Many Japanese people, including my wife, have told me that they have two faces. The mask at home and the mask they wear in society. At home, they often say it as it is. In public, they will do their very best to not be rude to you, no matter what you say or do.

In this sense, they are all acting when out in public. They're natural actors in the sense that they are taught from a very young age to not show their feelings when out in public and to be quiet, conform and fit in.

An aside: Of course this is a good starting point, as actors do need to show their emotions.

Another interesting point is they naturally play down their surprise when responding to people who say something that is a surprise to them. They do this by slightly leaning backwards and saying, "wayyy" (that's how it sounds). A direct translation of "wayyy" is "I see" in English. So, when a Japanese actor gets in one of my classes and I bring up surprises, we both laugh as we see they can play one surprise in their repertoire, the "wayyy", very easily and very well.

My best advice to Japanese actors is to let go of the social mores (the social ways of behaviour), as much as they can when they commence to create character, make choices and act as that character.

That's because, taking risks, standing out, being different, is a good way of getting noticed as an actor, especially in their culture.

I continue to learn from Japanese people, culture and actors today and from other countries in the world too, if and when I am lucky enough to travel there.

By talking a little about Japanese culture, social mores and behaviour, as well as training Japanese actors, I believe we are all culturally better for it. I list a number of Japanese actors whose work I love in this book in the next chapter.

Learning Point Number Eight:

- Being humble and respecting teachers is the way to go
- As a Japanese actor you should not follow the Japanese custom of wanting to not stand out and stay quiet when working as an actor
- Take the space
- Step out from the crowd
- Try to think, as a culture, we are already natural actors as we are taught to hide our emotions in public

Above: Paul with some of the actors in his on camera acting workshop over 3 days in Tokyo, Japan in 2022. Paul is also pictured with Kyoko Kudo san, who Paul trained for 9 years and Kyoko san has booked film, television and film with Paul's coaching. Below: Headmaster Shinji Betchaku san from Stone Wings Acting School in Tokyo is translating the lesson plan content onto the whiteboard for Paul's class that day.

March 26, 2023

I am writing to appreciate Paul Parker for his outstanding work as an acting teacher. I have had the pleasure of hosting Paul for eight workshops at the WIAS acting school in Japan, where he has consistently impressed me with his teaching skills and personable nature.

Paul's workshops have been met with resounding enthusiasm from the Japanese actors who have participated. His approach to instruction is not only effective but also engaging, which is reflected in the overwhelmingly positive feedback we have received from our students. Many of them have commented on how much they learned from Paul and how grateful they are to have had the opportunity to work with him.

Beyond his teaching abilities, Paul is a joy to work with. He is professional, reliable, and personable, and always goes above and beyond to ensure that his students are getting the most out of his workshops.

I wholeheartedly endorse Paul Parker as an acting teacher of the highest caliber. His extensive experience conducting three-day workshops over the span of eight years at WIAS has consistently garnered praise and appreciation from the participants.

Sincerely,

Shinji Betchaku

Shinji Betchaku
Headmaster
WIAS(Wings International Acting School)

Part 2
Practice

Chapter 9: On-camera research

Teach yourself to analyze successful actors' work

This chapter is about established actors and their skills on screen. I think this will inspire you and help you learn how to analyze actors' work and eventually your own work. Let's look at some popular actors, and some of whom are my favourite actors.

The best actors' work is there for you to see. This is because film and television programs are recorded, played and then archived, hence reviewing and analyzing actors' work in these mediums is constantly available.

You can rent the DVD of the film, purchase it online or watch online with your streaming platform. You can also watch re-runs on television or YouTube.

What I recommend you do is simply watch actors on film and television and see them work. You will find that it is easier to teach yourself to learn to analyze actors' work if you turn the volume down on the television or film.

This is because, with the volume up, the editing, acting, directing, lighting, costume, set dressing, in short, all the things that make up the story of the production, influence you. But without the sound, you are less likely to get drawn in by the story and these production values.

This then puts you in a better position to be able to watch the acting. Watch actors and see what they do well. Then try to copy what they do.

I would like you to think, why do we like them? What are their major skills on screen? I've listed below what I think are their greatest gifts on screen. You can write your own list.

Actors who work a lot generally:

- Are still. They are still especially with their head and face when in a mid-shot or a closer shot for drama
- Listen really well
- Know how to keep their eyes and face, in general, in the frame
- Make impact with their face and eyes both vertically and horizontally in the frame
- Often have a loose jaw
- Often have their mouth slightly open so there is not tension on their face or head, especially when listening
- Use a variety of reactions
- Use the frame to their advantage. For example, they present their best side or angles
- Use their eyes well inside the frame
- Have their feelings come across on their face which is visible in the frame
- Control their mannerisms so they don't distract the viewer
- Move slowly. Slower as the camera goes closer
- And much more

Australian

Nicole Kidman

I am thinking of her work, post 2002. Kidman's greatest skill is having a look on her face that personifies how it would feel to receive the news that she has just received. Her strength, for me, is clearly in this area. When something is said to her, her character feels it and we clearly see it on her face. This is beautifully personified when she is playing her character in the television series *Big Little Lies* and in her portrayal of Virginia Wolf in the feature film *The Hours*.

Seeing this skill happens for most of the best actors on screen. Kidman is now one of them. As is **Toni Collette**, who does this so very well too.

Sam Worthington

Mr. Worthington's greatest skill to me is his ability to begin scenes in a neutral state. His face, the look on his face, is open and ready to explore. For me there is no surprise that his success has come in action-adventure films like Avatar as he explores and takes us on his characters' journey.

Mel Gibson

We don't know what Mr. Gibson is going to do next. His manic state as a performer is very watchable. Lots of actors do this. Also think Aussie, **Jacqueline McKenzie**. We don't know what these actors will do next and it is very watchable.

Cate Blanchett

I believe Blanchett's strength is in the detailed characterization of her characters. She is very versatile. Her deep, resonating voice is also a huge strength of hers.

Russell Crowe

Crowe's greatest strength on screen is his ability to personify the brooding man and the man who is about to be aggressive or violent. This is all done in the most important camera shots.

British

Sally Hawkins

I love Hawkins' characterization and her wonderful ability to play surprises. She is also a brilliant listener and watcher of other people's body language.

However, her greatest gift on screen is her ability to put her face, in fact, her whole body, into a state of anticipation. I have not seen any actor who can do this as well as Hawkins.

She draws us in beautifully because of her ability to have a look on her face of *what are you going to say* or *what are you going to do* or *what do you want me to say or do* – this is a rare gift. Sally is a magical actor on screen. Her work is sensational.

Dame Judi Dench

Dame Judi's greats skill on screen is in the sheer weight of female strength that is in most of her characters. It is simply her presence. In addition, it is also in the tonal use of her voice. Her tone of voice is so beautiful. She could cut toast with it! She also has piercing and direct eyes. So important for the screen.

Carey Mulligan

When I first saw Carey Mulligan in the film **Never Let Me Go**, I was spellbound by her character portrayal. I believe her greatest gift on screen is how relaxed she looks. Totally believable. Love her work.

Jodie Comer

My latest watch. This actress is simply breathtaking in her character portrayal and ultimately in her performance in the television series *Killing Eve*.

American

Stanley Tucci

The greatest American male character actor on screen of all time. What skills. Tucci's ability to transform himself into different, variable characters is only somewhat reached by some of the best British actors like John Hurt and Gary Oldman.

Al Pacino

Pacino's strongest gift is how he carries what he is thinking on his face, most importantly, through his eyes. He is also the master of subtext. It always looks like something is going on behind what is going on.

Robert De Niro

I love the way De Niro uses his body. He moves so well. Of course, he plays subtext too and has a look that says, something aggressive or violent is going to happen soon.

Allison Janney

Janney is the master of the use of her body. Oh my, what a delight to watch. Just watch her in the *West Wing* with the sound turned down.

Kiefer Sutherland

Sutherland's greatest gifts are the look of panic on his face, the tone of his voice, and his subtext playing. I suggest you watch his work in the film *A Few Good Men*.

Morgan Freeman

Freeman has a strong ability to carry a film. He does this by his looks. His looks are so specific that two things come to mind. Firstly, his ability to look calm and relaxed as he turns his head and body in the direction that he wants us, the audience, to look. Secondly, his eyes. Freeman's eyes move in a way that shows interest, shows anticipation, shows him looking, trying to discover things, looking at something that he wants us, the viewer, to follow. This is why he is a leading man and also why he has played many detective characters.

Tommy Lee Jones

Speaking of playing detectives, Jones has two incredible skills on screen. The first is his ability to use the frame with his eyes and face. He has learnt how to naturally cross the screen with his eyes and it is indeed a skill. As an actor, you simply must have no fear and feel free to cross the screen, cross the lens of the camera with your eyes. Jones does this so well.

Secondly, he has the ability to deliver mundane, sometimes boring lines really well. Well enough that we are interested in what he is saying and it also sounds interesting and/or educational. Think of his speeches in feature films *The Fugitive* and *US Marshals*. Think of his ability to move the audience with his voice as personified beautifully with his narration in *No County For Old Men*. And like Judi Dench, it is the vocal use of his tone.

Brad Pitt

Pitt is a highly underrated actor by some people. An actor with *je en sais quoi*. He is a terrific character actor, and I love his work. His greatest strengths are his listening ability, his ability to help incite interest in what his character is doing and the characters that we see that he has created.

Meryl Streep

I believe Stanley Tucci is *the* American male character actor of our time and Meryl Streep is the American female character actor of our time. There seems nothing Streep cannot do, and she looks natural at all times. Her development and use of different accents is exceptional. I say this as she can act in so many different accents.

My mentor Reg Evans worked with her in Australia on the tragic Lindy Chamberlain story turned into a film called *A Cry In The Dark*. Reg said, when they shot reverse shots of other actors, on her days off, Streep would sit, on set, on the stand in the courtroom scenes and be an eyeline for the other actors and would sit there in character, giving the actors something to perform back to. What a gift. Many, many, many celebrity actors do not do this. This is an example of Streep's commitment to her work.

Japanese

Koji Yakusho

Yakusho san is the master of looking grounded. This actor looks so centred, like a Buddhist monk. Everything revolves around his character's axis. He is mesmerizing on screen. Watch him in the film *Memoirs of a Geisha*.

Satoshi Nikaido

Nikaido san's strength is in his ability to constantly play surprises that are watchable, as well as his ability to carry a scene. He moves the film or TV episode forward with his looks, similar to the way Morgan Freeman does. Watch him in the feature film *Babel*.

Rinko Kikuchi

Kikuchi san is a risk-taker. Especially in her work where she speaks in Japanese. Like Mel Gibson, we don't know what she will do next. She is captivating on screen. Watch her in the feature film Babel.

Haru

I love watching this actress. Haru san looks so calm, so relaxed on screen. She is a young version of the female Everyman. She is Everywoman. Watch her in the NHK television drama *Asa ga Kita*.

In closing, go grab a film you love, that you've already seen and enjoyed, put it on, turn the volume down and watch the acting. Try to pick what the actors' wants are. See what they are doing. See them look sideways in the frame. See them play surprises – both good and bad. See what they do. See them work.

Observing other good actors is great because you can copy or steal what they are doing and try to emulate their work. Any good work that you see from the likes of Jack Nicholson, Russell Crowe, Cate Blanchett or Meryl Streep, you can take. You can make it part of your repertoire. Who says, you can't, right?

Observations of some excellent on-screen acting

As an acting coach, actors ask me a lot, *"Who are some of the best actors that you like on screen?" "What actors should I watch?"*

As a teacher, it is important for me to show my students actors personifying what I teach. I do this with most things that I teach on screen. Some of the topics or exercises that I teach I have made up myself, one I use from elsewhere (surprises) and will always acknowledge the source, as best as I can. For example, surprises came from Richard Sarell.

I am about to draw your attention to some video scenes on YouTube. I will do this for you to see the quality of actors acting as well as actors personifying some of the things that I teach. *If you have purchased this book as an e-book*, you can easily go to the external YouTube links that I'll list. For those readers with a hard or soft copy of this book, simply copy the links into your search engine or YouTube.

A disclaimer before we start: I cannot be held to account, if you, the viewer, do not like the content of what I am going to draw your attention to. There is no nudity in any of these links. But, some of the topics shown in the YouTube links may be best suited to adult viewing.

So please show caution if you are under the age of eighteen and reading this book. Perhaps ask your mum and dad to look at the videos first? Some of the chosen scenes show dramatic circumstances. For me, all these scenes have been chosen based on the acting on screen.

I also cannot be held accountable for whatever advert YouTube chooses to display prior to the scene or any other video clips that are in line to be played next as a video. As this is all totally under the control of YouTube and will change from time to time and from country to country.

Character and reactions

Let's start. Please watch some scenes from a 2003 episode of US cable TV show *The Shield* by Shawn Ryan. There are two terrific female actors at work, **Melanie Lynskey** from New Zealand and **CCH Pounder** from America.

These are the two phrases that spring to mind when watching these two ladies work – character driven – totally believable with their reactions. I am lucky enough to have met CCH Pounder three times. What an actor she is. I love her work. Melanie Lynskey is underrated and generally unknown by many. Love her work.

https://www.youtube.com/watch?v=hHL_M1AoWi8

Surprises and characterization

Let's watch some male actors, **Noah Wyle** and **Kiefer Sutherland**, creating a character and playing what I teach, called surprises, from the film *A Few Good Men*. Note the acting through the eyes and the stillness of the muscles on the face of Kiefer Sutherland and as a consequence, the camera comes into an extreme close-up on him.

So you know, these two scenes are the ones that actors are viewing while I am talking about their acting in Chapter 2 of this book – the transcription from acting classes in Hollywood.

https://www.youtube.com/watch?v=N16YkjFVAyE

https://www.youtube.com/watch?v=m_bVhTvCkBY

Now let's watch this magnificent performer on screen – **Cate Blanchett** – as she plays surprise after surprise in *Notes On A Scandal*

https://www.youtube.com/watch?v=XR4geqHuy9c

Caution: there is a gun shooting in this scene below; ending with the killing of a character in the film. Let's watch **Barry Shabaka Henley** play a really long surprise in the film *Collateral*. Start watching two minutes in.

https://www.youtube.com/watch?v=IejpzbxKUZE

Helen Hunt plays surprises all the time. Some good, some bad, some are just a confused surprise look. She is very good at them in *Mad About You* and *As Good As it Gets*.

My preferred video link of Helen Hunt has not been listed here, so please YouTube her. The video I often used has recently been taken down.

Acting through the eyes

Let's watch some eye acting by **Anne Heche** and **Harrison Ford** in the film *Six Days Seven Nights*

https://www.youtube.com/watch?v=C84amEercRc

https://www.youtube.com/watch?v=oGA3ajkJPNQ

Then, watch **Aden Young** in the TV show *Rectify*. My preferred video link has recently been taken down, so please YouTube him.

Then **Krysten Ritter** in *Breaking Bad*

https://www.youtube.com/watch?v=4hOoljr-XIs

Let's watch the master doing it.

Al Pacino – Fredo must die – *The Godfather*

https://www.youtube.com/watch?v=kzpivoNuISg

And more Pacino:

https://www.youtube.com/watch?v=jYnRBX2Trtk

Characterization

Let's watch some great character creations. We'll start with **Philip Seymour Hoffman** in *Capote*

https://www.youtube.com/watch?v=zXroRe—2QM

If you wish you can look at interviews with the real Truman Capote here

https://www.youtube.com/watch?v=atPaVIilEqk

https://www.youtube.com/watch?v=TiSiNgaQBYE

Then Philip Seymour Hoffman's work in *Magnolia*

https://www.youtube.com/watch?v=7k0-pSCwcx4

https://www.youtube.com/watch?v=UFFkSeKGnxk

Here are snippets from ten performances of Philip Seymour Hoffman

https://www.youtube.com/watch?v=8spDQQXxTYQ

Here's **Forest Whitaker** in *The Last King of Scotland*

https://www.youtube.com/watch?v=F7_aagPOpUU

Compare his character creation to the real man, Idi Amin

https://www.youtube.com/watch?v=dvVIkXPvp-4

https://www.youtube.com/watch?v=phPMSCcpb40

Here's **Gary Oldman** in *The Darkest Hour* playing Churchill

https://www.youtube.com/watch?v=1YpDd1nVthI

https://www.youtube.com/watch?v=skrdyoabmgA

Churchill and his secretary

https://www.youtube.com/watch?v=JwlhFfOC5Zo

Then listen to the real Winston Churchill

https://www.youtube.com/watch?v=s_LncVnecLA

The real Winston Churchill video

https://www.youtube.com/watch?v=5ROGkn4a_O4

The best of British for me here. Watch the amazing characters created by **Sally Hawkins.**

Eternal Beauty

https://www.youtube.com/watch?v=NiqwtgZzbds

Chapter 9: On-camera research | 235

Maudie

https://www.youtube.com/watch?v=wCZ_guQTGNw

Paddington

https://www.youtube.com/watch?v=jFoE6Qw8RGw

The Shape of Water

https://www.youtube.com/watch?v=PQyLNxWJkx0

Happy Go Lucky

https://www.youtube.com/watch?v=Pqj6w0yW_Xc

Happy Go Lucky – driving lesson

https://www.youtube.com/watch?v=QmUn89F0jNQ

Blue Jasmine (with Cate Blanchett)

https://www.youtube.com/watch?v=JFT2VNJ0eAo

Stanley Tucci

The Lovely Bones

https://www.youtube.com/watch?v=M-APah17AQA

The Devil Wears Prada

https://www.youtube.com/watch?v=HSPYgwP9R84

The Hunger Games

https://www.youtube.com/watch?v=plMyVJnmdGg

Captain America

https://www.youtube.com/watch?v=V4C7IAmiUgs

Meryl Streep

Her voices

https://www.youtube.com/watch?v=aPUedwHP_Ro

Kramer v Kramer

https://www.youtube.com/watch?v=80UzhoD-RBs

Doubt

https://www.youtube.com/watch?v=ThsZ8wfhJpk

Big Little Lies

https://www.youtube.com/watch?v=4GnlVd4l_5Y

Cate Blanchett

Notes on a Scandal

https://www.youtube.com/watch?v=XR4geqHuy9c

10 characters

https://www.youtube.com/watch?v=naZ3bVWOuNk

Blue Jasmine (with Sally Hawkins)

https://www.youtube.com/watch?v=JFT2VNJ0eAo

Carey Mulligan. Watch her here in *Never Let Me Go*

https://www.youtube.com/watch?v=ZsAfPCmTD5g

https://www.youtube.com/watch?v=07WGEJDAF9Q

10 performances

https://www.youtube.com/watch?v=J2cjxdkz4qc

Love the **Fanning sisters'** work

Dakota Fanning

https://www.imdb.com/name/nm0266824/?ref_=fn_al_nm_1

Elle Fanning

https://www.imdb.com/name/nm1102577/?ref_=fn_al_nm_1

Never forget this amazing character performance by **Jessica Lange** in *Frances*

Frances trailer

https://www.youtube.com/watch?v=TcaT7L9Xj04

The actor of our time, on screen: **Daniel Day-Lewis**

Lincoln

https://www.youtube.com/watch?v=1qjtugr2618

There Will Be Blood

https://www.youtube.com/watch?v=GX-9wXFQRgA

My Left Foot

https://www.youtube.com/watch?v=oaBtXwbfgGI

Gangs of New York

https://www.youtube.com/watch?v=jrkw1UgX3q0

https://www.youtube.com/watch?v=Oro4ph7yTmc

The Phantom Thread

https://www.youtube.com/watch?v=fn5dXUu_qxM

Using the frame to great effect

Using the frame, personified beautifully, by Tommy Lee Jones in *No Country For Old Men*. Notice how nonchalantly he crosses the screen with his eyes. Imagine that on the big screen in the cinema. It looks very powerful. You too can do it.

https://www.youtube.com/watch?v=VXNfxK5Q2Qg

Drawing the camera in based on the internal work of the character

Casey Affleck – *Manchester By the Sea*

https://www.youtube.com/watch?v=J30cS-dusjI&t=24s

Kaitlyn Dever - *Unbelievable*

https://www.youtube.com/watch?v=p196J_c31dA

Look at this awesome performer, **Joshua Dela Cruz**, often acting to nothing there. The animation and imagery are put in later in post-production. He is natural, relaxed and entertaining. What skills he personifies as he moves in the frame in the kids' TV show *Blue's Clues*.

https://www.youtube.com/watch?v=iwIkjgL79Zs

Learning Point Number Nine:

- Studying successful actors' work can benefit your own acting training and practice
- Watch the examples I have given, but with the sound turned down for best results
- Write your own list of things that you like and try to copy them

Above: The poster for a pilot that was made for a TV series that Paul wrote, directed and produced through his production company in 2023. Paul's next project will be a feature film script that he has co-written. Paul states, "I'm still learning to write and direct my own projects for the screen. I'm trying".

Chapter 10: Acting exercises – a way of thinking

The non-verbal acting exercise

In acting classes, sometimes, I say to actors, I am going to do an exercise. This exercise is an exercise on observation and awareness. Your ability to watch detail and to emulate what I do as best as you can. It is a non-verbal exercise.

I ask actors to watch me: enter the room, pick up a book off a chair, sit and read a page or two from the book, get up, put the book down and then walk out.

After I do the exercise, I ask the actors, one by one, to copy what I did. What took place next was the following, from most, if not all, of the actors; they:

- Couldn't remember what I did
- Stepped out of the exercise and spoke to me and the other actors
- Did things I didn't do, such as:
  - Spoke
  - Laughed
  - Scratched their bums or elsewhere on their bodies
  - Performed it more obviously
  - Added action
  - Added dialogue
  - Mucked around
  - Overacted it
  - Gave up

At the end of the exercise, the first thing I said to the actors was, "In the pages that I read from the book that I was holding, when I did the exercise, I was reading about, blah, blah, blah" (blah, meaning the content). "What were you reading about?"

Nearly every actor in the room had no idea what was on the page, as, when it was their turn, they were not reading from the book at all. They were acting that they were reading.

How are your observational and awareness skills? They are very important for you as an actor. Your concentration, focus watching and reacting skills, and your ability to be in the moment, are all relevant with this exercise. Consider practising this simple exercise with family and friends.

The ultimate questions

When teaching at acting schools, or when teaching a new group of my own, when I start to train the actors I say to the group, "I would like all the actors in the room to stand over this side of the room and all the non-actors to stand over that side of the room." Every time, apart from once, not all of the actors have moved to the side of the room where the actors should stand.

I then follow up with another question. "I would like all the professional actors to stand on that side of the room and all the non-professional actors to stand on that side of the room." This gets them bamboozled every time. As actors always disperse to both sides of the room.

Here I am, training actors and yet some of them don't think they are an actor and many of them don't think that they are professional. I then say to them, "What you think, is what you will become. I want you all to think, right now, from this moment onwards, I am a professional actor." Then on we go into the lesson plan.

What sort of actor are you?

There are two types of actors:

1. An actor who, when given the scene and the direction, and then the work with a teacher or casting director – can create the world, using the five senses and their imagination
2. An actor who, when given the scene and the direction, and then the work with a teacher or casting director – cannot create the world, etcetera

Which one are you?

If you are one of the latter, I talk at length in my first book about the importance of your imagination and improvisational skills to help all actors.

The number 1 actor above should also be creative and smart and not care how they look or how they behave. They are a risk-taker.

The number 2 actor above is most likely coming from fear and afraid to let go, afraid to suspend disbelief in the character, doesn't use their imagination and waits for the teacher to give the details or instructions.

Following this train of thought, when actors are given direction by casting directors, there are basically four different reactions. The actors:

1. Don't do what is asked. Perhaps they didn't hear it
2. Did hear it but were afraid to do anything
3. Did hear it and did a little bit of the direction
4. Did hear the direction and really went for it

Number 3 above is common. I want you to do number 4 – always.

It is so much easier for a casting director or teacher or director to pull back your performance, than to push up your performance by asking for more.

So many actors come from fear:

- Fear of their choice
- Fear of their character

- Fear of what they do will not be liked
- Fear that their interpretation will be wrong

Try never to come from fear, always come from love. You can do well. You can achieve. You can take risks. You can be successful.

I constantly say to actors, casting directors know if you have the script; the full script. As generally, actors with lots of credits are the only actors who get sent the full script or episode.

If you are not one of these actors, after reading the synopsis, the breakdown, the one or two or three scenes, what you must do is make it up. Of course you use the script as a guide, but you must also use your imagination to create the back story for your character. Some actors don't know how to do this. They need help. Hence the importance of improvisation and imagination as discussed in my first book. Then, a lot of these actors don't trust. They don't trust the choices that they made. You must teach yourself to trust.

What sort of characters suit you best?

Here's a few to choose from:

- Leading
- The best friend
- Occupational – e.g. the plumber, the truck driver
- Everyman – the character actor who can play anything
- The romantic interest

It is good for you to think on this too.

What genre am I suitable for? Is it:

- Sitcom
- Soap opera
- Romantic comedy
- Period piece, set in, say, 1876
- Drama or comedy
- Horror
- Sci-fi

Everyman

Wikipedia defines "Everyman" this way:

"The term Everyman was used as early as an English morality play from the early 1500s: The Summoning of Everyman. *The play's protagonist is an allegorical character representing an ordinary human who knows he is soon to die; according to literature scholar Harry Keyishian he is portrayed as 'prosperous, gregarious, [and] attractive'. Everyman is the only human character of the play; the others are embodied ideas such as Fellowship, who 'symbolizes the transience and limitations of human friendship'.*

"The use of the term Everyman to refer generically to a portrayal of an ordinary or typical person dates to the early 20th century. The term everywoman originates in the same period, having been used by George Bernard Shaw to describe the character Ann Whitefield of his play Man and Superman.*"*

The Everyman actor is the actor who works a lot and can play your everyday roles. They look like every man or every woman. They are often referred to as an ordinary or typical human being.

Think: Mark Ruffalo, Tom Hanks, Stanley Tucci, Gary Oldman, John Hurt, Sam Neill.

Everywoman too. Think: Meryl Streep, Cate Blanchett, CCH Pounder.

This type of actor can play leading and supporting characters. They are often the protagonist.

Exercises you can do

Warm up: Movement – music – Mozart. Simply move to this music freely.

https://www.youtube.com/watch?v=uvRE2wIFbW8

or – Tchaikovsky

https://www.youtube.com/watch?v=7_WWz2DSnT8

Then do the foundation work from my Book One and/or some sort of verbal warm up with your lips, teeth and the tips of the tongue.

All working on your diction by playing with sounds as you work on and with the articulators in the mouth. The main articulators are the tongue, the upper lip, the lower lip, the upper teeth, the upper gum ridge (alveolar ridge), the hard palate, the velum (soft palate), the uvula (free-hanging end of the soft palate), the pharyngeal wall, and the glottis (space between the vocal cords).

Learning Point Number Ten:

- Consider the ways of thinking in this chapter when preparing to work
- Be observant. If you are trying to emulate what someone else is doing, simply do it. Don't overact it
- Know what you are selling. Know your type. Meaning, the types of characters that you naturally look like and can play well, create those types of characters
- Warm-up exercises are underrated. Please do them

Chapter 11: Improve movement

So many actors I train struggle in front of the camera because they don't know what to do with their bodies. They are self-conscious. They push. Their minds are distracted. They are self-doubters.

There is a lack of movement or they have poor movement or we see tension in the body, or there is a self-consciousness about what they are doing which derives from an actor worrying about how they look on screen.

I believe the root of the problem is that so many actors cannot get past the notion of how do I look on screen.

I am sure this relates to why so many Americans get cosmetic surgery. They get it because their focus is on the external and not the internal significance of people. They get cosmetic surgery because they want to look physically better or more pronounced, in the sense of a bigger chest or bigger lips.

I'll explain in this chapter what I do when I see an actor who doesn't know what to do with her body and it is showing in the actor's work. I generally do the following things:

- Talk to them about the thoughts in their head. Directly ask them why they are self-conscious. This interaction is often deep-rooted, embedded in psyche, culture and ways of thinking and behaving. It usually takes a lot of time to heal and grow in this area
- Give them positive ways to think, including positive affirmations, and talk to them about the words they use in life. That is, the language they use

- Work with them on movement. I generally do this because I can see, in their movement, they are either overacting with the use of their body, looking contrived with the use of their body, or afraid to do anything with the use of their body

Below is a list of things, in order, that I often do with actors using movement as growth for the actor.

1. Ask them to do a dance/movement warm up to a song that they like

2. Ask them to isolate parts of the body and move them one by one. Such as toes, then feet, then ankles, etcetera

3. Introduce the topic of *Moving with Purpose*. Give the actor an occupation. Such as:
    - Cocktail waitress
    - Tennis player
    - Policeman
    - Doctor
    - Teacher
    - Office worker

4. Then introduce an activity. Such as:
    - You are threading a needle
    - Reading a book
    - Folding napkins
    - Making a phone call
    - Rolling tobacco

5. Then I put the two activities together. Such as:
    - Traffic cop conducting traffic
    - Barmaid making cocktails
    - Dance teacher teaching students
    - Librarian putting books on a shelf
    - Doctor telling someone they have cancer
    - Clown at a kids' party

I then discuss the exercises with the students. Talking with them about how free they are and asking them how free they feel. I encourage them to watch people closely and take mental notes or notes on paper about people's use of their bodies in life.

6. I give them scenarios to work with. Such as:
   - You are a cleaner, cleaning, who at the same time, witnesses a fight
   - You are a new tradesman, proud of your new uniform, but you start to feel insecure
   - You are a student in love with another student and don't know what to do
   - You are an admin office worker who becomes nervous

All the while I am moving the actor towards using their body to help express things that are going on, just as we do in life. I encourage them as we go along and draw their attention to their freedom of movement.

I then say, now decide on some of these things for the character you are about to play in the scene. Think, what is their occupation? What are some things that that occupation does? Then do them. Create a little world for your character. Do this without the script first, add the script later. Actors usually improve dramatically with this movement work.

Sometimes I use the neutral mask work as described in my first book to help free them up. Sometimes I do acting technique teachers: Grotowski or Laban movement work. Sometimes I do my Character Development chart work. Over time, actors become more relaxed in front of an audience when on the stage, or in front of the camera when acting on screen.

As most actors want to work on screen, by using the movement of the body exercises as described in this chapter as well as seeing movement personified by such actors as Allison Janney, I reinforce the fact that the camera sees your tense body and face. The camera sees your locked jaw. The camera sees everything. So loosen it and use your body naturally.

An actor's work must be naturally fluid with movement, and loose and relaxed on screen, as well as on the stage. The relaxed, centred, still face and body on screen actually looks really good and is a great starting point for performing on screen, as mentioned when I talked about actor Sam Worthington in a previous chapter.

Learning Point Number Eleven:

- Many actors don't know how to use their bodies for effect
- The camera shows everything, especially tension on the face and the body of the actor
- The freer your body is, the better you will look
- You can make variable points with your non-verbal communication of your body
- You can help yourself be captivating on screen with the use of your body
- You must get to a point where you don't care how you look when performing on camera

Chapter 12: On-camera exercises

Teach yourself reactions

When I analyze the acting roles that actors are cast in – the *five-and-under, the two-liners, the co-star* roles in film and television – I generally see the following: the camera doesn't stay on the actor too long. The scene edits to them just as they say their line, or part of their line, and then edits to something else, such as the other actor(s), some action or location views.

This is generally because these types of roles are cast with up-and-coming actors who have not yet developed a lot of skills and confidence in front of the camera. The actors are also, generally speaking, not as relaxed as the actors in bigger roles.

However, every now and again, an actor will excel in one of these roles and the camera will stay on them longer. Perhaps simply a second or two or three longer. I believe that this is so because the actor uses their face and/or body well to respond to what is going on. They are comfortable enough to start to develop different facial reactions to what is happening, what is being said and/or what is being implied or happening through their subtext.

Consequently, I recommend that actors learn to develop reactions. Develop these facial expressions or facial poses and develop lots of them. Actors' reactions, generally speaking again, need to be applicable to the scene, the character they are playing, and what is going on. In other words, their reactions complement the action and dialogue in the scene.

I look for this when I watch film and television. I look for these actors that pop out at us, in minor roles, on the screen. These actors generally get noticed and soon get more work. They might get further work in the production that they are currently working on.

Actors, I encourage you to please create a character. Be alive, be active. Don't overact or step out of character. But simply learn to respond with your face and your body to what is going on. In other words – act! Have a variety of facial expressions that you can use when on screen, in the minor roles, as they will definitely help you get more work.

All the best actors started somewhere and do give the audience a variety of facial reactions or poses, so learn to do this.

I could give many examples of what I am talking about here, but I'll simply give one. Krysten Ritter absolutely blew me away with her character performance of the character Jane in the US television show *Breaking Bad*. Yes, she already had 20 IMDB credits before this, and yes, she became a recurring character for a while on this show. But I am using her as an example because of her ability to continually have reactions going on, all the time.

Ritter is continually alive in the world that her character is living in and this is one of the reasons why she is so successful and watchable.

She personifies the point of what I am talking about here so well. She was in nine episodes of *Breaking Bad*, and I encourage you to watch her.

I train my students to work on their reactions. You can see what I am about to introduce to my students here on YouTube. Here I am teaching in Hollywood:

https://www.youtube.com/watch?v=UdY5uEJtq2k&t=6s

In this video I ask actors to act through the face, especially the eyes, to the following words: anger, jealousy, love, forgiveness, insecurity, crazy, depressed, apathetic, kind, studious, caring, etcetera.

I simply want to see these responses, these looks in their eyes and to a lesser extent, on their faces. This exercise works and you can do it now too. You can practise in front of the mirror at home and/or by recording yourself with your phone and then watching it back.

Line-by-line responses

Here is another very good exercise to help you to learn to develop responses. I would like to preface this exercise by saying, when we are really listening, listening very astutely, we will naturally respond with our faces and eyes and then body and voice. If we are clearly in the moment and simply listening, with nothing else going on in our head, we will be in the moment.

Until you can get to this point, and/or if you continually have the same reaction on your face, it is a really good idea to learn to teach yourself reactions. They will help you get work and help keep the camera on you when you do get work.

Here is the exercise. Get a scene, a short one is good, make decisions on genre, style and character. For example, drama, in the style of a cop show and your character is a suspect who is guilty.

Write on a piece of paper, line one and so on, and reaction responses of a word or a few words. Like this:

Line 1 response... Your look is: *surprised*

Line 2 response... Your look is: *I don't believe that*

Line 3 response... Your look is: *I agree with that*

Line 4 response... Your look is: *Really?*

Line 5 response... Your look is: *You're crazy*

Line 6 response... Your look is: *Oh, come on*

Line 7 response... Your look is: *I'm going to ignore that*

Line 8 response... Your look is: *I think I'll leave now*

Then have someone read the lines that your character does not say, one by one. You now respond with your face performing the reaction response that you wrote down on a piece of paper.

This will generally be easy as scripts are written with challenges for the characters to overcome. What you are doing is simply making choices on how you feel you will respond. If there are many sentences said to you, try to write down two or three adjectives or phrases. Such as: *Will there be? I'm confused? I'm thinking about what that looks like? Are you having a go at me?* Etcetera.

I know these words are out of context; they are simply just adjectives and phrases for you to see that I have written something down.

Then, ask the reader to read the lines from the scene again. You respond to their line, non-verbally, thinking of the adjective or descriptive phrase that you have written down. You can say your next line back to them at the same time if you wish. In other words, the second time you do it, you are starting to move into acting mode and having fluidity with the reading of the scene.

Remember, you are responding to their line. You are taking the time to learn to teach yourself to respond, non-verbally, with your face and eyes. Hence teaching yourself *reactions*. Remember, this is not performing, this is an acting on-screen exercise.

Later, when you perform the scene for a workshop or class, or audition even, whatever you remember, you remember, whatever you don't, you don't care, you move on. I say this, as when we are performing – and I have already stated this many times – we must have a clear mind and let go, play, relax and trust.

In closing on this exercise, if you happen to record yourself doing this exercise, when you watch it back you will see yourself responding. You will see your character responding. You will enjoy it. You will see that your character is making decisions. The decisions could simply be *Will there be? Or I'm confused? Or I'm thinking about what that looks like? Or Are you having a go at me?*

This is very empowering for the developing actor. Enjoy the process.

An aside: Remember, one catch cry of casting directors in regards to the topic of choice or choices is *"Please make a choice"* or *"She didn't make a choice."* With this exercise, you will be sure to have made a choice.

As an actor you should practise all of the following things:

- Surprises – see the section on surprises in Chapter 1
- Act through the eyes
- Learn to control your facial muscles
- Perform in the V
- Mime the props or use of props supplied
- Stillness
- Be aware of your speed of movement in the frame
- Adapt your performances in all the most important shots

Movement and stillness

Some actors can't stop moving when acting. Others are afraid to move. When to move? When to be still? When is it right to move? When is it wrong to move? When is it right to be still? When is it wrong to be still? There's no set answer.

It all depends on five things:

1. The material
2. The type of character
3. What your character wants or is doing
4. The camera frame
5. You – the actor

Some teachers say "less is more". But what if your less is boring or self-conscious? The answer is, if the scene seems applicable for you to be still, you must be doing internal stuff while being still. Can you do this?

Stillness doesn't mean doing nothing

Try not to be lazy or overwhelmed by the occasion. Do stuff internally, such as, going for what your character wants. But be generally still while doing this stuff.

Some quotes I have heard from people in the industry are:

- The way you hide your feelings shows the audience the way you are
- It's the internal work that you do that draws the camera in
- It's the internal work that you do that makes you watchable
- Everything is working inside but you won't let it out

I like these quotes.

When to move and when to be still

As said, it all depends on these five things: 1. The material. 2. The character. 3. The character's choice. 4. The frame. 5. You.

1. **The material**
   - The genre you are auditioning for – e.g. sitcom (situation comedy) is fast movement. Drama is often not, depending on what's going on. This influences how much you move
2. **The character**
   - What sort of character are you making? Does that character move a lot or not? This influences how much you do move
3. **What does your character want or what are they doing?**
   - Your character's subtext or opinion or attitude or point of concentration. This influences how much you move

4. **The frame**
   - The frame shot affects everything that you will do. Often, especially in drama, the camera wants to move in on you, if it is not an action shot
5. **You**

   Generally what influences how much you move and/or be still falls into these categories:
   - Who you are as a human being. How you act is always a very good starting place as some actors move too much naturally, others the opposite
   - Age. Older people generally move less and move more slowly than younger people
   - Maturity and trust of the actor. The younger actor often hasn't found the knowledge that they can act. They don't trust what they do is enough. So, they don't trust and they move spasmodically
   - Physiognomy. How much you naturally move your head and face. Your manner. Your disposition. Your natural behaviour

Let's look at some examples. For people with hard and soft copies of this book, simply type the key words below into Google or YouTube.

Let's look at some actors being still and some moving when in film.

Stillness

Start 20 seconds in. Casey Affleck. *Manchester by the Sea*.

https://www.youtube.com/watch?v=J30cS-dusjI

Tom Hanks and Paul Newman – *Road to Perdition*

https://www.youtube.com/watch?v=fGFLyA3u_rw

Anthony Hopkins and Jodie Foster. *Silence of the Lambs*. Stop at 5 min 50 seconds in.

https://www.youtube.com/watch?v=QU8jKn7sMwU

Movement

Allison Janney – *The West Wing*

https://www.youtube.com/watch?v=vNb38k9oLkI

Bigger movement - comedy

Whoopi Goldberg – *Ghost*

https://www.youtube.com/watch?v=JII3c3DWIbU

Megan Mullally – *Will & Grace*

https://www.youtube.com/watch?v=AGWsCwTaRs8

Movement and stillness - together in the one scene

Morgan Freeman and Ashley Judd – *Kiss the Girls*

https://www.youtube.com/watch?v=QpxdbtnTXXY

Paul Dano and Daniel Day-Lewis – *There Will Be Blood*

https://www.youtube.com/watch?v=1B-L4xLWaUQ

Movement and stillness

Let's look at movement by these actors: Gary Oldman (106 IMDB) as Churchill and Stephen Dillane (74 IMDB)

https://www.youtube.com/watch?v=xA1Uz_TMzhs

Al Pacino – *The Godfather* – 1 min to 2 min

https://www.youtube.com/watch?v=ppjyB2MpxBU

Godfather 1 – end scene Diane Keaton and Al Pacino

https://www.youtube.com/watch?v=1zBwKbq02ds

Godfather 2 – start 1 min in

https://www.youtube.com/watch?v=znL8uYvohCw

Peaky Binders – UK TV

https://www.youtube.com/watch?v=1B9O6dHRGlU&feature=youtu.be

Duel

https://www.youtube.com/watch?v=PunLPMBpxGc

The Day of the Locust

https://www.youtube.com/watch?v=cmtXA6x6Jm4

Flight – Denzel Washington

https://www.youtube.com/watch?v=bEpL6Mt_jrk

Scene exercise: Prepare a scene and decide when to move and when to be still.

The start of the scene

What do you do at the start of the scene to establish where you are and what you have just been doing? Americans call this moment *the moment before*, but, many, many actors do not adhere to it. They don't have a start. They just start a scene. Unfortunately, often just standing or sitting in the centre of the frame.

To help yourself establish the start of the scene think about the location. What is it, and what does it look like? And what are you doing just before the scene starts? To help you get there, you have three options:

1. Use the five senses – sight, sound, taste, touch, smell

2. Emotional recall – think: when were you last there?

3. Use your imagination and make it up. Try simply, seeing it

Exercises you can do

Here is a list of things that I encourage actors to do. Write a list of twenty locations that you generally audition for. Then practise each location with the three options listed above. Then put them on video. Send them to yourself via email and watch them back. Which one was the most powerful?

For example: location – scene – beach

1. Perform a short scene using the five senses for the beach. Record it and email it to yourself and watch it

2. Perform a short scene using emotional recall (of when you were at the beach). Record it, send it via email and watch it

3. Use your imagination and make it up. Simply imagine being at the beach. Record it, send via email to herself and watch it

Then decide which looks best – 1, 2 or 3?

Then save that short start on your computer, under a folder called LOCATION STARTS. Have a subfolder called BEACH – then put the video there of the one you chose.

Then continue on down your list of the other nineteen locations chosen and follow the same routine as just explained above.

Then, next time you get an audition for the beach, you can simply go to your computer, to the folder LOCATION STARTS, then the subfolder BEACH and copy the start, or use it as inspiration for your current start for the new audition scene.

Then prepare your scene with a reader, and focus on the following:

- Establishing the start (the location). As said, copying or adapting your recently prepared start

- Showing vulnerability
- Having some movement and some stillness

Stillness: To help you be still

Why do many actors look like nothing is going on when they act or they look boring when they are still? For many, this is because they have not made internal decisions for their character.

In this instance, as an audience we don't see the actor's character or behaviour, their character's manner and we don't see the internal drama or conflict that is going on. As a consequence, the actor is not captivating.

On the other end of the scale, some actors do massive amounts of research and scene study, and either: still look like nothing is going on, or, they look like they are pushing or overacting.

This is generally because they:

- Don't know themselves well enough as a performer and so they don't trust themselves. They don't think they and their work are good enough
- They are used to bad habits
- They haven't understood/and or are unable to implement what acting for the screen is
- They don't realize that what they are doing is enough
- They don't perform for the camera. They perform for themselves or the audience in the room or for a theatre or mini theatre

You must keep practising in front of the camera to be sure of all of these things.

In support of this, and here's a paradox for some actors, I want you to think as the character. Not the actor. Be moved and affected by what is going on around you as the character. This helps you form manner and behaviour and this helps bring the audience in. And it brings the camera in too. This is what the actor of our time on screen – Daniel Day-Lewis - does on set.

Warm-up exercise

Practise doing the following in front of the camera:

- loosening tension from the jaw and mouth
- work on the eye lines and in the V
- do a movement exercise while in the frame
- do a stillness exercise while in the frame

Acting through the eyes exercise

Focus and concentration: pick a point and just look at it.

Thoughts or subtext on face: learning to have your thoughts and meaning on the face, especially through the eyes. Think of situations, adjectives, to help yourself with this exercise: Sad. Happy. Jealous. Guilty, all as previously mentioned.

Add the tone of the voice to sad, happy, jealous, guilty, etcetera.

Learning Point Number Twelve:

- Watch the strong performances of great actors, particularly in regards to movement and stillness
- Develop your techniques that help you be watchable on camera
- Practise the skills listed in this book
- Remember, if you listen brilliantly, you will often respond accordingly
- To help you have variety, although contrived in a workshop setting, doing the exercises in this chapter will help teach you to have more variety of response on your face and in your eyes in the frame
- A variety of expressions should be your goal on screen

Chapter 13: On-camera work: Conclusion

I encourage you to think like this:

What do I have to adjust in all the most important shots, the mid-shot, the medium close-up and the close-up shots? Such as physically move my body and face less? Or adjust my eyelines? Adjust my movement? Also, what will I do with my body, my props and the use of the five senses?

Also, as I move to mid-shot and close-up shots, should I physically slow down the pacing of my body? Act more with the eyes?

While always remembering to know where my frame boundaries are and work within these camera shots. Noting also that I can practise acting through the eyes and the movement of my face in front of the mirror. I can practise all the camera skills introduced in this book.

What other actors will I watch in front of the camera, in film, TV and commercials? What news readers, documentaries or reality television will I watch?

I can do my emotional exercises, do my technique work, breathe properly, play subtext, practise on-camera skills introduced in this book. Work on my physiognomy. Noting what I do with my head, face and eyes. I can practise looking sideways when I think. I can try to put my thoughts into my eyes and out towards the camera.

Some overall pointers to remember

- The five most important shots
- The closer the camera goes, the slower you move

- You especially, move slow in the frame in the mid-shot and closer shots (please watch actors in film and TV for reference)
- The closer the camera goes, the less you do externally
- You decide what shot works best for you. If not directed with or by the audition information
- Try to keep the body and head still
- The more the camera moves in, the stiller the actor is
- Number one thing we watch is the eyes, followed by the mouth
- The more the camera moves in, the more we focus on the eyes
- Learn to act with the eyes and with the tone of the voice, especially in mid-shot or closer shots
- You must try to get your thoughts across through the eyes
- Where to look? Look sideways as opposed to up and down
- The camera sees everything. Tension – keep the jaw loose, slightly open the mouth
- Learn to perform in the V
- Always ask the casting director and/or the director on set the size of the frame
- Remember, if you don't listen *really well*, you won't work that much

I suggest you do exercises focusing on the following

- The V. Go through the different camera shots
- Listening and anticipation: have someone tell you a tall story, listen to them and maintain a look of anticipation
- Play surprises. Using the information in Chapter 1, and put them on scripts
- When to move with head, face and eyes in the frame. Move your eyes sideways when you mention a person, place or thing in the script
- Practise passing the baton
- Tell a story looking in the frame. Adhering to the V, using anticipation, practising surprises and passing the baton

- Practise wants, opinion, attitude and colours
- Peak in the scene. Make a decision on what is the peak in the scene, then note it in preparation
- Perform for the shot. If it doesn't say what shot to do your audition in, or the teacher doesn't, ask yourself what shot do you do your best work in? Practise the scene in the shot you feel the most comfortable with and the frame where you know the guidelines
- Natural movements. Try to be as natural as possible when performing. Remember less is more. Remember the closer the camera comes, the less you do. The more internal it is. The speed in which you move, has to be slower as the camera comes closer. Glide around that frame
- Character: you need to look natural as you move your body as the character, as you gesture
- Character voice. Remember the importance of the tone of your voice in particular. But also use pacing, pausing, pitch and volume for effect

Your on-camera acting goal in life

The most powerful shot on screen is: the unedited camera moving shot that moves in on the actor from a three-quarter shot, all the way up into a close-up or extreme close-up, and then back again. Only the very best actors in the world get this kind of shot. For example, Daniel Day-Lewis in *Lincoln* and *There Will Be Blood* and Jack Nicholson in *A Few Good Men*.

Scene study creation from words

As discussed in the scene study chapter earlier in the book, you can break a scene down into sections and give that scene a short heading. Then you can fill out the scene study charts that include the questions you ask yourself about character.

Many actors think, how do I now create the character for this script? There are many ways that I help actors create characters. Here is an example of one. To help you I suggest you could do the following:

- First write down some phrases that describe how you are feeling about the character. Such as: *speaks their mind, been through a lot, has no filter, says what they think, is very frustrated,* etcetera.
- Ask yourself, can I relate to this character? Can I relate to these phrases describing what I think the character is about?
- Then write down some adjective words to describe the character. Such as:
  - educated
  - smart
  - impatient
  - outspoken
  - motivated
  - complainer
  - swearer
  - loud
  - blunt
- Ask yourself, do I know anyone like this?

Then start with movement. Think, how can I personify these words? How can I non-verbally use my body to express these words? Then start moving in your space to personify these words.

Then do verbal exercises with the words. Think how can I verbally personify these words. Play around with the following: tone, pitch, pacing, pausing and volume.

Then start saying the dialogue and trying to remember the non-verbal ways you used your body.

Then say the dialogue and try to remember the ways in which you used your voice.

Then record yourself on your phone and/or a camera and watch yourself back. Be kind to yourself as you explore.

Upon revision, ask yourself, how does it look how I am personifying what I am doing?

Then think, what effect does the location have on what I am doing? For example, am I at a train station, on the beach, or in an office?

Then think, how can the season or day of the week and/or time or the weather affect what I am doing. Play around with that.

Then record yourself on your phone and/or a camera again and watch yourself back. Be more specific with your observations and analysis now.

Then ask yourself, *is what I am working on looking clichéd?* Is it too much like someone famous? Or a character I have done before? How can I make this different? How can I make this character quirky?

Then start trying to do that.

In the end, with this exercise, you are trying to create a character that had its origins in adjectives, from words, as you work with the adjectives. I use this simple methodology a lot with my students and they find it easy to follow. In the end, they usually end up with characters that are different.

Learning Point Number Thirteen:

- Simply thinking about on-camera skills to work on will make you a better actor
- Really work on the checklist of on-camera skills
- Practice will make you better
- Learn to develop characters
- Remember, the use of voice and acting through the eyes are the most important things
- Stay in the frame
- Use the frame to your advantage
- Note down the things that you are working on, on a piece of paper and carry the notes with you throughout your day

Above: Paul with Tarnue Massaquoi at a social event in 2019, on one of Paul's teaching tours of the USA. Tarnue had no IMDB credits when he started working with Paul in 2003. As of September, 2023 Tarnue has 59 IMDB credits and 1 award win as an actor.

Chapter 14: Role-playing exercises

What is role playing?

Often confused with characterization, role playing is in fact altogether different. It is different because with role playing you simply take on a role, not a fully realised, three-dimensional character, that has evolved from character development. The role of a police officer, or a judge, or a caretaker, or a homeless person, or an office person, etcetera. Hence, simply, for the most part, think of occupations.

Working on your role-playing skills will help you:

- Improve your improvisation skills
- Play occupations
- With commercial auditions
- Create characters

This will all be beneficial due to the playing of roles that you are most likely going to audition for.

Role-playing exercises work on status, attitude, emotion, use of body and voice and language and more, to help you illustrate the role. Role playing is a lot of fun and an essential part of an actor's toolkit.

I would like you to follow this train of thought: actors get sent a script (called "sides" in the States), they read it and immediately think of the occupation that is usually given to them in the descriptions. Such as:

- Jesse is a scientist who is ...
- Betty runs the local bakery and ...
- Matt is a computer nerd who ...

What the actor is immediately doing is thinking of the role. They consciously and/or subconsciously think, "How does a scientist or baker or computer nerd behave?" It is natural to think this way.

Role-playing exercise work profoundly prepares you for this moment, for the commercial audition and the quick turn-around or, for the on-the-spot audition, where you don't have time to work with the script prior to performing.

From my experience in the professional industry, dating back to 1979, role playing is hardly taught anywhere. In fact, most people, including actors, do not even know what role playing is.

By working on role playing, you are in a perfect place to then create a character. Here are some role-playing exercises that you can do.

Role-playing exercises

I work with actors on role playing by doing the exercises listed below. Some of these exercises came from my studies in drama at university, but I can't remember the source. I am sorry; if I could remember the source, I would acknowledge it.

I begin by getting the actor to look at themselves.

I ask the actors to write down their measurements: their height, weight, eye colour, chest, arms size, collar, bust, dress size, hat size. Then their cultural background. Actors also write down if they feel they are physically different in any way and how.

Then, actors look at each other closely to help each other determine some roles. One by one they leave the room and then come back in and talk about anything, and, as they are doing so, they are watched by their peers.

Their peers write down the type of roles that they think they could play and or the type of roles casting directors would call them in for, for an audition. Then feedback is given back to the actor one by one in a circle.

Then actors write down the roles they have played in their lives. Then the roles they usually choose in an improvisation when given a free licence to do so. For example, were they always dominant? Were they the leader? Or were they submissive and the follower?

Then, in class, actors play the **Dominant and Submissive** game. In pairs I give the actors a location and some roles. For example, a car yard, door-to-door salesman, shoe salesman, complaints department. One actor is dominant, the other is submissive.

Then I ask the actors to do another improvisation where they switch the dominant and submissive roles. During the improvisation, the dominant becomes submissive and the submissive becomes dominant.

Then I ask actors to brainstorm the roles that exist on television in the following categories: Lead actor. Recurring role. Guest star/day player. Small role, five-and-under or walk-on roles. Then the actors do the same in the area of film.

I then continue working on role paying by introducing actors to the following topics: **Occupations** and **Status** and the *use of body and voice for the role.*

I also introduce **Emotions.** I give each actor an emotion and ask them to bring it into the scene. Actors must act out the emotion given. Here are a few main ones.

Emotions:

- *Fear* → feeling of being afraid, frightened, scared
- *Anger* → feeling angry. A stronger word for anger is rage
- *Sadness* → feeling sad. Other words are *sorrow, grief* (a stronger feeling, for example when someone has died)
- *Joy* → feeling happy. Other words are *happiness, gladness*
- *Disgust* → feeling something is wrong or nasty. Strong disapproval
- *Surprise* → being unprepared for something
- *Trust* → a positive emotion; admiration is stronger; acceptance is weaker

- *Anticipation* → in the sense of looking forward positively to something which is going to happen. Expectation is more neutral

For those of you reading an e-book - definitions of these words are given above with Wikipedia links.

I then give the actors scenarios, such as:

- Stranded on a desert island
- Car breaks down on a country road
- They enter a pub and then realize it's not a normal pub
- Actors waiting to audition outside the audition room

Then I introduce **Status**. Both high and low status. I pair students up and give them roles. Such as:

- Policewoman – homeless person
- Nurse – Doctor
- Complaints department: worker & customer

Then I introduce **attitude** and a list of different attitudes and put the students:

- On public transport
- At an outdoor BBQ
- In an office

Then I introduce the **relationship**:

What are the general rules in the relationship? I do this in the form of a question-and-answer activity that actors have to adhere to. For example:

- Doctor and nurse – work close together, nurse assists doctor and gives information. The doctor is the expert
- Policeman/woman and suspect – policeman is trying to solve the crime, out to protect the public, criminal is doing things for himself
- Teacher and student – teacher to help, student wants to learn from the teacher, teacher is there for the student, can be a mentor

- Actor and director – actor is trying to perform for the director, director is trying to make the best product he can

Then I introduce **symbols**: what are the symbols/gestures of the role? It is also good to think about what symbols or gestures you could use when you improvise. A wood chopper lifting up an axe. A traffic cop with white gloves conducting traffic. A doctor with a stethoscope, etcetera.

Then I introduce, **occupations**: let's play with some different occupations.

Then I introduce, what is the **class** of the role? Upper, middle or working class? Consider this and take it into account if you think it helps.

Then I introduce the question, "What does your particular role **value**?" It is important to consider that.

After that, I ask, "What is their **point of view**?" It is good to always have and express a point of view. In fact, we can assign points of view to actors and they can play them out.

So to recap, I work on the following areas in role playing:

- Dominant and submissive
- Emotions
- Attitude
- Status
- Purpose
- Relationship
- Language
- Symbol/gestures (including body language)
- Occupations
- Social class of the role: upper, middle or working class?
- What does your particular role value?
- What is their point of view?

Here's some sample short scene scripts from class.

Police officer

"I'm Senior Constable Blake. If you choose to be selfish and drink and drive and put others at risk, you are only thinking of yourself. The police will be enforcing more strict policies to stop those of you who decide to put other lives in danger. There'll be no excuses – don't drink and drive."

Nurse

"As nurses, we have become tired. We ask that those of you not wearing masks, not social distancing and not following the lockdown rules, to please help us out and do the right thing. Save lives and help keep us all healthy!"

Some other occupations to play with include: post office worker, professional athlete (e.g. AFL player), house wife/husband, council worker/road worker, computer office worker, TV presenter.

Your type of role for performance

Actors then choose a role that people said they were suitable for. They write a short commercial scene, prepare and perform it.

In the process they answer the following questions:

- Are they dominant or submissive?
- What's their emotional state?
- What's their attitude?
- What's their purpose with the role?
- What's their status?
- What's the language they will use that is suitable for the role?
- What symbols or gestures will they use suitable for the role? (This includes body language.)
- What's their relationship with the person they are talking to?
- What's their social class?
- What do they value?
- What's their point of view?
- What does your role value?

Checking in to see you are improving

I sometimes introduce a game called The Role Circle. In the game, actors take it in turns entering the circle and carrying out an investigation or an inquiry about a topic they decide upon and talk to the group in role.

The group are all the same person and respond when looked at. They pick up the pace after it has been going for a while. Of course the objective is to see the actor in the role and the person surrounding the actor to have to guess what role they are, with them not saying what it is. It's easy really. This exercise works really well with seeing how the actors are improving their role-playing skills.

The same goal can be achieved with the *Who Am I* activity. Actors take it in turns. One person leaves the room and the others decide their role. The actor who left the room comes back in and improvises. The rest of the class who didn't leave the room start talking and gesturing to the person who did leave the room, in the role that the remainder of the class collectively chose, without openly saying the role. At the end of the improvisation, the actor who left the room has to try to guess the role.

Then I give the actor some harder roles to play, such as:

- Insurance company representative
- CEO
- Politician
- Activist for demonstrations in public
- Dry cleaners' employee

Here's another activity that stretches the actor: I give actors a card with an occupation written on it and ask them to work on the use of their body for the occupation.

Actors are then given another card with an attitude on it and asked to work on the use of their body for the attitude.

Actors attach the attitude to the occupation. Each actor performs one of the occupational roles with attitude one by one (without speaking), and the rest of the class try to pick the occupation and the attitude.

Learning Point Number Fourteen:

- Role playing is different from characterization
- If you try to copy an occupation, on the surface, you are role playing
- Role-playing exercises help you when you have to play an occupation. Such as, when you are in a commercial audition and where you don't have long to prepare
- Practise them to help you in those quick turn-around auditions and especially for television commercial performances
- Try to play as many roles as possible
- Know your type, your brand, and practise these roles to improve your role-playing skills
- You are indirectly making yourself a better actor by doing things such as working on role playing, cold reading, etcetera.

Chapter 15: Cold-reading exercises

What is cold reading?

Like the term "scene study", cold reading is a generally used term in the acting world.

Los Angeles is loaded with what they call *Cold Reading* and *Scene Study* classes. From my experiences as an actor and a teacher and from what actors have told me, there is not much difference between these classes; especially in Los Angeles.

In these classes, actors arrive and are given a scene partner and a script. They are then told to go away and work on the scene with their partner, come back together as a group. Then, in pairs, the actors perform the scenes.

Maybe they get direction, maybe something is said to them about their acting ability and/or how to improve it; maybe not. Often, not much or nothing of substance is said to them. The actor and their partner then sit back down and watch ten to twenty other pairs of actors get up out of their chairs and do the same thing, two by two.

Cold reading, the Australian way, my way, is very different. My cold-reading classes are teaching the student how to cold read scripts, how to make impact with that script. All to help the actor at a cold read when they are in front of a casting director or director or producer who is considering them for a part. Of course an actor's ability to cold read is also good in acting classes as well.

Have you ever been at an audition and had the casting director say to you, "You are not right for this role, we can see that now that you are in here, but, can you take a look at this script and we will consider you for this other part?"

This scenario is more common than you may think. When in this situation, there is nothing the actor can do. They cannot appeal or contest the decision made by the casting person. They simply have to do what is asked or refuse it and ask to leave.

In this scenario, many actors do not empower themselves. From personal experience, as well as coaching actors, actors want to please everyone, often to their own detriment, and so they nervously and hurriedly read the new script over, try to make sense of it, usually under pressure and right in front of the casting director, and then say "I'm ready" and cold read audition the script. Generally, they are not ready at all. Generally, they do not do a very good job either.

The casting director, in most cases, has said words to the effect of, "How long would you like to prepare before we put you down on tape?" The actor, wanting to please, usually says, "Can I have a few minutes", or "I'll just read it and then I'll be ready". This is because the actor wants to appease the casting director and they don't want to *rock the boat*, as we would say in Australia.

I train my actors to say, "How long can I have to prepare?" If the casting director replies, "You can take a long as you want." I say to my actors, if it is Monday morning. I train them to say, "Can I come back Friday afternoon?"

You may be surprised to know, actors, that a lot of casting driectors actually say, "OK" to this. By asking for as much time as possible, the actor is giving themselves the best and most time availabe to do their preparation work. Of course, if the casting director says, "No you can't take that long, we need to submit all the actors work to the producers soon", my actors are trained to say, "How long can I have then?" Of course, the casting director then tells them.

In the above scenario, the time may not be a long time. In addition, what if the casting director says, "No I would like to see you read it very shortly." Meaning now. When these scenarios happen, an actor's ability to cold read scripts comes into effect immediately.

In my cold-reading classes, I teach my actors how to cold read the scripts. This is done by actors continually practising exercises that they are taught. Naturally they are also given a handout on the cold reading tips.

This is what I suggest you do.

Practising cold reading

My lesson plan course objectives for cold reading for students is as follows:

- Develop the actor's skills to improve their ability to quickly take the words off the script
- To build connection, trust, fun and creativity with the group
- To profoundly encourage participation, analysis and growth as an actor
- If they have read the script over prior to commencing, to make a decision and make impact with their performance
- Cold read so they are all at the same point to move on into the work as a team
- To begin to learn how to make impact with the performance
- For students to verbally participate in class to aid their development
- Analyze their capabilities and develop ways to work faster and more efficiently
- Develop skills to improve their cold reading ability
- Be given advice and share techniques on how to analyze a script's meaning
- Test a few different decision-making methods; such as subtext, attitude or comprehension

I commence with warm-up exercises and one short, simple how to take a sentence off a script exercise and then build the students up onto working on more sentences and short and then longer scenes that they can use to help them when auditioning.

I usually go into teacher in role to begin. Meaning, I step into the exercise by cold reading with a student. The student is usually amazed that when they are looking at me, I am looking at them. Sometimes this puts them off as they think, "He is looking at me every time I talk to him and then replying with the next line from the script. How is he doing this?"

I am simply doing it by looking at the script, quickly, every time the other actor looks at the script. I also often grab a few lines, and keep them in my head and reply when they stop talking.

If, as an actor, you are really listening, it generally will make sense as to which line is next.

What I introduce and practise with students

- How to stand with open body language
- How to hold the script at a height that makes it easy for you to take your eyes from the script to the other reader's eyes
- Which hand to hold the script in. This is influenced by the positions of the actors and/or the position of the camera, if you are being recorded
- How to hold the script with two fingers. This makes it easier to turn the pages
- How to turn the script from page one to two and so on
- How it doesn't matter if the script makes a noise
- How you can remove the staple if you wish, and drop each page after you are finished with it; it doesn't matter if the page falls onto the floor
- How to grab the first line and have it in your head as you begin
- When you look at the script, how to try to grab a line or a sentence or two and have the lines in your head

- How you can quickly look at the script while they are talking, but it is better to look at the script when they do
- How to try to keep your eyes on them as much as possible – this insures you make a connection and helps you make impact with them and your character

I generally do the above exercises with stone cold scripts. Meaning, the actor has not even looked at the script at all.

If they have looked at the script, I ask them, in addition to the above:

- To make a quick decision about what the scene is about
- To quickly make a character choice, displayed mainly through the attitude and tone of the delivery of their lines
- To decide if, and then if so, what is the subtext, opinion or point of concentration?

What does cold reading mean to you now, actors reading this? I suggest you practise trying the above points. Turn them into exercises that you can do. By doing so, you will be better prepared when given a script to quickly look over in the future.

In addition, you will impress the casting director or director or producer by your cold-reading skills, as every time they look back up at you, you will hopefully be looking directly into their eyes.

Also, if held right, your head and eyes will be up most of the time too.

Learning Point Number Fifteen:

- Cold reading is different in Australia to America
- Having cold-reading skills helps make you look very professional
- It is a skill to know how to hold a script in your hand and connect with the other reader
- Cold reading is learning how to take the words off a script easily and stay connected with the other reader
- Empower yourself if you are asked to cold read at an audition
- The points given here can be turned into exercises by you and this will improve your cold-reading skills
- These skills will help you in auditions and in acting classes if you are given only a short amount of time to look at the scene. As sometimes, no time is given
- Casting directors and directors alike love seeing cold-reading skills personified by actors

Chapter 16: Improve your charisma and attraction

Charisma and attraction on screen, to me, means developing your sassiness, your sexiness, your sex appeal for the screen.

Many actors do it. People generally don't often talk about it today, because for many people, we are always trying to be politically correct, not come across as sexist or rude.

Social media profoundly influences most of us too. All this is great, but actors should still work on their charisma and attraction and use them to their advantage.

When I teach this subject, I ask actors to do the following:

- I ask the students to extend their views or have an open mind and not be offended by what is said within the group and to talk openly about charisma, savvy, sexy and sex appeal
- Have a general and personal discussion about what savvy, sexy and charismatic mean
- Take both a general and personal look at what is savvy, sexy and charismatic on screen and in person
- Take a general and personal look at what is savvy, sexy and charismatic about them
- Introduce creating savvy, sexy and charismatic characters
- Teach them to discover their charisma and sassiness
- Develop their charisma and sassiness for the screen
- Clear bad habits on screen, that make them look unsexy or uncharismatic with them
- Develop a list of charismatic skills to work on in front of the camera

- Put their savvy, sexy and charismatic characters in an audition setting
- Invite into class a special guest actor who has charisma, sassiness and savviness on screen
- Explore, take risks and work more on their skills

Improve your charisma and attraction exercises

With this topic, in class I often start with research and for that I show actress Jennifer Tilly performing her character in the film Liar Liar. Tilly struts around with pouted lips, cleavage showing and wearing a tight skirt. She overdoes it, but it is a good starting point as everyone usually agrees that she looks sexy and sassy.

We then look at the following actors on screen: Marilyn Monroe, Krysten Ritter, Ashley Judd, Michele Pfeiffer, Brad Pitt, Sean Connery, Josh Hartnett, Ewan McGregor.

Then I read a definition, usually taken from Wikipedia. Sometimes it is taken from a dictionary.

- Sassy /ˈsasi/ adjective – lively, bold, and full of spirit; cheeky. "Toni was smart and sassy and liked to pretend she was a hard nut"
- Sexy /ˈsɛksi/ adjective – sexually attractive or exciting. "Sexy French underwear" very exciting or appealing. "Business magazines might not seem like the sexiest career choice"
- Style – a particular procedure by which something is done; a manner or way. "Different styles of management"
- Charisma /kəˈrɪzmə/ noun – Compelling attractiveness or charm that can inspire devotion in others. "He has tremendous charisma and stage presence"
- *Je ne sais quoi* – literally means "I don't know what" in French. The phrase was borrowed into English as an expression of a quality that makes something or someone attractive, distinctive, or special in some way, but is hard to put into words

Actors do a warm-up exercise by moving to music that sounds seductive or sexy; such as songs from Barry White or from the band Hot Chocolate, or I play the song, I'm too sexy for my car.

Actors can also move around the space personifying the following words: Confidence. Excitement. They smile. They walk with clarity of purpose. The sexy walk. They like themselves. I say, "Be aware of your body language, flirt, feel confident, feel free, feel like you have just won the lottery, etcetera."

I then move the actors into an exercise called:

The positive feedback improvisation

I like to play a game called The Maître D game. Each actor takes it in turn being the Maître D and having the rest of the group heap praise, verbal and non-verbal praise, on them.

Actors love it when I arrange this improvisation game because I ask them to exaggerate, to the highest order, the giving out of compliments to one another.

One actor at a time. Actor moves around the space. Teacher talks about embracing and accepting the personal qualities said to them by others. I say, "If you wanted to use these types of words and think this way, that is great. Casting directors or production houses reject you, but don't reject yourself." So actors absorb all the compliments said to them as they walk around the space. They love it!

Actors then list the qualities that they think each other actor in the class has that are sexy. They then list attributes that they think they could work on while being sexy. Actors do this privately at first, then share their thoughts with the group. Actors are encouraged to take on board and work with, the suggested qualities to work on, usually with a seductive or suggestive scene.

Actors start with a script of a television commercial monologue. Like *Sundance spa*. Actors sitting in a spa and looking and feeling relaxed and sexy. Their peers, not the teacher as much, highlight their qualities and their changes.

I usually add a few directorial words to help them to be sexy in their second take or second performances. I also usually put them somewhere where they can be sexy, like in a bar, a spa, etcetera. It sounds a bit smutty, but it isn't.

As a group we also discuss masculine and feminine. We also discuss charm, as shown often by George Clooney, the James Bond character actors and even historical actors like Cary Grant and Clark Gable.

I ask the actors to all walk around the room and to be as masculine/feminine as possible. I guide them with direction on their physicalness. For example, men are grounded and strong, women are feminine and light. Women turning their head and playing with their hair, men strong and firm in stance and then adding some things that men can do, like working out in the gym, drinking at a game, building or changing a tyre; and women preening themselves, like sunbathing on the beach, shopping. All clearly clichéd, some could say sexist stuff, I admit. But actors generally love it. Gay actors generally embrace it too, which is great.

We also discuss energy and aura. I talk about metaphysics, what you put out, you receive, what you are is what you see, the interchange of matter and energy, a consciousness, an energy that attracts people.

I then do a group improvisation where each actor enters the story and adds to it. The story is the most important thing, where not all actors are in space all at once. I ask them to make a strong choice, to listen, invent, don't block what is said to them. To just go with it. Actors use compliments from the above improvisations as they try to personify charm, sex appeal, sassiness, etcetera. Then actors share their thoughts with the group.

For homework, actors write a short monologue on being sexy or sassy or charismatic or imagining they have je ne sais quoi. Half a page to a page long and then they bring that script into class.

Actors then work on a seductive script. This could be a James Bond 007 script. I assist where necessary, offering advice and guidance.

Actors work in pairs to work on the aspects of each other's sex appeal. The class has a general discussion on sex appeal and flirting, then I assist where necessary. Offering advice and guidance.

Actors are often asking themselves and writing down what they did learn from doing the exercises. They take into account what other people say what they liked.

I also ask actors to give me their definition of sexy or savvy or charismatic. Actors list the different elements of sex appeal. For example, the body. A good body and also how to use/show your body to your best advantage. The mind. The eyes – flirting, language that you use and confidence displayed. Appearance – clothing, uniforms, jewellery, make-up, lipstick, cleavage, nationalities. Voice, accents, energy, metaphysical, aura, sex appeal, confidence, open body language, etcetera.

Actors work in pairs on a script they have written. They work on the aspects of each other's sex appeal. We continue to have general discussion on sex appeal and flirting, then the teacher assists where necessary. Offering advice and guidance.

To assist the improvisations or the performances with text, where necessary, I add things like:

- Believe you are sexy
- Animal energy and magnetism
- Trendy. You're hip
- Aloof
- Sensitive. A SNAG – a sensitive new age guy
- Walk around the space like you have a ticket to the Academy Awards in your pocket

- Walk around the space like you have a winning Lotto ticket in your pocket
- Then add thoughts of, let's say, all night love-making with your dream partner
- How you're reflected in other people's eyes
- How do you feel? Let that affect your posture, etcetera?

We also do a flirting exercise called The Flirting Game. A sexy pick-up improvisation game. Actors flirt and pick each other up in the improvisations, using all the above elements. Often set in a bar.

All culminating with me getting the actors to perform the given scene on camera. In pairs working on their skills.

We then review each actor's charisma and sexiness/sex appeal work in class. These classes are great fun and actors always enjoy working on these skills.

In closing, for more homework on this topic, I'll ask the actors to watch some more actors, such as:

Carey Grant https://www.youtube.com/watch?v=AhLR1SXjDmY
Chris Hemsworth https://www.youtube.com/watch?v=JOddp-nlNvQ
Audrey Hepburn https://www.youtube.com/watch?v=zahSEExjjFs
Ingrid Bergman https://www.youtube.com/watch?v=Do2olZ49M54

Learning Point Number Sixteen:

- Many actors have had successful careers by playing being sexy or sassy and/or using their charisma
- Done well, it can help you get work in drama as well as in comedy
- I've given you some exercises to help you improve your charisma and attraction skills
- The exercises are a lot of fun to do

Chapter 17: Case scenarios

As in my first book, I've included in this book some case scenarios because I believe that it will help actors with their training, as they might relate to the topics discussed.

Case scenario 1: The dancer

I have trained many dancers. I have tried many ways to try to take dance behaviour out of the actors' work as, most of the time, it is not relevant and is more of a distraction.

I try to do this because we want to see a character. We need to believe a character. If something distracts us, we step out of the scene. We step out of the production. Once this happens, we usually can't get back in.

Often the dancer cannot act without incorporating dance moves into their performance. Sometimes this is an obvious turn or hand gesture. Sometimes a pirouette. Sometimes they go up on one toe like a ballet dancer, as they are acting. Sometimes, simply, we see a perfectly constructed body posture pose that just looks contrived or fake.

In addition, I have also seen the following:
- The lifting of one foot up and pointing it into the floor as they act
- The swivel of the body as they turn
- The leg slowly stretching outwards
- Even, the deliberate cracking of a joint such as the neck or back or some other joint

All this while the actor is acting and performing a character in a scene for a commercial, film or television.

I've seen all this as the dancer is in training and wanting to work as an actor. Yet, for a lot of them, they cannot seem to let go of their slightly exaggerated, erect posture, their ways of turning, like they are about to plié and then jeté across the floor, to kiss the guy in a scene. In short, they can't stop their dance moves.

For this type of actor, in most cases, I work with them on trying to eliminate or profoundly reduce their use of body as best as I can. I do try to use things they naturally do, if at all possible. I try to get the actor to incorporate their use of body all in line with the character and the genre/style of the production that they are in.

But, it is often not easy. It is one of my greatest challenges I experience as a performing arts teacher, along with trying to get actors to eliminate bad habits.

I receive the best results by doing character creation and scene study work. I take the actor away from what they naturally kept doing.

In this, let's call it, area of the unknown, I encourage them to create characters who show differences in posture and body. If necessary, I draw their attention to their habits and say, "Let's try and not see that way of turning when you move over there." Or, "Try to use your body in a different way so we don't see that dance action."

English actress Gemma Whelan is an example of an actress who is also a professional dancer, who uses her body so well on screen and does not come across as a dancer.

For example, in an episode of the television series Killing Eve, Gemma Whelan's character, Geraldine, drops to the ground when she is upset by what her mother, character Carolyn, has just said to her in the family home. It is very powerful. It looks beautiful and artistic, but not contrived. Sorry I couldn't find vision of this on YouTube.

Case scenario 2: Character whereabouts for the start of the scene

Let's look at a case scenario for character whereabouts for the start of the scene. Making decisions based on the information below will also help you create the character. I have included this information as a case scenario because so many actors do not do what I am about to discuss.

Below is an excerpt from an audition script from 2021. From Hollywood. One of my students auditioned for this part.

Information given by the casting director: Character: Senior Forensic Officer.

What is a Senior Forensic Officer? Let's do some research. Wikipedia says this:

"A police forensics career requires a bachelor's degree in forensic science. Some may opt to specialize, and with a postgraduate degree they can become a DNA or toxicology analyst. Those who specialize can expect to be required to be certified, and to complete continuing education requirements.

"Scene of crime officers identifies and collect forensic, photographic and fingerprint evidence from crime scenes. Scene of crime officers (SOCOs – also known as crime scene investigators or CSIs) work alongside police officers to help solve crimes … dusting for fingerprints and searching for footprints."

For your audition, are you going to be the generic cliché forensic officer or a different type? What sort of character will you create? How are you going to create this character?

The excerpt from the 2021 audition script says: *"Mist hangs over the farm. Reveal teams of police and forensics, backed by the mountains. They string lines across the terrain. A helicopter flies overhead. Rain falls."*

Can you see the mist hanging over the farm? Can you picture it? You need to. Use the five senses to help you see it. Think, what does it look like? Smell like? Taste like? Feel like? Touch like? If you can't see it, do more improvisation. Work on your imagination as you need to see it.

All that really matters is when we watch your performance, it looks like you are there seeing these things. That's the art of acting. All that really matters in the end is that it looks like you are experiencing these things.

Few actors can do this without actually creating it with their imagination. Hence, I like to use the five senses.

They're six senses really, aren't there? The sixth sense is commonly known, but not often spoken of, as your feeling, the energy, the mood of the situation.

Sight, sound, taste, touch, smell, feeling. I want you to use these to help set the setting. Go through them one by one. I want you to make a decision on all six senses and how you will respond to them. I suggest you use two senses at the start of the scene and then deliver your first line. One is always sight. Then choose another. Then improvise using your imaginations in the space.

With the use of your imagination:

- Look at the farm from a distance. Remember it is raining
- See the police officers and forensics people walking about
- Acknowledge some of them. Who do you like? Dislike?
- Acknowledge in some way the helicopter flying over

Then perform the scene bit by bit. Then put all this in the start of the scene and then, in your own time, say the first line, which in this scene begins with "We will be ..."

Then try to perform it. In different ways. Just simply, try to do everything differently. This is made so much easier if you do not start the scene the same way.

There you go, you are on the way to creating a character performance where the character has come from somewhere else. (Like we all do in life. We are always coming from somewhere else.)

I went through this scene with one of my actors in one of my Audition Preparation & Training classes, and the actor got a call back for the paid job. That validated our smart thinking, our choices and our work.

Learning Point Number Seventeen:

- If you are a dancer/actor, be prepared to let go of some of your manner
- The character whereabouts case scenario is an example of how you can step out from the clichéd norm, and or, of *doing nothing*, and use your imagination and the five senses to help you create a sense of the location, as given for each scene. As all scenes on all film and television scripts have the location written on the top of each scene before the dialogue or action starts with each scene
- Smart actors who make interesting choices book work and get call backs

Above and below: Paul with some of his favourite USA students: Chris Ivan Cevic and Cyanne McClairian, shown above. Both are award winners. And with Robin Leabman and Sara Davenport and Cyanne below. Paul taught these actors over many years in Hollywood, LA.

Above: pics from Paul's 2018 USA teaching tour. Celebrity actress Jeannetta Arnette (95 IMDB credits as of September, 2023) is front left of camera, (in a blur) in the first pic and far back in the group shot. Paul has trained Jeannetta on and off since 2009.

Chapter 18: Self-evaluation form

I recommend that you learn to analyze your work.

This self-evaluation form is a precarious document. Precarious in the sense that some actors lose confidence in their own skills because they see their own replies either: lack an answer or clarity, or are not of a high standard when they answer the questions below. I believe, though, it is an important document.

This document is a self-reflection for actors on where they are at. This is a sample document of mine with actual student comments written on it in italics.

NAME: AGE:

1. **How well do you think you act in front of the camera?**

    Student example answer taken from class:

    I think I act a decent amount in front of the camera. I know at times that I have a habit of shifting my eyes too quickly out of frame, that's also because until recently I wasn't 100% sure of the frame on camera I was working with. I'm definitely working with the frame now but still need to get the hang of it.

2. **In regards to acting in the frame, what do you feel you know you are good at?**

    Student example answer taken from class:

    I think I'm good at being relaxed in front of the camera rather than looking stiff in the frame.

3. **In regards to acting in the frame, what do you think that you are not good at?**

   Student example answer taken from class:

   I think I still need to work on where I place my eyeline within the frame, not outside of it. Sometimes I focus so much on acting within the frame that I forget to really listen to the reader and maintain being in the moment rather than my body already knowing what is coming next.

4. **Do you feel that you are creative and imaginative with your acting? If yes, please describe how you are? If not, why not? Please describe why?**

   Student example answer taken from class:

   I do feel that I am creative and imaginative in my acting. I come from a theatre background, specifically physical theatre, so I think naturally I can be in my body with my acting, however I do sometimes worry that I act more towards theatre than for the camera as I am used to theatre.

5. **What are your biggest concerns when acting in front of a camera?**

   Student example answer taken from class:

   That I am acting for theatre when I'm on camera rather than acting for the camera/frame. Also coming across flat through the frame.

6. **Do you know how to make an impact in front of the camera? If so, how?**

   Student example answer taken from class:

   In some ways yes by making sure you're grounded within your body and listening to your reader in order to play moment to moment with everything that's thrown your way. I could also learn more on how to make an impact in front of the camera.

7. **Do you know how to cold read? If so, list some things you know you do well?**

   Student example answer taken from class:

   I don't know what cold reading means.

8. **In regards to script analysis, what do you feel you know you are good at?**

   Student example answer taken from class:

   Guessing what is going on in the scene.

9. **What are your biggest concerns when it comes to script analysis?**

   Student example answer taken from class:

   I worry if I am doing it right. Everyone else seems so creative. I feel I am making the obvious boring choice and I wonder if the casting directors will like my choices.

10. **What would you like to work on in these classes with me?**

    Student example answer taken from class:

    Being comfortable self-testing and working within the frame. I definitely also want to work on making sure I am not flat within a scene on camera, both vocally and with my expressions.

Learning Point Number Eighteen:

- Be diligent in your self-assessment
- Be as professional as you can be
- Learn, learn, learn and improve
- Other actor replies to the above self-evaluation questions personify that many, many actors have the same concerns about their own ability

Chapter 19:
A checklist of your professionalism

This chapter is all about you taking a professional approach to your acting career. It is about how you can take action and try to get as much control of your career as you can.

Consider taking action on these topics

- How professional are you? Do you see your career as a business? Do you set yourself goals?
- How effective is your current headshot?
- How does your CV look?
- Should you create your own showreel?
- Should you create your own website?
- How to help yourself get work or more work, including creating your own work
- Finding representation with agents and managers
- Doing a performance for an agent/manager
- How to help yourself get seen by casting directors
- Targeting producers/directors
- How to help yourself get into the USA pilot season
- USA - Union and non-union work
- USA – when to join the SAG (Screen Actors Guild) or AFTRA (American Federation of Television & Radio Artists Union)
- When to join IMDB Pro
- Things you can do when your agent is not getting bites when they submit you to casting directors for paid work
- Taking advantage of the digital world to help you find work

I will talk about some of these topics.

Character description

Please write ten or so words that people use to describe your commitment to your acting work.

For example, as a teacher in the workplace, here are some words that people use to describe me:

Passionate – Committed – Smart – Organized – Brilliant – A thinker – Creative – Diligent – Talented – Perceptive – Articulate – Experienced – Professional – Honest – Caring – Supportive

Performance skills

What performance skills do you have? List them?

Business

Remembering it is *show business*. Show is the acting. Business is you as a business. As an actor, you are a brand for sale. What are you selling? Look at your resume, headshot and showreel, and get to know your type. If necessary, create your own showreel.

What business plan do you have? List the things that you want to work on?

Business plan: Create a plan for the phases of your Career:

- One-month plan
- Three-month plan
- One-year plan
- Two-year plan
- Five-year plan

Please write three to five achievable things for each section.

For example:

One-month plan:
a. Re-do my resume

b. Research potential agents/managers

c. Experiment with camera

d. Research monologues for my type

e. Write to three agents/managers

Three-month plan:
a. Learn two monologues for my type

b. Research top casting agents in the city I live in

c. Get background

d. Go to at least one networking event

Six-month plan:
a. Write to ten agents

b. Write to ten managers

c. Have had one meeting with manager

d. Have had one meeting with agent

e. Have at least one new IMDB credit

One-year plan:
a. Have website up

b. Have reel

c. Potential new headshots

d. Have played at least three roles that give me IMDB credits

e. Have an agent

Two-year plan:
a. Create my own work

b. Review all my marketing

c. Review my representation

d. Write targeted letters to people I want to work with

Five-year plan:
a. Be a working actor

b. Have 20 IMDB credits

c. Have an agent who I really connect with

d. Have a role that really connects with my soul

e. Have worked in both TV and film

Attitude and self-sabotage and procrastination

Are you ready for this career? Based on my teaching of actors dating back to 1990, many actors are not. Questions to ask yourself: do you self-sabotage? Procrastinate? Is there some laziness going on? If so, you must work on trying to eliminate these things.

Communication

How well do you communicate with people? Your teacher? Your family? Your agent? Casting directors?

Re the teacher: are you late for class? Are you late back after the break, or you don't always turn up? You don't reply to the teacher's email or social media message? If so, what message are you sending to your teacher? Do you think teachers don't remember these things? These are examples of your professionalism.

Here is another example:

The two Australian casting directors who have cast television show *Neighbours* over the past twenty-five years in Australia, have said to me in the past. I will paraphrase here.

- Jan Russ – casting director – if you are late or give negative comments or attitude to anyone, you often get crossed off the *To Be Considered* for the part list
- Thea McLeod – casting director – we check actors' social media. Making sure their posts are politically correct

Agent/manager and location

What city should you live in? Melbourne or Sydney? Los Angeles or New York? Or Atlanta? Or San Francisco? Or Tokyo or Osaka? Or London or Brighton? I suggest you live in the city that produces the most film and television work. Google this to find this out if necessary.

Do you know how to write a letter to an agent? As it is not about you just introducing yourself. It is also about what you can give them. Do for them. Practise writing a letter. Hit your topics in this order: your brand – work done – auditions had or having – training had or having. Then your details of height, weight, contact details, special skills including cities that you are a local hire in. For example, Melbourne and Sydney in Australia? Perhaps both Los Angeles and New York in the USA? Local hire in any city listed means that the people who employ you don't have to pay to put you up in a hotel – you have your own accommodation.

Write something creative and smart as you introduce yourself to an agent or manager. For example, you can research the agent/manager and then comment positively about projects that they have worked on as a producer. (Noting many agents and managers work as a producer too.)

When is the right time to go for representation? To go for an agent or manager?

In summary, here are your options:

- Wait – train to get better and obtain some credits

- Prepare a submission

In regards to whether you feel prepared to do a submission and approach an agent:

- Do you feel ready? You are an actor with some training. Do you have some success?
- You feel your ducks are in a row, meaning you have everything ready?
- You feel you have a performance video or some scenes to show them?
- You feel your future work will give the agent money?
(Their percentage of your booked work.)

Many actors ask me, is it possible to get an agent with very little acting experience? Yes, it is. Because for a small percentage, it is possible. If an agent takes you on in this circumstance, generally speaking, it is because the *actor's look and/or ethnicity* is of a particular look that the agent doesn't already have.

If any particular agent does already have your look (you've checked their website and seen the actors' headshots), then it may be harder to get representation. Then, the best way to secure an agent is to have a very good showreel where you can demonstrate that your acting skills are high.

Doing student films or up-and-coming filmmakers' films will help you get going in the industry and give you footage of your acting.

Many actors try to get representation when they are not ready. They are not good enough yet. I have experienced this, more than ever, in the past ten years. I believe this is because we are now living in a time where we all want it and we all want it now. We can't wait.

Unfortunately for some, many actors lose the only chance they had with that agent or manager by approaching them too soon. Make sure you are ready and are very good at acting and have headshot, resume, reel and your pitch ready before you approach agents.

When preparing a submission, many actors are ego driven and don't see the bigger picture. If you always remember that acting is not about you, that is a good start. If you come from a performance and business philosophy that your job is to serve the story as you create a character and interact with others to tell the story. You are a story teller. A small part of the bigger picture. Then you have a good starting point that will influence your approach, including in writing, when you contact an agent. Think, what can I give them? What characters can I personify? How can I help them market me? How can I form a team between us?

Approaching agents

How do you approach an agent? In Australia you can download a list of agents from the MEAA (the Media Entertainment Arts Alliance) website for free. In America you can buy list booklets that contain the names and addresses of the people printed on labels that you can stick onto envelopes. I'm sure there are some other ways to obtain lists like this, so please Google it.

Many actors don't know where to start and/or what to do to try to get an agent. I guide my students.

If they have booked a job of worthiness, I usually pick up the phone and encourage an agent to take the actor on.

If not, I talk to the actors about different strategies.

One strategy goes like this.

With any agent's office, remember the receptionist's main role. They are a conduit for calls and people who walk into their office; usually with an appointment. Noting some offices have locked doors keeping the general public out. In the entertainment industry, generally speaking, one of the receptionist's jobs is to get rid of unrepresented actors who walk in the door.

I have a technique that I have used for a long time and I encourage my students to try it. It goes like this. You are about to approach an agent's or manager's office, after doing research on all things relating to that agency and on the main people who work there, I suggest you try getting the agent's assistant's name. You do this by calling the office and asking for the agent's or manager's assistant's name, then saying "Thank you" and hanging up. Often the receptionist will give you the agent's assistant first name only. That is good enough. Sometimes you get both names.

An aside: If the receptionist asks you, "Why do you want to know?" Consider saying, "I have a package to deliver." Yes, I know this is a white lie. But it is not that harmful of a white lie, is it?

Next you must know what you want to talk about. Plan it. In preparation, even write your speech and proposed interaction and then go into the office and ask to speak to your target *agent*. Then when the receptionist says to you, "No, they're busy, unless you have an appointment." You then ask to see the assistant, using the assistant's name.

This can often get you seen by the assistant to the person that you want to see at the company. Then, be ready to sell yourself. Listing what you can offer them and that you want to create a team. You have done research. You know they are *blah blah blah's* assistant and you are there to create a business team.

Have your headshot and resume and, preferably, your showreel in your bag, but only leave it with them as a last option. Clearly state your goal and say to the assistant that you want to get in front of the agent (or manager).

Many actors that I know have gotten in front of the person they want to see by doing this approach. Best of luck.

Here are a couple of closing thoughts on trying to seek representation:
- It is much easier to reject someone who applies to an agent or manager in writing in an email. Remember that

- Remember, you can make much more of an impression face to face. Better that than the generic email reply rejection, right?
- You must be one hundred per cent polite and courteous in all your dealings with prospective representation
- Many people have talked themselves into getting anything they wanted in life by being bold. Remember that too

The worst thing that can happen to you is they say "No". Or they say, "Get out of the office or we'll call security." If they do that, you simply leave. They said no, so what? You move onto the next person on your list to contact.

When is the right time to meet casting directors?

Most actors rush into everything. We're in the world of *I want it and I want it now*. But, are you ready now? Many actors are not.

Whatever work you put in front of a casting director, in person or online, you better be good. Casting directors are smart, perceptive people-watchers and very good with the use of psychology. They are also used to seeing very good work by actors.

Whatever acting work you put in front of casting directors, when given the chance, they will re-direct you in a different way. That's their job. To see that you can take direction. You have to be ready for this.

Many actors cannot take the direction given to them by the casting director. Instead, they simply do the same thing again or a slightly modified version of what they just did. Casting directors politely say "Thanks for coming in" and let you leave. And, in these circumstances, you most often, did not make an impression.

A good thing to remember is this. Whatever they ask you to do, or change, you really do it. You really go for it. You change. You risk take. You try to give them what they want.

This is because, generally speaking, casting directors know that it is easier to pull someone's performance back a bit as opposed to keep pushing them up to give them more.

The online world and social media

In the digital world, actors can help themselves and their career by applying for jobs. They can also market themselves through these platforms.

I've listed the main ones below. You can market yourself on:

- Facebook
- Instagram
- LinkedIn
- Showcast
- Star Now
- Casting Networks
- Actors Access
- Breakdown Services
- Backstage
- Craigslist
- NY Casting
- Mandy.com
- TikTok
- Your website

Do you know how to operate in social media platforms and how best to market yourself?

Many successful actors have two Facebook and two Instagram accounts. One for family and friends and one for work. With Facebook, they often create a *following* page where you can follow them.

I encourage all my actors to create two accounts on Facebook and Instagram. Even if they are just starting out as an actor.

Casting directors are known and quoted for saying, "We will check your social media before we cast you." I know of many people who have lost all sorts of jobs, not just acting jobs, because of things they posted in social media.

Having a website and being in the appropriate acting business websites is the way to go. *Actors Access* in the USA and *Showcast* in Australia, you should be on these.

You should also be on IMDB Pro too when you start to book work and want your headshot by your name on your page.

Many people, not just actors, are making money by their posts and product placements in online platforms such as TikTok and Instagram. So much so that there are now agents representing actors mainly in these platforms.

The choice is yours if you wish to go down this avenue.

Be aware though, I know of actors' agents who have asked their clients to stop doing commercials for products on TikTok and Instagram or they will stop representing them. In scenarios like this, the actor has to decide which way do I want to go and which agent do I want? The social media agent or the acting agent? Some actors have both, some do not or cannot.

Always be professional in all your online postings, including the images you post.

Learning Point Number Nineteen:

- Be diligent in your self-assessments
- Be as professional as you can be. Create a Business Plan and set yourself goals
- Every day's a school day - learn, learn, learn – improve
- When ready, market yourself as best you can
- Create your own work
- Be bold. When ready, take the big steps to help ignite your career
- Form a team
- I encourage all my students to empower themselves. This helps eliminate the thoughts of "woe is me", self-pity, resentment or jealousy

Chapter 20: Review of your audition

Remember your goal in an audition is to be interesting, different and impactful. You make enough impact where the casting people want to see more of you.

You don't need to be perfect or accurate. Go down the creative route, not the accurate route. Be an individual. Get rid of the control and perfect elements of performance, and embrace the freedom in the audition. Start with the character, don't start with the rules. Look at the rules last. This allows you to be creative in your preparation and in between the takes.

Mental health topics and issues are much more talked about in today's world with actors. I would like to talk a little about some common concerns and mental health issues that I have experienced and worked with, with some of my students.

How to deal with performance anxiety and other issues

Strategies for dealing with performance anxiety, self-doubt or low self-esteem

- Breathe into the body. Focus on breath. Maybe close your eyes to help you focus on your breathing
- Drink a glass of water
- Write down what you think the trigger is
- Start the positive affirmations I have given you below
- Do the self-hypnosis practice that I taught you in Book One

- Write the problem or issue down on a piece of paper with your dominant hand. Move the pen to the non-dominant hand and answer. Keep going. Other parts of your brain will open up and give you some answers
- Have two chairs – move between the chairs asking yourself the questions in one chair and giving yourself the answers by sitting in the other chair
- Talk to a doctor or psychologist about your concerns and strategies

Strategies for dealing with Post-Traumatic Stress Disorder

If you have been officially diagnosed with PTSD, make sure you take any medications you have been prescribed. Because very often there are medications involved in the treatment of PTSD.

- Do all of the above strategies if you wish and if you feel they will help you
- Talk to a doctor or psychologist about your concerns and strategies

Affirmations

Give positive comments to yourself, for example: my acting teacher of thirty-three years, as of 2023, a qualified teacher, says that I have talent. Or, more importantly, the following:

- I'm good enough and I can do well
- Whatever I do is okay
- I'll prepare, or I prepared, the best I can/could in the timeframe permitted
- I'll come from love and not fear

You can say your affirmations many times a day. You can print them off and place them prominently around the house. Such as, in the bathroom or kitchen or even in your car, in your purse, wallet or handbag. Then when you open the kitchen cupboard to take out cereal (or on the wall in the shower, etcetera), you see the document. All to remind you of your positive affirmations.

Audition preparation and training – a checklist

Things have changed: personal computers, phones, internet, Google, YouTube, social media, etcetera. We live in a world of I want it and I want it now! We can't wait. My mentor, Reg Evans, used to say, "Wait, wait until you are really, you are really good and ready to wow them in the audition room."

I see many, many actors audition when they are not ready.

As a professional actor you need to know what this language below means:

- What does – take the space mean?
- What does - are you ready to step up to the plate mean?
- What is a risk? And how do you take risks?

You need guidance and training if you think or mention to someone, either in class or privately, any of the following:

- I can't learn the lines
- I can't stay focused
- I don't have a technique to follow
- I don't know the importance of breathing and how to use my voice
- I don't know how to create characters
- I don't know how to cry on cue or be vulnerable with my work
- I don't know how to perform on camera
- I have performance anxiety
- I can't concentrate
- I can't trust
- I don't know how to make impact
- I don't know how to do the audition different
- I can't take direction
- I get flustered
- I'm scared
- I'm afraid
- I'll sabotage
- I can't book work

As said, many actors do say these things. I believe it is because we live in a world of, *I want it and I want it now!* We can't wait.

Remember, many acting teachers and schools will just take your money. They don't care. A former employer said to me dozens of times, "Actors pay the rent. Only five per cent of them in any year are going to work; the rest just make the school look good and pay the bills." Which category of student do you fit into? Are you just making up the numbers at any acting school or class?

You have to ask yourself: Are you ready to take the space? Are you ready to step up to the plate? Are you prepared to be a risk-taker? Because if not, you will most likely not make an impact in the audition room.

If you do not make an impact, your headshot and resume may be put into an office drawer or cupboard for the next year or two or three to five years.

You need to have an empowered state of mind. In other words, you should empower yourself in all circumstances.

Your audition checklist

The list below is particularly for film and theatre, but most of it relates to television too. The time that you have between getting the script and having the audition will influence your preparation work.

As a teacher teaching actors, I believe there are three areas to work on: 1. Structure. 2. Make decisions. 3. Relax, let go, trust and play.

In short, **Structure** relates to the topics you work on to improve your acting. **Make decisions** is about the scene study questions and back story to character and creating your character, and **relax, let go, trust and play** is what you will do when you perform.

Preparation – after you get the audition script

- Print a copy or two of the audition scene as soon as you can
- After you have read the scene, immediately turn the scene over and write down your first impressions of what is happening in

the scene and what is happening with the character that you are auditioning for
- Let other people you know read the scene and give you their interpretations of the scene
- If technique works for you, use a technique with the scene (noting: a decided upon technique usually works for most actors)
- If technique works for you, do back story to scene and character (noting: a decided upon technique usually works for most actors)
- Make a decision on what has just happened prior to the start of the scene
- Consider tapping into one of the five senses at the start of the scene
- Make a decision on subtext or opinion or attitude for your character
- Make a decision on where you can take a risk with the scene and/or the character (don't simply make the obvious choice for most large roles in theatre and film in particular)
- Practise positive self-talk: for example, look into a mirror and give yourself compliments, remind yourself of the importance of listening and your choices made
- Learn the lines
- Don't over-prepare or over-rehearse the audition scene
- Start doing the self-hypnotherapy of seeing yourself achieving a positive result
- Do research on the show or the production
- Do research on the casting directors in that office and what they cast
- Decide before you get there if you will talk to people or sit quietly
- Have a professional-looking headshot on your resume that looks like you
- Consider what you will wear that gives a hint of the character that you will be portraying
- Prepare and practise a speech about what you have accomplished in your career

When in the foyer

- Arrive at the audition early
- Have a copy of your headshot and resume and the script with you
- Empower yourself when you walk in the foyer room
- Have open body language and a smile
- Be polite and courteous and respectful to everyone you see
- Be confident
- Don't complain about anything
- If a casting assistant or associate is there, thank them for bringing you into the audition
- Be professional. Leave your negative comments or attitudes in the car/on public transport
- Make a decision on whether you will talk to other actors while you wait
- Don't let anyone distract you or psych you out in the foyer. Say "I will talk to you after I have had my audition" if you have to

When in the audition room

- Empower yourself when you walk in the room
- Have open body language and a smile
- Be polite and courteous and respectful to everyone you see
- Acknowledge/introduce yourself to everyone you see
- Don't offer to shake hands, but do shake hands if they offer
- Don't apologize for being there
- Thank them for bringing you into the audition
- Try to get a sense of the mood or feeling in the audition room. For example, are they really stressed or busy?
- If a camera audition – ask the shot or what is my frame
- Ask a question about the scene which evokes interest, but preferably not one that will affect what you have prepared in a negative way
- Really listen (limit your caffeine, sugar and corn syrup intake)
- Put yourself in a state of anticipation

- State your name and agent with personality

If the casting people ask you, "What have you been up to?", this usually means your acting career and not your personal life. So, talk about your career – bookings, auditions, training. In that order.

When auditioning

- Communicate if you would like to do something quickly as the scene starts
- Look into the eyes of the reader or the casting director before you start
- Perform for the camera shot if there is a camera
- Use the frame or the shot. Feel free to move around the frame slowly or be side on in the frame for a small time, usually at the start of the scene, to give variety
- Put yourself in a state of anticipation
- Take a risk. Don't just do the obvious choice
- Trust your choices and play surprises
- Really listen
- Try not to nail it
- Try not to sit on your shoulder watching yourself
- Try not to do it perfectly (perfection is subjective)
- Don't say, "Scene", immediately after you have finished acting

When given direction

- Slowly move off the mark and closer to the casting director when given direction
- Say the direction that is given to you out loud as you move back to the mark
- Readjust your body language for the second read after the direction has been given to you
- Always make sure the second read is different – don't just do the scene one way

- If they don't ask to see your work a different way – consider asking them politely, "Can I do it another way for you today?" (your choice)

When leaving the audition room

- Empower yourself when you leave the room
- Have open body language and a smile
- Be polite and courteous and respectful to everyone
- Don't apologize for what you did
- Thank them for bringing you into the audition
- Thank them or the reader for reading with you
- Don't ask them, "When will I hear if I get a call back or the part?"
- Remember their name

Additional information for a theatre audition

- Have a few monologues ready
- If you prepared the work, always audition your best and most appropriate work
- Stand in the space so you can make the most impact. Generally, three-quarters of the way back in the space from the people auditioning you, and in the middle of the room
- Know your upstage and downstage
- Know your stage left and right
- Move across the stage/space leading with the appropriate foot
- Look around so you know how much you must project with your voice
- Look around so you know how much you must use your body
- If applicable, align yourself with the other actor or actors when on stage
- Remind yourself to not upstage anyone or let anyone upstage you
- If applicable, make a stage entrance and use it to your advantage
- After the initial greeting, turn around and face the wall and then turn back around to do the audition piece and then turn back after the piece is finished

More audition tips

- Be prepared for the part that you are auditioning for
- Be on time
- Be polite to all other people
- Turn off mobile/cell phone
- Dress properly – appropriately
- Show flexibility
- Be humble
- Don't swear
- Follow instructions
- Don't flirt with the casting people (well, only if you know you can get away with it)
- Speak clearly
- Don't disrupt others' preparation
- Never criticize fellow actors who audition their work during your audition. As you may have a reader reading opposite you or you may be auditioning with another person or in a small group – which is common in commercial auditioning
- Own your mistakes
- To follow up, send a thank you card
- Ask if it is okay to drop in some time to say hello. Is it okay to just turn up? What is their office's policy?

Preparation

- Have a story or bio about yourself/sell yourself
- Do research on the play you're auditioning for and the theatre group
- Know your craft/practice makes perfect
- Have a few monologues under your belt
- Budget your time accordingly
- Be centred, know how to focus
- Know what you're auditioning for
- Have your script/sides prepared

- Know location and address beforehand
- Be ready for surprises
- Believe in yourself
- Always have extra headshots and resumes
- Make sure your contact info is up to date
- Bring a pen

How to believe, stand out and audition well

I'd like you to watch this audition video on YouTube on making it as an actor and how to audition:

https://www.youtube.com/watch?v=YlqafzWTirQ

It is a collection of insights from successful actors that's been put together and produced by Evan Carmichael. It's organised into ten points discussed with movie stars such as Matt Damon, Bryan Cranston and Christian Bale. I do not know and have never met Evan Carmichael, but I like what the actors say in these interviews.

As mentioned earlier in the book, I wish to remind the viewer that I cannot be held accountable for any type of advertising that appears on YouTube either before, during or after you watch this video.

The points discussed by successful professional actors can be summarized like this:

- believe
- take the long view
- stick to your guns
- stand out from the crowd
- break through the discomfort
- do it to the hilt
- know what your job is
- don't give yourself boundaries
- be yourself
- work hard

In closing on the topic of auditioning, here are a few ways of thinking that I strongly encourage you to think and behave:

- **Accept judgement**
  Accept that your work is going to be judged in a workshop with casting directors or when performing for an agent or manager or for any submission for a casting job

- **Be fearless**
  Being fearless is so much easier said than done, but remember things like the little kid who performs and sings and dances in an uninhibited way in front of an audience. Was that you when you were a child? All that little child has done is ... grown up. Just because there are money and a career attached to the job now, doesn't mean you can't be fearless.

- **Hold your energy**
  Do not give your power or energy anyway to anyone. For example, really attractive people, or people who have *je ne sais quoi*, are looked at all the time and people are also wanting to touch and/ or be with these people.

  These people are either consciously or subconsciously sapping up *your* energy and consequently building their resources. Don't give anyone your energy. My Book One talks more about this in the section on auditioning.

- Feel and enjoy the self-empowerment as you take risks, have an arc in your performance (meaning some sort of growth or change occurs), show vulnerability, relax, trust your choices, change, let go and play.

Yah! (One of my favourite students, seven times acting award winner on stage - Cyanne McClairian/Martin - likes to say "Yah!".) So, go actor! Enjoy it!

Learning Point Number Twenty:

- Self-reflection will make you a better performer
- Be diligent in your self-assessment
- Be as professional as you can be
- Please believe me when I say, if you empower yourself in auditions, you will get more callbacks and more bookings
- As Bryan Cranston says in the YouTube video link above, look at every audition as a performance. They accept the work and book you or they don't. Move on

Above: Paul teaching one of his students from Hollywood on Skype on his laptop. Paul now has a lovely large Mac personal computer, where his students in class can be seen like they are on film or television.

Appendix 1
Handouts

My school's curriculum offers classes that are diverse, challenging and have an international flavour. The curriculum has been devised deliberately to give actors all-round training. Within that, the handouts are very important.

On camera – tips list

Here is a list of things to help your work on camera in the areas of physiology, psychology and physiognomy.

- **Facial expressions:** What to control and how to control the face
- **Head and body acting:** How and where to look
- **Work the technique:** e.g. dropping in the text
- **Creating characters:** How to develop characters. Develop one, they're fun
- **Facial expressions:** Have control and awareness of raising eyebrows, frowning and forehead moving. When you look off to think, try to look sideways as opposed to up and down. Controlling as best you can – the eyebrows, forehead and frowning. Keep a loose jaw and relaxed head, face and neck
- **Passing the baton:** The exchange of energy. The give and take between actors. Sometimes physical, e.g. you give a book. Listening is the key. Status often changes
- **Peak in the scene:** What is the most important line?
- **Surprises:** We hear it, decide whether it's good or bad, do we change our want? Then respond. This is profoundly watchable. Good surprises are generally big: you laugh, you move quickly, you are louder, your face has external expression. Bad surprises are more internal: you hold your breath, stare, gulp, stiffen your

body, drop your jaw, go red in the face, look surprised, upset, disappointed or mad; especially in the eyes
- **Wants/opinions/attitudes:** Wants are separate from the text, hard to achieve and off or to the other person. See the Wants handout later in this Appendix for the list of Wants
- **Add colours:** Add a colour to your want. Go through what colours mean to you and then add them to your work to give it something else. For example: red for passion and excitement or jealousy. White for purity. Green for envy. Blue for peaceful. Brown for muddy
- **Always do something:** Even if it is just listening
- **In the moment:** Stay in it
- **Know what you are doing:** e.g. what is happening in the scene? How to move in the shot/frame?
- **Letting it land:** What is said to you
- **Natural movements:** What we do naturally
- **Playing the changes in the scene:** Influenced by surprises and what is said to you as well as the gear shifts within the story. Should you take time to respond and then move on? Or respond quickly? Did you acknowledge that change in the scene? Did you change your status? Noting: this is often referred to as having an arc in your performance. Meaning some sort of growth or change occurs for your character
- **Listening:** Listen like a hawk – always!
- **Anticipation:** Put yourself in this state as much as possible. As much as you can, have a look on your face of "What are you going to say to me?"
- **Risk taking:** Verbal and non-verbal
- **Start of the scene/Sensory work:** Do something to tap into the five senses to help establish where you are
- **The lead in the movie:** Knowing how to carry the movie – e.g. looking off to things happening, deciding what to do next, introducing new people and plot points

- **Performing for the shot:** Practise in the ¾ shot, mid-shot, medium close-up, close-up, extreme close-up
- **Performing in the V:** Depending on the shot, put your arms out in the shape of a V. Your body is the back of the V. Put your hands up by your chin for the extreme close-up
- **Acting with the eyes:** Learn how to show expression and make impact through the number one thing we watch on camera – the eyes
- **Acting with the tone of the voice:** Learn how to use your voice to make impact with tone and flavour through the number two thing we watch on camera – the mouth
- **Student self-analysis chart:** Student evaluates how they're feeling and what is going on in their mind

On camera – actor or teacher evaluation chart for student

ACTOR: DATE:

Preparation

- preparation for work – excellent / very good / good / fair / poor / not applicable

The actor's mind

- relaxed – yes / no / sometimes

- concentration – excellent / very good / good / fair / poor

- self presentation – excellent / very good / good / fair / poor

The actor's skills

- really listening – yes / some / not really / poor

- understanding of script – excellent / very good / good / fair / poor

- choices made – excellent / very good / good / fair / poor

- risk taking – yes / no / some

- subtext evident – yes / no / some

- were there other things taught by Paul Parker in action – yes / some / not really / poor

Development of character
- yes / some / not really / poor

The actor's on-camera skills

- knowledge of skills required for camera – excellent / very good / good / fair / poor

- presence on camera – excellent / very good / good / fair / poor

- ability to perform in the shot – excellent / very good / good / fair / poor

Variety in performance
- yes / some / not really / poor

Taking direction
- attempt to implement direction given – yes / no

- implementation of things taught – excellent / very good / good / fair / poor

Mark/score
- overall performance – excellent / very good / good / fair / poor

- if a mark was given out of ten – what would it be?

On camera – student evaluation chart - Theory Questionnaire

STUDENT NAME: **DATE:**

Prior to each advanced camera class, actors are to fill out this questionnaire:

- How do you feel when the camera is pointed at you?
- How do you feel you look in front of the camera?
- What skills do you know about acting on camera? List them?
- Do you know how you can help make yourself as captivating as possible on camera? If so, how?
- What things would you like to work on most to improve your work on camera?

Scene study – quick audition assessment sheet

- What is this scene about?
- Where is the change in the scene? Or shift in focus? Or peak in the scene? Or the joke?
- Create a brief back story to your character here
- What decisions will you make?
- What will you do that will be different than other actors?
- What subtext? Or opinion? Or attitude? Or point of concentration will you have?

It's often good to think "What does my character want in the scene?" Or what is my character's opinion or attitude in this scene? You can determine their opinion or attitude from the script, but if you choose to play with wants; here's a few to consider.

WANTS

Choose a want separate from the text, (meaning not in the scene), hard to achieve, and you want it off or you are doing it to - the other person

TO THE OTHER PERSON	FROM THE OTHER PERSON
Belittle	Acceptance
Convince	Affirmation
Control	Appreciation
Deceive	Attention
Dominate	Be desired
Humiliate	Be held
Hurt	Commitment
Influence	Compassion
Intimidate	Confession
Kill	Confirmation
Make the other person laugh	Cooperation
Manipulate	Empathy
Provoke	Encouragement
Resist	Forgiveness
Reject	Freedom
Seduce	Friendship
Strike fear	Happiness
	Honesty
	Intimacy
	Love
	Lust
	Peace
	Pity
	Power
	Recognition
	Remorse
	Respect
	Revenge
	Satisfaction
	Sex
	Submission
	Sympathy
	Understanding

To Coach - To Educate - To Empower

Creating characters

Below is a sample of one of the charts that I use to help actors create characters.

Character Development Chart

Use of Body

- Gait, mannerisms
- Affected by: war, pregnancy, emotions/thoughts, occupation, missing limb

Use of Voice

- Centre of breath, voice, accent, tone, affectation, volume, pitch, flavour

Use of Mind / Back Story (has correlations with Stanislavski technique)

- Character background information from Scene Study I classes included in this book
- Your characters want, opinion or attitude?

Laban Influence

- B – Body E – Effort S – Shape S – Space
- Effort Dimension – Space, Time, Weight, Flow
- Actions – Punch, Slash, Press, Wring, Float, Glide, Flick, Dab

Animal Influence (has correlations with Grotowski technique)

- What animal? How does it influence the body?

Imitation (has correlations with Brecht technique)

- Copying, imitating someone as best you can
- Drawing attention to what you're doing (Brecht's "Estrangement effect". Also known as "Distancing or Alienation Effect")

Stimuli

- Props/costumes, visual images, stream of consciousness, adjectives, observation

Appendix 2
Lesson plans

I ask you, the reader reading this book, as an actor do you really want to be taught things? Things that you know or believe will work? Or do you simply just want to be taught by a celebrity or someone who has entertainment industry credits?

I firmly believe that you should be taught by a qualified teacher. Learning to be a teacher takes time, education and practice. I studied at university for four years to be a teacher. While in teacher training, I went out and taught (called teaching rounds) at many different schools. From private schools to middle and working-class schools. I taught drama and English at these schools.

Many actors who have bought my first book have mentioned to me that they loved how I spoke about real qualified teachers teaching, as opposed to anyone who calls themselves a teacher or coach, teaching actors.

I understand we all have to find a niche somewhere and I guess people who create acting schools or classes, and teach (but are not qualified teachers), need to make a buck somewhere. I just know from my experiences, actors are often being poorly taught and often abused and ripped off; in Australia, the USA, Japan, China and South Korea.

I am a strong believer in lesson plans. Meaning the teacher plans for the teaching lesson. Lesson plans that come from a curriculum. Lesson plans that have each class's objectives for the students clearly listed.

I often tell the students the lesson plans' objectives for each class. I also tell or give the students a handout with the assessment criteria for each lesson's objectives on it.

The basis for the lesson plans should come from the school's curriculum, which comes from the philosophy, vision and mission statement and the general ways of teaching of each particular teaching body.

This could also include the influences and requirements from the educational government body that oversees them.

All good teachers should leave room to improvise and digress from the lesson plans. This is because things will undoubtedly come up in class that you didn't expect, and it is really important for the teacher to address those things and digress for a moment or two perhaps to make some other points; or let some other things in class evolve.

The following lesson plan information is taken from the first page from my On Camera 1 lesson plan. The number 1 doesn't mean it is for beginners. It is simply my number 1 from my many camera classes. All taken from my different levels of my curriculum.

Lesson Plan Level One – on camera 1

Premise: I have been teaching on Skype and Zoom for twelve years as of 2023. I have ongoing students in five countries in the world as of the writing of this book.

Classes with this curriculum are consequently now on Skype or Zoom. Except when I travel and guest teach in Australia, America and Japan. This course takes approximately four to five classes of one hour's duration. All to help improve an actor's awareness and skills.

This course is usually taught around the time the student works on other courses: Australian Techniques 1, Scene Study 1 and Improvisation 1.

Scenes are given by the teacher: initially the monologue from Australian Techniques 1, then a two-person scene is given where the actor acts opposite the teacher.

Here is a sample of some of the content from a camera class.

Lesson plan introduction
Handouts to be given out over the classes:

- On Camera 1 – checklist handout. Listing twelve things that are introduced and worked on in the classes
- Wants, opinions, attitude sheet handout
- Scripts

Actors are also drawn attention to actors' work that the teacher wants them to watch in selected scenes online on YouTube.

Lesson Plan – Week One

Teacher/lecturer: Objectives of lesson, for students to:

- Feel comfortable and relaxed
- Learn about the importance of performing on screen
- Learn how to perform on screen by doing exercises
- Watch well-known actors personify what I teach
- Rehearse and perform selected scenes with the lesson plan objectives personified by the student

Students are given an overall philosophy on acting on screen and principles of what the course is about (briefly – I do not talk for a long time) and what will happen in the classes. Then I begin the warm-up exercises and actors get to work.

Appendix 3
People who influenced my teachings in Book Two

Surprises: Richard Sarell – television director, Melbourne, Victoria, Australia.

Parts of the Scene Study charts and Impulse exercise: Konstantin Stanislavski – Russian theatre practitioner – and Lindy Davies – actor, director, teacher, Australia.

Appendix 4
Successful students

In Book One, I wrote a detailed list of many of my successful students. In this book, I will talk about a few of my students – a kind of case study review on selected students and their training.

Below is a small list of some of the thousands of actors that I am proud of and have trained over the years. Please feel free to put their names into the International Movie Database at www.imdb.com to read about their achievements.

Jeannetta Arnette: I trained Jeannetta over a few years since 2009 and audition prepped her for some of her film and television roles. She now has 95 IMDB credits as of September 2023.

Gerald Webb: IMDB says 13 award wins and 10 nominations. I trained Gerald for 2.5 years. He now has 97 IMDB credits as of September 2023.

Naama Kates: IMDB says 6 award wins. I trained her for many years over a fifteen-year period. Firstly, as a teenager in New York and later in Los Angeles. Naama now has 19 IMDB credits as of September 2023.

Preston Jones (1V)

https://www.imdb.com/name/nm1171144/?ref_=fn_al_nm_1

IMDB says 1 award nomination. I trained Preston for many years over a five-year period. He now has 47 IMDB credits as of September 2023.

Elina Madison: IMDB says 6 award wins and 1 nomination. I used to train Elina in her apartment in Los Angeles in and around 2002–2003. I would audition prep Elina for some of her film roles. She now has 105 IMDB credits as of September 2023.

Chris Ivan Cevic: I trained Chris for many years over a ten-year period. He now has 21 IMDB credits as of September 2023 and 13 credits and 2 wins as a producer.

Patrick Censoplano: I trained Patrick for many years over a fifteen-year period. He now has 17 IMDB credits as of September 2023.

Nicole Dionne: I trained Nicole for five years from 2002. She now has 44 IMDB credits as of September 2023.

Cyanne McClairian: a 7-times award-winning actor on stage. I have trained Cyanne over a fifteen-year period. She now has 24 IMDB credits as of September 2023.

Tarnue Massaquoi: Award-winning actor. I trained Tarnue for many years over a fifteen-year period. He now has 59 IMDB credits as of September 2023.

Mike Larose: I trained Mike for many years over a fifteen-year period. He now has 21 IMDB credits as of September 2023.

Kat Ludley: Award-winning actor. I am still training Kat, firstly in 2018, then ongoing from 2020. Kat now has 16 IMDB credits as of September 2023.

Appendix 5
Paul Parker Curriculum Vitae

In Book One, I included my full curriculum vitae. In Book Two, I will just mention the most important points.

Teacher

USA - England - Australia - Japan - South Korea - China

Paul started teaching actors in 1990 while still at teachers' college. Still teaching today, Paul has taught, ongoing, in person, in Chicago, Los Angeles, New York and San Francisco in the USA, Osaka and Tokyo in Japan, in Adelaide, the Gold Coast, Melbourne and Sydney in Australia, and guest lectured at Universities in Beijing and Hainan in China. As of now, Paul has also taught online in Brisbane and Perth in Australia, London in England, Seoul and other cities in South Korea and many other US states. Paul has also taught at universities, TAFE colleges and acting schools in Australia, and acting schools in the USA and Japan.

www.aidaacting.com

Judge / Adjudicator

USA

Paul was one of the entertainment industry judges, including prominent Los Angeles casting directors, agents and managers, that were judging actors work on screen, for IPAC – the International Performing Arts Conference – in Los Angeles, USA, from 2007 to 2010. Paul also opened these four conferences with a one-hour acting class, to an audience of over a thousand people.

Australia

Paul was also the adjudicator at the One Act Play Festival in Ararat, Victoria, Australia in 2014.

Director

USA – Australia – Japan

Paul began directing for the stage in 1991 and for the screen in 2015. Paul has directed theatre in the USA, Japan and Australia. Paul has directed film in Japan and Australia.

www.player-productions.com

Above: Paul overseeing editing with editor Katsuya Sakane san, on Paul's short film Die San Vacuum Cleaner in Tokyo, Japan, in 2018.

Actor

International Awards

Best Actor – Winner in an **Ensemble Cast** for **The Love Of Freedom** in NAACP Theatre Awards, Los Angeles, 2001.

Best Actor and Runner Up to Best Actor in a television role, Ballarat South St., Eisteddfod, Australia, 1998.

Tally of productions Paul has been in as an actor:

FILMS: 33
TELEVISION: 14
TELEVISION COMMERICIALS: 4
THEATRE: 16
COLLEGE & COMMUNITY THEATRE: 18
STAND-UP COMEDY: various places, over many years

Paul's IMDB

https://www.imdb.com/name/nm1296339/?ref_=nv_sr_srsg_0

Education

National Institute of Dramatic Art (Director – Winter Program)

Deakin University/Victoria College – Rusden (Bachelor of Education)

Paul Parker's third book will focus on performance and presentation skills that he teaches, from time to time, to people from various professions. Clients simply come to Paul or are referred to him. Among the clients he has taught are doctors, psychiatrists, witnesses in court cases, teachers, University students and tutors, scientists, chiropractors, real estate professionals, CEOs, heads of departments, small business owners, professional athletes, farmers, nurses and many other professions.

PERFORMANCE IN BUSINESS PRESENTATION

With International Performance Teacher:

Paul Parker B.Ed.

Learn How To Make Impact At:

- Conferences / Staff meetings / Staff workshops
- In front of the camera / On set in a TV studio
- With your clients / your students
- And much, much more...

www.ingramcontent.com/pod-product-compliance
Lightning Source LLC
Chambersburg PA
CBHW071954290426
44109CB00018B/2012